# ENERGY CRISIS IN PAKISTAN

## Origins, Challenges, and Sustainable Solutions

# ENERGY CRISIS IN PAKISTAN

## Origins, Challenges, and Sustainable Solutions

MUHAMMAD ASIF

Foreword by
MUHAMMAD YUNUS
Nobel Laureate

OXFORD
UNIVERSITY PRESS

# OXFORD
### UNIVERSITY PRESS

Great Clarendon Street, Oxford OX2 6DP

Oxford University Press is a department of the University of Oxford.
It furthers the University's objective of excellence in research, scholarship,
and education by publishing worldwide in

Oxford New York

Auckland Cape Town Dar es Salaam Hong Kong Karachi
Kuala Lumpur Madrid Melbourne Mexico City Nairobi
New Delhi Shanghai Taipei Toronto

With offices in

Argentina Austria Brazil Chile Czech Republic France Greece
Guatemala Hungary Italy Japan Poland Portugal Singapore
South Korea Switzerland Turkey Ukraine Vietnam

ISBN 978-0-19-547876-1

Typeset in Adobe Garamond Pro
Printed in Pakistan by
Kagzi Printers, Karachi.
Published by
Ameena Saiyid, Oxford University Press
No. 38, Sector 15, Korangi Industrial Area, PO Box 8214,
Karachi-74900, Pakistan.

The book is dedicated to

### *Quaid-i-Azam Muhammad Ali Jinnah*
The Father of the Nation—a man of principle, dignity and
determination; who single-handedly fought on numerous fronts to
create Pakistan; who sacrificed everything for the cause of Pakistan

### *Brave Souls*
The unsung heroes: the honest, dedicated and courageous energy
officials who manage to defeat the fears and resist the temptations
imposed by the prevailing corruption within the system; who dare to
say the truth rather than what their superiors want to hear

### *Contemplative Pakistanis*
Who are suffering from the energy crisis despite having paid all their
taxes and utility bills; who are the victims of the rampant injustice in
the society at the hands of the influential and 'untouchable' ruling elite

# Contents

# Foreword

One can but doubt the paramount significance of energy as one of the most basic human needs. Its utility has greatly evolved over the last century. The whole gamut of human activities including dwelling, transportation, industry, trade and commerce, and agriculture has become ever more dependent on energy. Globally, energy prosperity has become crucial to overcoming fundamental social problems such as poverty, hunger, disease, and illiteracy. Paradoxically, the growing human reliance on energy is paralleled by a string of challenges that are both local and global in nature. On the one hand, energy prices are surging, and on the other, the vast majority of the population in the developing countries is living without access to electricity—one of the most commonly utilized forms of energy. The United Nations duly acknowledges that a much greater access to energy services including electricity is essential to addressing developmental issues such as achieving the Millennium Development Goals. There is an increasing understanding that ensuring 'availability of sufficient, affordable, and environmentally friendly energy' is amongst the major challenges that the world faces in the twenty-first century.

Dr Muhammad Asif is a young and prolific academic with extensive research interests in the area of energy. In his book, *Energy Crisis in Pakistan: Origins, Challenges, and Sustainable Solutions*, he has skilfully exploited his research expertise to reflect upon the energy scene of Pakistan. The book furnishes a wealth of information on the subject of energy, assuming no prior knowledge, therefore being approachable to people from diverse backgrounds. Although the main focus of the book is on the energy scenario of Pakistan, it also proficiently covers the global spectrum of energy. The critical discussions on the policy issues and on the role of the relevant stakeholders are particularly thought provoking. I hope that the book will help its audience develop a holistic understanding of the energy issues of Pakistan and inspire them to play an active role in achieving a sustainable energy future for the country.

Muhammad Yunus
Winner of the 2006 Nobel Peace Prize
Founder of Grameen Bank, Bangladesh

# Preface

The rampant energy crisis has made the hapless Pakistanis live in a modern stone age. The year 2010 has dawned upon them as they face up to 20 hours of electricity and gas load-shedding along with frequent disruptions in transportation fuel. The intense shortfall of electricity—crossing the 6,000MW mark and recording an over 40 per cent deficit in the demand and supply equation—has left them struggling even to meet the fundamental needs like lighting, water, cooking and protection against extreme weather conditions. The resulting sleepless nights, disfigured daily routines and exacerbated financial conditions (also depriving over four hundred thousand from their jobs) have made life all but a set of continuous physical, financial and psychological torture for them. This is indeed not the reward the conscious citizens deserve in lieu of the taxes that they pay to the government.

In Pakistan, there is a great scarcity of information and knowledge on the subject of energy. The absence of think-tanks and almost nonexistent research and development infrastructure in the pertinent departments, academia and industry is an obvious indicator of the across the board vacuum of the fundamental understanding of energy. Consequently, the perception and approach of the common man towards this precious commodity is as weak as that of the policy and decision-makers'. In the backdrop of the ongoing energy crisis, there is an ever greater need to uplift the degree of all-round awareness in this field amongst the wider segments of the society. This book is therefore a much needed scholarship that aims to educate the concerned stakeholders—including the policy and decision-makers, industry, local and foreign investors and businessmen, academia, civil society, NGOs, and international donors and aid agencies—on the indispensable role of energy in the existence of modern societies, and on the vital dimensions of the energy sector of Pakistan with particular reference to the prevalent energy crisis.

The present energy crisis is intense, costly and multi-layered and is having enormous economic, socio-political and strategic ramifications for the country. The inconvenient truth is that it has not taken the country by surprise but has been fostered by the bankrupt policies on the part of the successive regimes over the last three decades, though the greatest responsibility rests with the Musharraf–Shaukat era. Compelling evidence begs to prove that concepts like proactive initiatives and sustainable solutions are unheard of in the corridors of power. The usual modus operandi is to let issues crop up and to grow into storms either by design or due to incompetence. The acknowledgment by the federal minister for defence production in a TV show in December 2009, 'Yes we commit corruption and it is our right to do so', however, speaks volumes of the underlying issues. This book has unearthed some of the most prominent and deadly setbacks inflicted to the energy sector, interestingly all by the policy and decision-makers including the top most executives in the country. As a matter of fact, a complete account of the financial and administrative irregularities at the hands of the concerned authorities— which have contributed to the downfall of this sector and are not the main focus of this scholarship—would easily require a separate book of a much greater volume.

   To live the present and dream the future, the past has to be healed. This is precisely the way out—the distorted policies and decisions that have led the energy sector to this crisis need to be rectified. The traditional approach of buying haphazard and unviable solutions is only going to add to the complexities of the situation. A good example in this respect is that of the rental power projects. The electricity from these power projects will be of no use to the household, industry, agriculture, and commercial sectors if it is beyond their purchasing capacity. It is, however, bound to impose colossal implications upon WAPDA and the already fragile economy of the country. The rental power programme is like adding unnecessary, dreadful and heavy burden on an already fragile infrastructure. It must be understood that in order to bring a positive change in the energy sector, the root causes of its miserable condition—lack of commitment, incompetence and most importantly wide-ranging corruption—are absolutely imperative to be addressed. The situation requires evolutionary as well as revolutionary measures in order to save the energy sector from the verge of a complete destruction. To ensure light at the end of the tunnel, the policy and decision-makers have to truly act as 'servants of Pakistan' as Quaid-i-Azam referred them in his first address to the Constituent Assembly on 14 August 1947. The energy challenges, no matter how big they are, can surely be addressed as long as there is clear intent, right strategy and due commitment on the part of policy and decision-makers. With pragmatism and resolve the challenges can be converted into opportunities.

Despite the current dismal state of the energy sector, there are some valid grounds to be optimistic about the energy future of Pakistan. The country is fortunate to have the necessary ingredients—healthy and diverse energy resources and capable manpower—required for achieving energy sustainability. In terms of energy resources, the best hopes for Pakistan rest with hydropower, coal and renewable energy like solar energy and wind power. Meaningful exploitation of these resources can provide sufficient and affordable energy to indigenously meet the national requirements on a long-term basis. To ensure a prosperous and secure energy future for the country, the concerned stakeholders have to play their respective role in a just manner.

The book encompasses a wide scope of the subject of energy. In the first two chapters, it discusses the contemporary pivotal status of energy by highlighting its various dimensions. In the third chapter, it presents an overview of the energy base of the country in terms of resources and intuitional infrastructure. Having described the anatomy of the current energy crisis, in Chapter 4, the book reflects upon its implications for the country, particularly in the socio-economic and geo-strategic contexts. With the help of a historic outlook furnished with relevant data, the factors that contributed to the present crisis have also been comprehensively analyzed. In this regard the performance of the crucial stakeholders i.e., policy and decision-makers, energy departments, industry, and academia has particularly been examined in Chapter 5. Finally, also foreseeing the challenges the country is likely to face in future, in the last two chapters, the book provides a set of solutions to address the existing energy crisis and to achieve a sustainable energy future for the country. Reflecting upon the key strengths of the energy base of Pakistan, a number of potential technologies have been discussed. In this respect, guidelines for the aforementioned stakeholders have also been produced.

The book predominantly constitutes of the author's analysis of broader dimensions of Pakistan's energy scenario, based upon his academic research and on-ground experiences. It is also furnished with the views of a good number of senior energy officials, investors and entrepreneurs, politicians and bureaucrats, and foreign experts and consultants. The author owes a great deal to his beautiful homeland, Pakistan, for everything it has endowed him. This book is an attempt to pay his motherland back for its favours.

# Acknowledgements

It would not have been possible to write this book without the help and support of sincere and kind people around me. Above all, I am indebted to my parents for their ever present love, prayers, support and encouragement without which my accomplishments in life would not have been possible.

My thanks go to Mr Shams-ul-Mulk, former Chairman of the Water and Power Development Authority (WAPDA), Mr Javed Nizam, ex-Member of WAPDA and Mr Syed Tanzeem Hussain Naqvi, ex-Chairman of the Karachi Electric Supply Corporation (KESC) for sharing their invaluable experiences. I also feel obliged to Dr Pervez Butt, former Chairman of the Pakistan Atomic Energy Commission (PAEC) who presently serves as a Member on Energy in the Planning Commission of Pakistan for sharing his valuable insight on the policy and decision-making process with regards to the energy sector. I am also thankful to an ex-Deputy Chairman of the Planning Commission, several former as well as existing senior energy officials, politicians and bureaucrats who have provided me with important data along with sharing their insights on the energy sector while preferring to remain anonymous.

I would also like to acknowledge my other family members, colleagues and friends for their well wishes and moral support that made this huge task easier for me. Deserving my gratitude are my senior colleagues—Professor Tariq Muneer and Mr Bill Pollock—for waging constructive discussions with me on some of the issues discussed in the book. I would also like to appreciate my friends Dr Sajid Ali, Dr Hussain Shaheed, Dr Shahid Pervez, Dr Abdul Jabbar and Dr Qasim Khan for their motivation and keen interest in seeing this book materialize.

I am also grateful to a number of newspapers and magazines in particular the publishers of the *Dawn* and *The News* that have frequently published my articles on the subject of energy during the last five years. My thanks also go to the readers of my articles for playing an important role in motivating me to write this book through their appreciative feedback and calls for a detailed examination of the energy problems facing the country. I would also like to thank the newspapers *Express* and

*Jang* for permitting me to use their photographs to reflect upon the energy crisis.

Last but not the least, my very special compliments are reserved for my wife and my sons—Ibraheem, Musab and Qasim—who have been very accommodating with my two-year-routine of working on the book for long hours during the evenings, weekends and even holidays. It has been a remarkable sacrifice on their behalf. My sons have also been a source of inspiration for me and I hope that they carry the torch of knowledge, righteousness and endurance high in their lives also, to the benefit of Pakistan and the wider society.

# Acronyms and Abbreviations

| | |
|---|---|
| ADB | Asian Development Bank |
| AEDB | Alternate Energy Development Board |
| BSP | Biogas Sector Partnership |
| CNG | Compressed Natural Gas |
| CCP | Competition Commission of Pakistan |
| CFL | Compact Fluorescent Lamp |
| CIA | Central Intelligence Agency |
| EIA | Energy Information Administration |
| ENERCON | National Energy Conservation Centre |
| ESD | Energy Services Delivery |
| EU | European Union |
| GOP | Government of Pakistan |
| GSP | Geological Survey of Pakistan |
| GWh | Gegga Watt hour |
| GS | Grameen Shakti |
| HDI | Human Development Index |
| HDIP | Hydrocarbon Development Institute of Pakistan |
| HEC | Higher Education Commission |
| HSD | High Speed Diesel |
| IMF | International Monetary Fund |
| IBP | Indus Basin Project |
| IPP | Independent Power Producer |
| IESCO | Islamabad Electric Supply Company |
| JJVL | Jamshoro Joint Venture Limited |
| KAPCO | Kot Addu Power Company |
| KESC | Karachi Electricity Supply Corporation |
| kWh | kilowatt hour |
| LCDC | Lakhar Coal Development Company |
| MDG | Millennium Development Goal |
| MENA | Middle East North Africa |
| MFI | Micro-Finance Institution |
| MIT | Massachusetts Institute of Technology |
| MNRE | Ministry of New and Renewable Energy |

| | |
|---|---|
| MTOE | Million Tonne Oil Equivalent |
| MW | Mega Watt |
| NASA | National Aeronautics and Space Administration |
| NGO | Non-governmental Organization |
| NTDC | National Transmission and Despatch Company |
| NIST | National Institute of Silicon Technology |
| NWFP | North-West Frontier Province |
| OAPEC | Organization of Arab Petroleum Exporting Countries |
| OECD | Organization for Economic Co-operation and Development |
| OGDC | Oil and Gas Development Corporation |
| OGRA | Oil and Gas Regulatory Authority |
| PAC | Public Accounts Committee |
| PAEC | Pakistan Atomic Energy Commission |
| PAPCO | Pak-Arab Pipeline Company Limited |
| PARCO | Pak Arab Refinery Limited |
| PCAT | Pakistan Council for Appropriate Technologies |
| PCRET | Pakistan Council of Renewable Energy Technologies |
| PEPCO | Pakistan Electric Power Company |
| PPA | Power Purchase Agreement |
| PPIB | Private Power and Infrastructure Board |
| ppm | parts per million |
| PSO | Pakistan State Oil |
| PV | Photovoltaic |
| Rs | Rupees |
| SDO | Sub-Divisional Officer |
| SEC | State Engineering Corporation |
| SHS | Solar Home System |
| SIS | Secret Intelligence Service |
| SME | Small and Medium Enterprise |
| TWh | Terawatt hour |
| UPS | Uninterrupted Power Supply |
| UK | United Kingdom |
| USA | United States of America |
| US$ | United States Dollar |
| USSR | Union of Soviet Socialist Republics |
| VIP | Very Important Person |
| WAPDA | Water and Power Development Authority |
| WHO | World Health Organization |
| WWF | World Wildlife Fund |

# 1

# Energy and its Wider Dimensions—I

## 1.1. Energy and Sustainable Development

Energy is the backbone of human activities. The accomplishments of civilization have largely been achieved through the increasingly efficient and extensive harnessing of various forms of energy to extend human capabilities and ingenuity. Providing adequate and affordable energy is thus essential for eradicating poverty, improving human welfare, and raising living standards worldwide. The per capita energy consumption is an index used to measure the socio-economic prosperity in any society—the Human Development Index (HDI) of a country has a strong relationship with its energy prosperity.[1] A direct correlation between access to electricity and economic well-being in a range of countries, for example, has been indicated in Figure 1.1.[2]

Throughout the course of history, with the evolution of civilizations, the human demand for energy has continuously grown. At present, the key factors driving the growth in energy demand include an increasing human population, modernization, and urbanization. According to the United Nations, the world population, 6.5 billion in 2005, is to grow to 9.1 billion by 2050.[3] Other estimates suggest that the world population is expected to double by the middle of this century.[4] Most of the population growth will take place in the developing world—Asia and Africa. The increment in the number of human beings on the planet is bound to have a knock-on effect on the global demand for energy. The International Energy Outlook projects strong growth for worldwide energy demand up to 2025.[5] In the IEO 2005 mid-term outlook, the emerging economies account for nearly two-thirds of the increase in world energy use, surpassing energy use in the mature market economies for the first time in 2020. In 2025, energy demand in the emerging economies is expected to exceed that of the mature market economies by 9 per cent. Much of the growth in energy demand among the emerging economies is expected to occur in emerging Asia, which includes China and India;

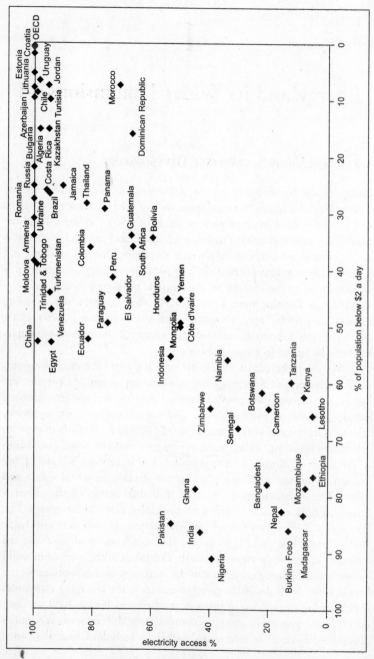

Figure 1.1: Relationship between economic prosperity and availability of electricity

demand in this region is projected to more than double over the forecast period. Primary energy consumption in the emerging economies as a whole is projected to grow at an average annual rate of 3.2 per cent up to 2025. In contrast, in the mature market economies—where energy consumption patterns are well established—energy use is expected to grow at a much slower average rate of 1.1 per cent per year over the same period. In the transitional economies of Eastern Europe and the former Soviet Union, growth in energy demand is projected to average 1.6 per cent per year. The total world consumption of marketed energy is expected to expand by 57 per cent over the 2002–25 time period.[3]

Global urbanization trends are complementing the growth-trends of population and energy demand. Statistics suggest that during the twentieth century the urban population in the world experienced a rapid growth as shown in Table 1.1.[6]

**Table 1.1: Urbanization in the world over the last century**

| Year | World population (Billion) | Urban population | |
|---|---|---|---|
| | | (Billion) | % of the World total |
| 1900 | 1.6 | 0.22 | 13.8 |
| 2000 | 6.1 | 2.8 | 46.0 |

By the end of 2008, world population grew to over 6.7 billion.[7] It was for the first time in history that nearly half of the global population lived in urban areas. By 2030, out of the total estimated population of around 8 billion, 5 billion would be living in urban areas. Figures also indicate that most of the urbanization is set to take place in the lesser developed part of the world—by the same time, the towns and cities of the developing world will make up 81 per cent of the urban population.[8]

Poverty, hunger, disease, illiteracy, and environmental degradation are amongst the most important challenges facing the world. Poor and inadequate access to secure and affordable energy is one of the crucial factors behind these issues. Electricity, for example, is vital for providing basic social services such as education and health, water supply and purification, sanitation and refrigeration of essential medicines. Electricity can also be helpful in supporting a wide range of income-generating opportunities. Although, during the last twenty-five years, over 1.3 billion people living in developing countries have been provided access to electricity, more than 1.4 billion people—over 21 per cent of the world's population—don't have access to it.[9] Furthermore, around 2.4 billion people rely on traditional biomass, including wood, agricultural residues and dung, for cooking and heating. Statistics also suggest that more than 99 per cent of people without electricity live in developing regions, and four out of five live in rural areas of South Asia and sub-Saharan Africa.[10] The leading countries in the world in terms of population without access to electricity are shown in Table 1.2.[9]

There appears to be a global consensus that the provision of secure, affordable and socially acceptable energy services is a prerequisite for eradicating poverty in order to achieve the Millennium Development Goals (MDGs). The Earth Summit 2002 strongly urged the nations to:

> Take joint actions and improve efforts to work together at all levels to improve access to reliable and affordable energy services for sustainable development sufficient to facilitate the achievement of the MDGs, including the goal of halving the proportion of people in poverty by 2015, and as a means to generate other important services that mitigate poverty, bearing in mind that access to energy facilitates the eradication of poverty.

The United Nations also acknowledges that 'without increased investment in the energy sector, the MDGs will not be achieved in the poorest countries'.[11] It is estimated that if the MDGs target is to be reached, 500 million more people would need to be electrified by 2015.[1]

**Table 1.2: Countries with a large population without access to electricity**

| Country/region | Population without electricity | | | |
|---|---|---|---|---|
| | 2000 | | 2008 | |
| | Millions | % of world total | Millions | % of world total |
| India | 579.10 | 35.4 | 487.2 | 34.6 |
| Bangladesh | 104.40 | 6.4 | 96.2 | 6.8 |
| Indonesia | 98.00 | 6.0 | 101.2 | 7.2 |
| Nigeria | 76.15 | 4.7 | 71.1 | 5.0 |
| Pakistan | 65.00 | 4.0 | 71.1 | 5.0 |
| Ethiopia | 61.28 | 3.8 | 60.8 | 4.3 |
| Congo | | | 53.8 | 3.8 |
| Myanmar | 45.30 | 2.8 | 45.1 | 3.2 |
| Tanzania | 30.16 | 1.9 | 34.2 | 2.4 |
| Kenya | 27.71 | 1.7 | 29.4 | 2.1 |
| World Total | 1,634.20 | 100.0 | 1,410 | 100.0 |

With the growing world population and people's innate aspirations for improved life, a central and collective global issue in the new century is to sustain socio-economic growth within the constraints of the Earth's limited natural resources while at the same time preserving the environment. This target—sustainable development—can only be met by ensuring energy sustainability.

## 1.2. ENERGY RESOURCES: STATUS AND TRENDS

The energy resources presently being consumed in the world can be broadly classified into three broader groups: fossil fuels, nuclear power, and renewable energy. In future, however, hydrogen is being deemed to be at the heart of the energy infrastructure.

### 1.2.1 FOSSIL FUELS

Fossil fuels, deposits of once living organisms, principally consist of carbon and hydrogen bonds. Since the advent of the industrial revolution, fossil fuels, in their various forms, have been the main source of energy supply. Fossil fuels are primarily classified into following three types: coal, oil and natural gas. Coal is the solid form of fossil fuels and is a hard, black coloured rock-like substance. It powered the industrial revolution in the nineteenth century that transformed human civilization. It is usually extracted from mines and comes in three main types: anthracite, bituminous and lignite. Towards the end of the nineteenth and early twentieth century, as human creativity exceeded expectations, fossil fuels saw their refined liquid phase, oil, that is more efficient than coal. Crude oil consists of many different organic compounds which are transformed into a wide range of products through a refining process. Oil is extracted from the earth through a drilling process. More recently, the world became familiarized with natural gas, the gaseous phase of fossil fuels, that is even more efficient. It is mainly composed of methane ($CH_4$). Natural gas is normally found entrapped in the earth's crust at varying depths and may or may not be in association with oil. Like oil, it is extracted through a drilling process. Natural gas is more attractive than coal and oil because of its higher calorific value and lower carbon dioxide emissions as shown in Table 1.3.

**Table 1.3:  Comparison of different types of fossil fuels in terms of energy content and carbon dioxide emission**

| Fuel | Specific energy content (kWh/kg) | Specific $CO_2$ emission (kg/kWh) |
|---|---|---|
| Coal | 6.7 | 0.37 |
| Crude oil | 12.7 | 0.26 |
| Natural gas (at N.T.P.— 0°C & 1bar) | 15.3 | 0.19 |

## 1.2.2 NUCLEAR POWER

Nuclear power is the energy derived from controlled nuclear reactions and is broadly classified into two types: nuclear fission and nuclear fusion. Nuclear fission is the splitting of a heavy atom into two or more parts, releasing huge amounts of energy. In nuclear fusion process energy is released as several small nuclei are combined to make a larger one whose mass is slightly smaller than the sum of the small ones. It is the same process that empowers the sun, where hydrogen nuclei are fused to form helium. However, nuclear fusion power is a future technology and all of the nuclear power being capitalized at present comes from the fission process. It is believed that in terms of energy yield, fusion would be a much richer process than fission. The research on nuclear fusion is at an early stage and it may take a good number of decades before it can be utilized for human energy requirements.

The world entered into the nuclear age on 2 December 1942 when nuclear fission reaction was successfully triggered for the first time in a research lab at the University of Chicago. The initial focus was to develop weapons for the Second World War. After the war, attention was paid to developing nuclear power for peaceful civilian application. Electricity was created from it for the first time in 1951, while the first commercial nuclear fission power plant became operational in Pennsylvania in 1957. In nuclear power plants the energy produced by splitting atoms of enriched uranium is capitalized to produce steam which in turn drives steam turbines to produce electricity.

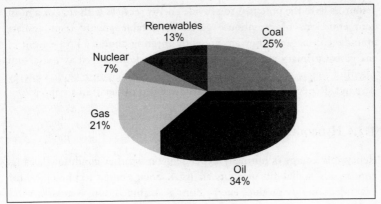

Figure 1.2: World primary energy supplies by fuel type, 2008

Nuclear power has played a major role in reducing the world's use of oil for electricity generation in recent decades. As of 2008, there were more than 430 nuclear power plants in operation in 31 countries across the world.[3] Nuclear power makes a contribution of nearly 7 per cent in the global primary energy supply mix as shown in Figure 1.2. In terms of electricity it contributes to over 15 per cent of the global generation.[12] Some countries greatly depend on it to meet their electricity demands. In 2007, France, for example, from its 59 nuclear power plants, produced around 78 per cent of the country's total electricity.[13] The United States has the largest number of nuclear power plants in the world—currently there are 104 power plants supplying around 20 per cent of the overall electricity in the country.[3]

### 1.2.3 RENEWABLE ENERGY

Renewable energy, as the name implies, is the energy obtained from natural sources such as wind power, solar energy, hydropower, biomass energy and geothermal energy. Renewable energy is considered to be one of the most prominent solutions to future energy challenges, i.e. growing energy demand, depleting fossil fuel reserves, energy insecurity and global warming. Renewable energy sources have also been important for humans since the beginning of civilization: Biomass, for example, has been used for heating, cooking and steam production; wind has been used for moving ships; both hydropower and wind have been used for powering mills to grind grains. Renewable energy sources that use indigenous resources have the potential to provide energy services with zero or almost zero emissions of greenhouse gases. Renewable energy resources are abundant in nature. They are presently meeting almost 13.5 per cent of the global primary energy demands and are acknowledged as a vital and plentiful source of energy that can indeed meet the entire world's energy demand. Renewable energy has been discussed in detail in Chapter 7.

### 1.2.4 HYDROGEN

Renewable energy is normally dependent on weather conditions and its continuous availability remains an issue. Solar energy technologies, for example, can only produce energy during sunshine hours. Similarly, wind turbines can be effective only in the presence of a certain degree of wind speed. Hydrogen, in the capacity of energy vector, is expected to be the optimum solution for intermittency and storage of energy produced by renewables. Apart from its storage and transmission characteristics, hydrogen is also suitable for end uses.

In coming decades, the world is expected to witness the dawn of a new economy, which will use hydrogen as an energy carrier. The paradigm shift will alter the nature of financial markets and political and social institutions, just as coal and steam did at the beginning of the Industrial Age. The vision of building an energy infrastructure that uses hydrogen as an energy carrier—a concept called the 'hydrogen economy'—consists of an economic system in which energy is supplied by renewable resources and hydrogen is used as the energy vector, medium of energy storage and transportation as represented in Figure 1.3.

The transition of the world energy system to hydrogen as a fuel is quite logical and becomes clearer when one takes a look at the historical energy production sequence. Each successive transition from one source to another—from wood to coal, from coal to oil—has entailed a shift to fuels that were not only harnessed and transported more economically, but also had a lower carbon content and higher hydrogen content. It is also evident that at each step greater energy density is being achieved. The third wave of decarburization is now at its threshold, with natural gas use growing fastest, in terms of use, among the fossil fuels. The fourth wave, the production and use of pure hydrogen, is also on the horizon. Its major drivers are technological advances, renewed concern about the security and price of oil and gasoline, and growing pressure to address local air pollution and climate change.

Hydrogen is the simplest and one of the most plentiful elements in the universe. Despite this, hydrogen does not occur naturally as a gas. That is, it always combines with other elements. Chemically bound hydrogen is found abundantly on Earth: in water, fossil fuels and all living things. Yet, it rarely exists in free-floating nature. Instead, it has to be extracted from water or from hydrocarbons. Hydrogen can be primarily produced through reformation of natural gas, electrolysis of water, or partial oxidation of heavy fossil fuels such as diesel. In the 'hydrogen economy' scenario, energy produced from renewables will be utilized to carry out electrolysis of water to yield hydrogen.

Hydrogen's potential use in fuel and energy applications includes powering vehicles, running turbines or fuel cells to produce electricity and generating heat and electricity for buildings. Hydrogen is a unique fuel

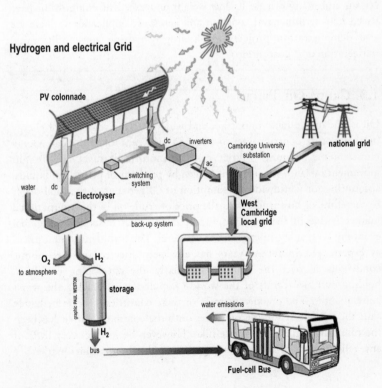

Figure 1.3: An impression of the hydrogen economy vision.
Courtesy Cambridge University

with unmatched properties, one of them being its ability to produce electricity electrochemically in fuel cells with high efficiencies. In addition to having high (75–80 per cent) efficiencies, hydrogen fuel cells are much cleaner (the only by-product being water) and quiet (i.e. no moving parts). They are versatile, as they can be used for large-scale power generation in central power plants, as well as for small-scale electricity production in the distributed mode. As such, there is no doubt that hydrogen fuel cell generation capacity will grow rapidly.

Around the globe, there are a large number of hydrogen-based national and international programmes that may be quoted here as examples of activity on this front. Owing to its unique properties, hydrogen has become a suitable fuel for motive power and has gained the attention of many leading automobile companies. Hydrogen-fuelled vehicles are being produced by BMW, Ford, General Motors, Honda, Toyota, Mazda, Nissan and many others. Its low weight and excellent combustion have paved its way into naval, aviation and aerospace applications. There are also demonstration projects for hydrogen-hydride air conditioning, refrigeration and heat pumps.

## 1.3. Crude Oil Prices

Oil is one of the most important and widely serving resources of energy in the world, contributing to over 34 per cent of the total energy requirements. Around 95 per cent of motorized travel and freight movement by land, sea and air is fuelled by products of petroleum liquids, accounting for worldwide consumption of 60 per cent of the total oil. It is, therefore, of no surprise that the price of crude oil in the international market is one of the most important factors that influence the global economy both at the micro- and macro level. The turbulence in oil prices as experienced in recent years has adversely affected socio-economic conditions all over the world. Particularly, the developing countries, holding over two-thirds of the world's population, are facing the worst consequences. The practice in most of these countries is to immediately shift the burden of surging oil prices onto the common man as has been the case during the recent price-hike. However, he receives very little, if any, relief in case of a slump in oil prices in the international market.

## 1.3.1 Price-Volatility

Oil prices in the international market have been extremely volatile over the last few years as can be seen from Figure 1.4. As a matter of fact, oil prices have been making headlines for a rapid growth since 1999. The average annual price of Organization of Petroleum Exporting Countries (OPEC) crude oil, standing at US$12.3 per barrel in 1998, reaching US$36.1 barrel in 2004, hit the US$69.1 mark in 2007. Since the latter half of 2007, oil prices experienced an unprecedented fluctuation. The price of a barrel of oil, standing at US$67 in June 2007, crossed the psychological landmark limit of US$100 per barrel for the first time in history on 3 January 2008. The continuously swelling oil prices reached as high as US$147/barrel in the second week of July in 2008.[6] This wave of surging oil prices, recording a nearly 120 per cent increment in almost a year, was being regarded as the second oil shock after the 1973 oil embargo saga. Shortly afterwards, in the aftermath of the ongoing credit crunch that has hit the whole world in general and the developed countries in particular, oil prices started to crash. Despite this slump, the annual average price of oil managed to grow as much as US$94.5/barrel. Since the beginning of 2009, oil prices are again on the rise—the monthly average price had grown to US$71.7/barrel in August 2009 from US$38.6 in December 2008.[14]

The recent dip in oil prices is reported to be a consequence of speculative trading, as was the case with the preceding price-hike. The price-volatility vividly indicates the increasing fragility of the global oil market. There is already enormous pressure on the oil producers' cartel OPEC from some of its member states to curtail production capacity in order to maintain the oil price over US$100/barrel. Some of the major producing countries are taking the stance that a price below US$100/barrel is not 'sustainable'. Therefore, it is clear that oil prices are set to rise further in the future. It is fair to say that over the last six decades, the world has cherished an extraordinarily 'cheap oil age'—a closer examination suggests that from 1948 to 1998, in an inflation-adjusted scenario, oil prices actually came down by 37 per cent.

It is also vital to understand that there is no more primary oil left in the world. The oil recovery is, therefore, becoming much more complicated and expensive. Regardless of the recent price-slump, amongst the concerned circles, the perception of oil has amazingly changed—five years ago, an oil price above $60 per barrel was unthinkable. Today, oil prices below $100 are regarded as being 'cheap'. It is interesting to note that in March 2005, when the crude oil price was around US$55/barrel, hardly any one could believe it when the US investment bank Goldman Sachs predicted that oil could reach US$100/barrel. As per European Union Energy Commissioner Andris Piebalgs, 'everyone took it as a joke.' Having seen it happen within three years, he issues the warning: 'We can't rule out USD 200/barrel because in the last two years, all of us have been completely mistaken, thinking that what is in fact happening now was impossible'.[15]

## 1.3.2 PRICE-HIKE: DRIVING FACTORS

Apart from economic and trade agreements on the part of oil cartels, there are a number of factors that have traditionally been driving oil prices. These include a growing demand for oil across the world especially in emerging economies such as China and India, receding excess production capacity and weak position of the US dollar. Political unrest, military conflicts and extreme weather events are also amongst the factors that have traditionally played their role in causing rapid rise in global oil prices.

### 1.3.2.1 Geo-strategic Conflicts

Man-made issues such as international geo-political and geo-strategic conflicts resulting in full-fledged military attacks and wars, and sabotage and terrorist activities on a relatively smaller scale have traditionally resulted in higher oil prices. The Persian Gulf region, housing nearly over 65 per cent of the world's oil reserves, as a whole suffers from quite a volatile geo-political situation as it has seen a number of conflicts over past few decades. The track record of oil prices indicate that several such issues like Yom Kippur War (1973), Iranian Revolution (1979), Iran/Iraq War (1980), First Gulf War (1991), unrest in Venezuela (2002) and Second Gulf War (2003) have all contributed to a rapid increment in crude oil price.[16] There are serious reservations regarding the security of oil production and supply channels of some of the Middle-Eastern and African countries—sabotage activities in Iraq and Nigeria are amongst the major challenges that are presently haunting the international oil market.

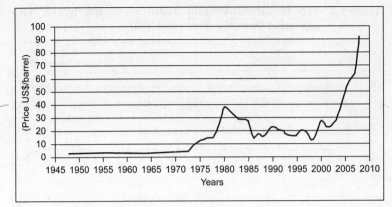

Figure 1.4: Growth in average annual oil prices since 1948 (nominal)

### 1.3.2.2 The China–India Factor

The rapidly growing oil demand from China and India is adding to the pressure on the international oil markets. China and India are the two countries with the highest rate of growth in oil use, whose combined populations account for a third of the world total. In particular, the Chinese industrial boom is pushing the country's demands for an increased proportion of global oil—China has already surpassed Japan to become the second highest consumer of oil in the world as shown in Table 1.4. In the next two decades, China's oil consumption is expected to grow at a rate of 7.5 per cent per year and India's at 5.5 per cent (compared to a 1 per cent growth for the industrialized countries).[6] The role of the two countries is set to become even more crucial in the days to come. The Energy Information Administration (EIA) projects that China's demand for oil will more than double by 2025, reaching 14.2 million barrels per day, of which more than 10.9 million barrels will be imported. As a result, China's net imports will have increased by 8 million barrels per day since 2004.[17]

**Table 1.4: Top 10 oil consuming countries in the world, data extracted from IEA Statistics 2007[18]**

| Country | Consumption (million barrels/day) |
|---------|-----------------------------------|
| USA | 20.9 |
| China | 7.0 |
| Japan | 5.2 |
| Russia | 2.7 |
| India | 2.7 |
| Germany | 2.6 |
| S. Korea | 2.3 |
| Canada | 2.3 |
| Brazil | 2.2 |
| Mexico | 2.1 |

### 1.3.2.3 Natural Catastrophes

Natural catastrophes such as earthquakes, floods and hurricanes can also lead to supply disruptions thus pushing oil prices. Offshore, both fixed and floating facilities are prone to be hit by hurricanes. Similarly, onshore exploration and refining facilities can also be impacted by severe weather conditions, i.e. tropical weather systems, and the flooding that often accompanies them. For example, the August 2005 hurricane, Katrina, shut down large portions of oil and gas production in the Gulf of Mexico at a time when worldwide energy output was already stretched thin. While the storm's impact was most acute in the United States, it also sent fuel costs higher around the globe, squeezing consumers. Katrina caused prices to rise to an all time record high, almost US$72/barrels.

### 1.3.3 DEPLETING OIL RESERVES

A combination of constrained production capacity and growing fears of a rapid depletion of oil reserves in the world is also an important factor that has been playing a role behind-the-scene in pushing oil prices up. In recent years, the global oil infrastructure, particularly with regard to extraction- and refining-capacity, has been stretched to the limit. The production capacity of various oil rich countries in the world, such as Iraq and Venezuela, has also been curtailed. The aspect of depleting oil reserves, despite its critical role, for various reasons, is not being publicly acknowledged by market forces.

The world's ultimate conventional oil reserves are estimated at 2000 billion barrels. This is the amount of production that will have been produced when production eventually ceases. The demand for oil has grown rapidly over the last few decades as shown in Table 1.5.[19] The surging demand for oil has already stretched production to the limits—in mid-2002, there was over 6 million barrels per day of excess production capacity, but by mid-2003 the daily excess capacity was below 2 million barrels which further skewed to less than one million barrels by 2006.[3]

**Table 1.5: Growth in World Oil Demand**

| Year | World population (Millions) | Average daily oil demand (Million barrels/day) | World average per capita consumption (barrels/year) |
|------|------|------|------|
| 1965 | 3,310 | 31.23 | 3.65 |
| 1968 | 3,520 | 39.04 | 4.05 |
| 1971 | 3,750 | 51.76 | 5.04 |
| 1974 | 3,990 | 59.39 | 5.44 |
| 1977 | 4,200 | 63.66 | 5.53 |
| 1980 | 4,410 | 64.14 | 5.31 |
| 1983 | 4,650 | 58.05 | 4.56 |
| 1986 | 4,890 | 61.76 | 4.60 |
| 1989 | 5,150 | 65.88 | 4.67 |
| 1992 | 5,400 | 66.95 | 4.52 |
| 1995 | 5,610 | 69.88 | 4.54 |
| 1998 | 5,870 | 72.92 | 4.51 |
| 2001 | 6,140 | 75.99 | 4.53 |
| 2004 | 6,400 | 82.35 | 4.67 |
| 2007 | 6,610 | 87.45 | 4.82 |

Different countries are at different stages of their reserve depletion curves. Some, such as the United States, have passed their midpoint and are in terminal decline, whereas others such as UK and Norway are close to midpoint. However, the five major Gulf producers—Saudi Arabia, Iraq, Iran, Kuwait and United Arab Emirates—are at an early stage of depletion and can exert a swing role, making up the difference between world demand and what others can supply.

There is a consensus among experts that the world's midpoint of reserve depletion will be reached when 1,000 billion barrels of oil have been produced—that is to say, half the ultimate reserves of 2,000 billion barrels. It is estimated that around 1,000 billion barrels have already been consumed and 1,000 billion barrels of proven oil reserves are left in the world.[20] According to a BP statistical review of oil reserves in 2008, the reserve to production ratio for North America, Southern and Central America, Europe and Eurasia, Asia Pacific, Middle East, and Africa were 14, 50, 22, 14, 79, and 33 years, respectively. The reserve to production ratio for the whole world is reported to be equal to 42 years.[21] In the backdrop of a continuous growth in oil demand—as according to the US Department of energy, by 2025 the global demand could be as much as 110 barrels/day[22]—the global reserves are actually going to run out much quicker than 42 years.

A growing number of opinions among energy experts suggest that global oil production will probably peak sometime during this decade, between 2004 and 2010 as indicated in Table 1.6.[23]

**Table 1.6:  Various projections of the global oil reserves and the peak year (billions of barrels)**

| Author | Affiliation | Year | Estimated ultimate reserves | Peak Year |
|---|---|---|---|---|
| Hubert | Shell | 1969 | 2,100 | 2000 |
| Bookout | Shell | 1989 | 2,000 | 2010 |
| Mackenzie | Researcher | 1996 | 2,600 | 2007-2019 |
| Appleby | BP | 1996 | | 2010 |
| Invanhoe | Consultant | 1996 | | 2010 |
| Edwards | University of Colorado | 1997 | 2,836 | 2020 |
| Campbell | Consultant | 1997 | 1,800-2,000 | 2010 |
| Bernaby | ENI | 1998 | | 2005 |
| Schollenberger | Amoco | 1988 | | 2015-2035 |
| IEA | OECD | 1998 | 2,800 | 2010-2020 |
| EIA | DOE | 1998 | 4,700 | 2030 |
| Laherrere | Consultant | 1999 | 2,700 | 2010 |
| USGS | International Department | 2000 | 3,270 | |
| Salameh | Consultant | 2000 | 2,000 | 2004-2005 |
| Deffeyes | Princeton University | 2001 | 1,800-2,100 | 2004 |

A siren call regarding energy security was also raised in a speech recently made by the British Ambassador to the US, Sir David Manning. He eloquently put forward the case thus: 'The International Energy Agency predicts that, if we do nothing, global oil demand will reach 121 million barrels per day by 2030, up from 85 million barrels today. That will require increasing production by 37 million barrels per day over the next 25 years, of which 25 million barrels per day has yet to be discovered. That is, we'll have to find four petroleum systems that are each the size of the North Sea. Production from existing fields is dropping at about 5% per year'. Only one barrel of oil is now being discovered for every four consumed as highlighted in Figure 1.5. Globally, the discovery rate of untapped oil peaked in the late 1960s. Over the past decade, oil production has been falling in 33 of the world's 48 largest oil-producing countries, including six of the 13 members of OPEC.[24]

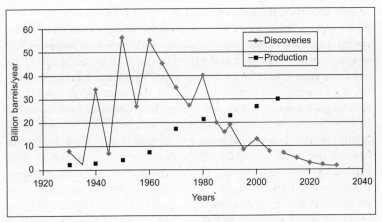

Figure 1.5: An overview of global oil discoveries and production

## 1.3.4 SOCIO-ECONOMIC RAMIFICATIONS OF SURGING OIL PRICES

The volatile oil prices are having serious implications for global economy. An analysis of global energy statistics reveals that more than 90 per cent of the countries in the world are net importers of oil. The higher and unstable oil prices place the economic prosperity of oil-importing countries, especially the poorest developing countries, at major risk. All aspects of the modern age, i.e. dwelling, education, health, manufacturing, trading, transportation, and agriculture having become energy intensive and more expensive. The cost of living thus rises exacerbating the poverty level in the world. In future, the combination of substantial rise in oil prices and disruption in supplies is going to be fatal—disruptive supplies and higher oil prices resulting in a combination of higher inflation, higher unemployment, lower exchange rates and lower real output would adversely affect the economies of oil-importing countries over the long term. The most important thing to be concerned about is the reality that when people have to spend more money on oil, this would mean that there is lesser to spend on other needs such as food, and other living and recreational expenses. The poor will face the heat of the consequent economic crisis first and the hardest, both nationally and internationally. Nevertheless, eventually, all would be affected.

The rising oil prices would also impact the global food scenario as the recent food crisis in the world was also linked to the surging fuel prices. In many parts of the world including USA, Brazil, India, and Southern African countries, the growing trend of biofuel production at the cost of food crops is being regarded as one of the key phenomenons having contributed to the food crisis especially with regard to the price hike of wheat, maize and rice. These price hikes in turn are being considered to have triggered the inflation in food prices.[25] Professor John Beddington, the chief scientific adviser of the UK, has also suggested that the global rush to grow biofuels was compounding the problem of food crisis.[26]

From a macroeconomic perspective, with increased oil prices, the balance of trade between countries and exchange rates would also change. Net oil importing countries would experience deterioration in their balance of payments, putting downwards pressure on exchange rates. Consequently, imports would become more expensive and exports less valuable, leading to a drop in net national income. Higher oil/energy prices are going to result in budget deficits in oil-importing countries across the board.

## 1.4. ENERGY AND GLOBAL WARMING

The global environmental scene has changed dramatically over the last century. Global warming is one of the biggest challenges humanity is facing. The energy sector has played a key role in global warming. Energy, during its production, distribution and consumption, is responsible for producing environmentally harmful substances. Particularly, fossil fuels have been considered to be the prime source of Greenhouse Gas (GHG) emissions. Greenhouse gases naturally blanket the earth and trap a fraction of the heat of the sun that enters the earth's atmosphere producing the greenhouse effect. This phenomenon of an increase in the global average atmospheric temperature, as a consequence of this greenhouse effect, is referred as global warming that leads to climate change. Estimates suggest that since the advent of the industrial revolution in the nineteenth century, the level of greenhouse gases in the atmosphere has grown from 280 parts per million (ppm) carbon dioxide equivalent ($CO_2$e) to 430ppm $CO_2$e. Scientific circles believe that in order to avoid catastrophic implications, the level should be limited to 450–550ppm $CO_2$e.[27] The growing concentration of greenhouse gases in the atmosphere has increased the global average temperature by 0.5°C over the last century. It is predicted that the global mean temperature may further rise by as much as 4.5°C by the end of this century.

Energy systems vary in terms of their potential to generate greenhouse gases. Table 1.7 provides a comparison of $CO_2$ emissions from different energy systems.

Energy consumption is regarded as an index to measure the contribution towards global warming. The average value of the per capita energy consumption in industrialized and developed countries is almost six times greater than that in developing countries. The former US Vice President Al Gore, in his famous work on global warming that won him the 2007 Noble Peace Prize, heavily criticized the United States of America for turning a blind eye to the issue of global warming. According to him the US stance on the Kyoto Protocol is unfavourable despite the fact that it alone is responsible for more than 30 per cent of the world GHG emissions. He concludes that a US citizen emits nearly six times greater amount of GHG as compared to the world average emission as indicated in Figure 1.6. Whereas, compared to African or South East Asian countries such as Pakistan, India, and Bangladesh, the per capita carbon emission in the US is around 22 times higher.[28] According to the World Wildlife Fund (WWF), in terms of echo footprint, an index of sustainability, the excessive consumption of natural resources by the developed countries is imposing serious implications on the eco system of the planet.[29] This evidence indicates that the responsibility for the disturbance in the global ecosystem, leading to the phenomenon of global warming and climate change, rests to a great extent on the shoulders of the developed and industrial countries of the world.

Global warming is leading to a pattern of more frequent, more erratic, more unpredictable and more extreme weather events that are affecting

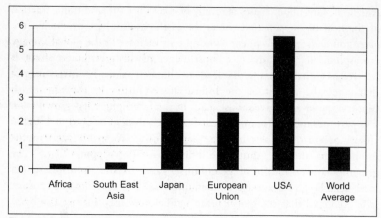

Figure 1.6: Annual per capita carbon emission in tonnes

more people. The UN panel on climate change expects increasing deaths, injuries and illness from heat waves, floods, storms, forest fires and droughts, as a result of global warming.[30] Evidence suggests that weather-related disasters have quadrupled over the last two decades. According to a recent report from a leading international charity, Oxfam, from an average of 120 disasters a year in the early 1980s, there are now as many as 500, with the rise to be attributed to unpredictable weather conditions caused by global warming. The year 2007 has seen floods in South Asia, and across the breadth of Africa and Mexico that have affected more than 250 million people. The number of people affected by disasters has risen by 68 per cent, from an average of 174 million a year from 1985 to 1994 to 254 million a year from 1995 to 2004.[31]

Several hundred million people in densely populated coastal regions—particularly river deltas in Asia—are threatened by rising sea levels and the increasing risk of flooding. More than one-sixth of the world's population lives in areas affected by water sources from glaciers and snow pack that will very likely disappear.[32] The number of people at risk of flooding by coastal storm surges is projected to increase from the current 75 million to 200 million by 2080, when sea levels may have risen by more than one foot. In the United Nations' list of countries under severe threat by global warming, Bangladesh is on the top. Being a low-lying and densely populated country, Bangladesh would be worst hit by any rise in the sea level. Coastal areas will experience erosion and inundation due to intensification of tidal action. A rise in seawater will enable saline water to intrude further inland during high tides. Destruction of agricultural land and loss of sweet water fauna and flora could also occur. The shoreline will retreat inland, causing changes in the coastal boundary and coastal configuration. The process will also shrink the land area of Bangladesh. Worst scenarios suggest that by the year 2050, one-third of the country could be under water, making more than 70 million people homeless.[33]

**Table 1.7: Comparison of $CO_2$ emissions from different energy systems**

| Type of power plant | Fuel/type of energy | CO2/(kg/kWh) |
|---|---|---|
| Steam power plant | Lingnite | 1.04-1.16 |
| Steam power plant | Hard coal | 0.83 |
| Gas power plant | Pit coal | 0.79 |
| Thermal power plant | Fuel oil (heavy) | 0.76 |
| Gas turbine power plant | Natural gas | 0.58 |
| Nuclear power plant (pressurised water) | Uranium | 0.025 |
| Thermal power plant | Natural gas | 0.45 |
| Solar thermal power plant | Solar energy | 0.1-0.15 |
| Photovoltaic power plant | Solar energy | 0.1-0.2 |
| Wind power plant | Solar/wind energy | 0.02 |
| Hydro-electric power plant | Hydropower | 0.004 |

The impact of global warming on human health is also immense. The World Health Organization (WHO) estimates that global warming is already causing about five million extra cases of severe illness a year and more than 150,000 extra deaths. By 2030, the number of climate-related diseases is likely to more than double, with a dramatic increase in heat-related deaths caused by heart failure, respiratory disorders, and the spread of infectious diseases and malnutrition from crop failures. Countries with coastlines along the Indian and Pacific Oceans and sub-Saharan Africa would suffer a disproportionate share of the extra health burden. According to WHO experts, many of the most important diseases in poor countries, such as diarrhoea and malnutrition, are highly sensitive to climate. Also, that the health sector is already struggling to control these diseases and climate change threatens to undermine these efforts.[3]

Although global warming is a threat to the whole planet, its intensity is not uniformly distributed. One of the significant heartbreaks of global warming is that developed and industrialized countries are acutely responsible for the phenomenon but the heavier price is to be paid by the poor and developing nations. In the backdrop of the trajectory of the issue, the Kyoto Protocol urges the industrialized countries to reduce their collective emission of greenhouse gases by 5.2 per cent compared to the year 1990. However, compared to the emissions levels that would be expected by 2010 without the Protocol, this target represents a 29 per cent cut. The goal is to lower overall emissions of six greenhouse gases— carbon dioxide, methane, nitrous oxide, sulfur hexaluoride, HFCs and PFCs—calculated as an average over the five-year period of 2008–12. National targets range from 8 per cent reductions for the European Union and some others to 7 per cent for the US, and 6 per cent for Japan. The developing countries of the world have been spared emission reduction obligations not only in the Kyoto Protocal but also in its predecessor accords such as Agenda 21.

Professor Jonathan Patz of the University of Wisconsin in Madison, the lead author of a study on global warming published in the world famous scientific journal, *Nature* says that it is incumbent on those countries bearing the greatest responsibility for climate change to show moral leadership. He goes on to say: 'Those least able to cope and least responsible for the greenhouse gases that cause global warming are most affected. Herein exists an enormous global ethical challenge.'[35] Sir Nicholas Stern, a former chief economist of the World Bank, in his much respected and publicized report on climate change produced in 2006, also acknowledges that the developed countries should realize their responsibility towards addressing global warming. In his set of findings, known as the 'Stern Review', he concludes that climate change is the greatest and widest-ranging challenge mankind has ever faced. All countries will be affected by climate change, but the poorest countries will suffer earliest and most. Loss of biodiversity is another inevitable consequence—more than 40 per cent species are likely to face extinction. He further urges that climate change should be fully integrated into development policy, and rich countries should honour pledges to increase support through overseas development assistance.[36]

To tackle global warming, a radical change in human attitude towards environment and consumption of natural resources is required. A major shift in energy consumption practices—from the reliance on currently employed environmentally dangerous resources to the environmentally friendly ones—would be imperative to attain sustainable development. To safeguard the future of coming generations, the world thus has to move towards low-carbon energy systems.

## References

1. Energy and Development, World Energy Outlook 2004.
2. Gordon Weynand, Energy Sector Assessment for US Aid/Pakistan, United States Agency for International Development, June 2007.
3. M. Asif and T. Muneer, 'Energy Supply, its Demand and Security Issues for Developed and Emerging Economies', *Renewable & Sustainable Energy Reviews*, Vol. 11, issue 7, September 2007.
4. I. Dincer, M. Rosen, 'Energy, Environment and Sustainable Development', *Applied Energy*, 64, 1999.
5. International Energy Outlook 2005.
6. M. Asif and M.T. Khan, 'Surging Energy Prices: Socio-Economic Implications for the Under-Developed Countries', presented at the conference 'Nature' Knowledge, Power, Uppsala, 15-17 August 2008.
7. Half of the world's population to live in cities by the end of 2008: UN, United Nations Radio, 26 February 2008.
8. UNFPA State of the World Population 2007.
9. Human Development Report 2007-08, UNDP.
10. Poverty, Energy and Society, Energy Forum, The Baker Institute, Rice University.
11. Energy Services for the Millennium Development Goals, UNDP/World Bank, 2006.
12. Factsheets and FAQs, IAEA.
13. Mycle Schneider, The reality of France's aggressive nuclear power push, *Bulletin of the Atomic Scientists*, 3 June 2008.
14. Reference prices, Organization of the Petroleum Exporting countries, http://www.opec.org/Home/basket.aspx
15. 'EU energy commissioner says oil could reach 200 dollars a barrel', AFP, 3 March 2008.
16. M. Asif and M.T. Khan, 'Possible US-Iran Military Conflict and its Implications Upon Global Sustainable Development', *Journal of Sustainable Development*, Vol. 2, No. 1, in March 2009.
17. China's Oil Consumption, *The Washington Times*, 19 April 2006.
18. IEA Statistics, 2007.
19. Andrew McKillop, Oil Shock and Energy Transition, Vertus Sustineo Asset Management, New York, Former Expert—Policy and Programming, Divn A-Policy, DGXVII-Energy, European Commission Presentation to POGEE Conference, Karachi, May 2008.
20. M. Asif, J. Currie and T. Muneer, 'The Role of Renewable and Non-Renewable Sources for Meeting Future UK Energy Needs', *International Journal of Nuclear Governance, Economy and Ecology*, Vol. 1, No. 4, 2007.
21. BP Statistical Review 2008.
22. International Energy Outlook 2006.
23. Salameh M., 'Oil Crises: Historic Perspective', *Encyclopedia of Energy*, Vol. 4, Amsterdam: Elsevier; 2004.
24. British Ambassador Sir David Manning Discusses Energy: A Burning Issue for Foreign Policy at Stanford University, British Embassy, Washington D.C., 3/17/2006.
25. John Vidal, 'The Looming Food Crisis', *The Guardian*, 29 March 2007.
26. James Randerson, 'Food crisis will take hold before climate change, warns chief scientist', *The Guardian*, 7 March 2008.
27. 'Stern Report: the key points', *The Guardian*, 30 October 2006.
28. *An Inconvenient Truth*.

29. Living Planet Report 2004, WWF.
30. Volker Mrasek, Climate Change Impact More Extensive than Thought, *Spiegel Online International*, 3 February 2007.
31. *Reuters*, 25 November 2007.
32. Climate Change 2007: Impacts, Adaptation and Vulnerability, International Panel on Climate Change.
33. Human Development Report 2007-2008, UN, November 2007.
34. The Environment in the News, UNEP, 17 November 2005.
35. Steve Connor, 'Climate Change Linked to 150,000 Fatalities', *The Global Report*, 23-30 November 2005.
36. 'Stern Review: The Economics of Climate Change', HM Treasury, UK.

# 2

# Energy and its Wider Dimensions—II

## 2.1. THE BIRTH OF THE OIL-AGE

In the early days of the industrial revolution, forests and coal resources were in abundance and were sufficient to meet energy demands. However, as human creativity exceeded expectations, producing a more efficient energy technology was needed. The world, therefore, saw a switchover from wood and coal to oil that is a more efficient form of fuel than the other two. Oil is one of the most vibrant resources of energy the world is familiar with. It was initially discovered during the first half of the nineteenth century and the first modern oil well in the world was drilled in Baku (Azerbaijan) in 1847 at Bibi-Eybat oil field.[1] In 1857 and 1858, oil wells were drilled respectively in Bend (Romania) and Ontario (Canada). The first commercial oil well, however, was drilled in 1859 in Pennsylvania (USA). Within a decade there was tremendous progress in USA in terms of oil discoveries, its refining and trading. Contemporarily, there were quite significant developments in other parts of the world, particularly in Azerbaijan, then controlled by Russia. Shortly afterwards the oil business rapidly flourished. Some of the landmark developments the last quarter of the nineteenth century witnessed include: formation of oil companies (including some of the major companies of today i.e. Royal Dutch/Shell, ExxonMobil) and trading exchanges, construction of refineries, foreign investments in oil exploration and processing, initiation of international trading, and development of oil-based combustion engines. In the form of oil, the world found a more efficient form of energy to accelerate industrial and economical growth. In 1885, Gottlieb Wilhelm Daimler, a German engineer, developed the initial model of the world's first internal combustion engine-based automobile. Towards the end of the 1890s, the appetite for oil was on a rise within the industrialized world, above all Britain, that was still the predominant political, military, and economic power in the world. With the advent of the twentieth century, oil started to replace coal as the principal fuel to propel economic, industrial and military developments across the world.

## 2.2. LOCALIZED EXISTENCE OF OIL AND GAS RESERVES

Natural gas is the most recent of the three forms of fuels to be capitalized. Although natural gas was commercially utilized for the first time in 1821 in New York, it started making a considerable impact on the international energy markets by the middle of the 20th century.[2] Currently oil and gas are jointly contributing to around 56 per cent of global energy requirements and they play a major role in technological and economic advancement across the world. In terms of existence, both oil and gas are extremely localized by their very nature. Vast majority of their resources are found in relatively confined regions. For example, as of 2009, more than 88 per cent of the world oil reserves exist within 10 countries. The Middle East is the oil headquarter of the world. A detailed analysis suggests that only five countries in the region: Saudi Arabia, Iran, Iraq, Kuwait and the United Arab Emirates hold 64 per cent of the world oil reserves as highlighted in the Figure 2.1. The situation with natural gas is even more intense. Statistics indicate that of the remaining known gas reserves in the world, equivalent to 6,260 trillion cubic feet (tcf), around 57 per cent are shared by only three countries: Russia, Iran, and Qatar as shown in Figure 2.2. The top five countries jointly hold 64 per cent of the total reserves.[3]

The localized existence of oil reserves is a phenomenon that is not new but dates back to the early days of the oil-era. Figures suggest that the annual oil production in the world, 300 tons in 1850, had grown to around 22.5 million tons in 1891.[4] Although oil was being produced in several other countries, particularly the Dutch East Indies (now known as Indonesia) and Romania, over 90 per cent of the world production came from USA and Azerbaijan. Of the total production of 22.5 million tons, 9.5 million tons came from the US and 10.9 million tons from Azerbaijan.[4]

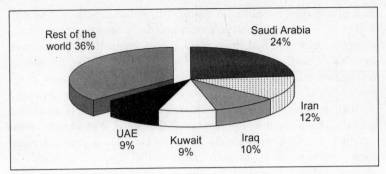

Figure 2.1: Remaining oil reserves in the world, 2009

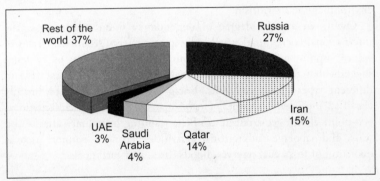

Figure 2.2: Remaining natural gas reserves in the world, 2009

## 2.3. ENERGY SECURITY

Energy security is the new addition in the catalogue of the challenges facing the global energy scenario. Energy security means consistent availability of sufficient energy in various forms at affordable prices. These conditions must prevail over the long term if energy is to contribute to sustainable development.

Human dependence upon energy has substantially increased in recent decades and the trend is continuous. Energy has attained the status of an indispensable strategic commodity, and ensuring its availability is one of the important responsibilities of governments across the world. Failure to ensure robust provision of interruption-free and affordable energy may result in serious financial, economic, and social losses. Breach of energy security is also prone to lead to national instability. A great number of countries in the world, particularly the industrialized mature economies, have placed energy security on top of their national policies. The high degree of multi-disciplinary inter-dependency amongst nations makes energy security vital both from national and international perspectives. In 2007, the German Foreign Minister Frank-Walter Steinmeier emphasized this fact by stating that maintaining global security in the twenty-first century will 'inseparably also be linked to energy security'.[5] At their summit in Brussels in March 2007, EU leaders adopted a roadmap, highlighted in the statement: 'Energy is what makes Europe tick. It is essential, then, for the European Union to address the major energy challenges facing us today and in future'. Similarly, the 2006 G8 summit held in St Petersburg had energy security on top of its agenda, to the surprise of many, as it was ahead of issues like education, health, trade, environment and terrorism.[6]

Owing to a great degree of dependency upon oil and gas, the international energy market generally gauges energy security in terms of secure supplies of these two commodities. The balance of evidence suggests that the present international energy market is vulnerable to different types of security risks. Energy security risks can be broadly classified into two categories. Firstly, man-made: such as international geo-political and geo-strategic conflicts resulting in military attacks and wars, and sabotage and terrorist activities. Secondly, natural: such as depletion of fossil fuel reserves, floods, fires, and earthquakes.

### 2.3.1 RISK ASSESSMENT

As with the supply of any commodity, the security of energy supply depends on the availability, size, and location of the reserves. The availability and the size of the reserves, and their location then determine the supply line: the exploitation, transportation and utilization arrangements. Conversely, the security of the exploitation, transportation and utilization arrangements then determines the security of energy supplies. Using a very simple model the major components of the risk can be identified. These are:

- the number of potential disruptive events
- the probability that given a potential disruptive event the supply line will be successfully disrupted
- the potential consequences of such a disruption

The contingency strategy could have three possible prongs. In order to decrease the risk, the number of potential disruptive events must be made as low as possible. Similarly, the probability that such an event will result in disruption must also be minimized. Finally, contingencies must be in place to successfully survive such a disruption.

The effect of human errors can be minimized by proper education and training of the operators, and by an ergonomically suitable design. Energy companies have always strived to achieve this, but failed spectacularly on a number of occasions, such as Windscale in the UK, Chernobyl in the Ukraine or Three Miles Island in the USA. However, based on past experience, the probability of human error can be estimated with relative accuracy. To determine the probability of sabotage or a military attack is difficult, since it depends upon various political and economic considerations. Nevertheless, it can be observed that such events are more frequent in unstable countries with many unresolved internal and external conflicts. Finally, the probability and severity of natural disasters can be, once again, estimated for various locations, based on geographical, geological, and historical data.

In order to minimize subsequent disruptions, or the effect of potentially disruptive events, defence systems or protection and safeguard systems are employed. These systems have been well-developed, and in order to maximize their effectiveness, they use the principles of defence in depth, redundancy, and diversity. All energy companies are geared to deal with human error and natural events, but problems can be encountered when dealing with sabotage or military attack. To minimize the impact of sabotage and military attack, security services must be called for assistance. These services are generally able to deal with these problems domestically in countries without serious internal and external conflicts. However, in countries with serious internal and external conflicts, the internal security forces can either be ineffective, particularly in remote locations, or their loyalty can be divided. In these cases, the governments sometimes require security support from other countries, which, while improving the defences, may make the internal conflicts worse and lead to an increasing frequency of attacks. Hence, stable countries, where the probability of an initial attack is already low, can, generally, protect their installations, but countries with significant internal and external conflicts, where the probability of an initial attack is already high, cannot, generally, protect their installations.

All developed countries have contingency plans in place to deal with the effects of supply disruptions in the form of strategic stock reserves as shown in Table 2.1. These plans used to be based on the diversity of the energy supplies, and the availability of strategic stocks. Due to the reliance on oil and natural gas by the developed countries, the principle of diversity of energy supplies holds less and less. All developed countries now deal with potential problems primarily by maintaining strategic reserves of oil supplies. By definition, the strategic reserves would be only available for certain activities and a certain period of time. This selectivity and time limit would prove a serious blow to the economies of developed countries if the reserves had to be used for a significant period of time.

**Table 2.1: Strategic oil reserves for selective OECD countries and region**

| Country/Group | Number of days the reserves can sustain |
| --- | --- |
| Japan | 123 |
| Germany | 92 |
| France | 83 |
| US | 80 |
| Canada | 76 |
| Italy | 72 |
| UK | 63 |
| Korea | 37 |
| OECD Europe | 82 |
| Average OECD | 80 |

Many of the world's leading oil-producing countries such as Iraq and Nigeria are politically unstable. The Middle Eastern region as a whole has quite a volatile geo-political situation and has experienced frequent conflicts over the last one hundred years. There are serious reservations regarding security of oil; production and supply channels of many countries are regarded as legitimate targets of radical elements because of various internal and external conflicts.

Getting oil from the well to the refinery and from there to the service station involves a complex transportation and storage system. Millions of barrels of oil are transported every day in tankers, pipelines, and trucks. This transportation system has always been a possible weakness of the oil industry, but it has become even more so in the present volatile geo-political situation. The threat of global terrorism has made the equation more complex. Tankers and pipelines are quite vulnerable targets. There are approximately 4,000 tankers employed, and any of them can be attacked in the high seas and more seriously while passing through narrow straits in hazardous areas. Pipelines, through which about 40 per cent of world's oil flows, are no less vulnerable and due to their length, are very difficult to protect. This makes pipelines potential targets for terrorists. In recent years there has been an increased number of pipeline sabotages in different countries particularly Nigeria and Iraq, sending shockwaves in international energy markets.

The above analysis indicates that the present situation is not sustainable, and that it cannot guarantee secure supplies of energy. There is thus an urgent need for diversity at the supply end, as the former British Prime Minister Winston Churchill once described the security of oil as: 'Safety and security lie in variety and variety alone'.[8,9] Given the challenges and opportunities, the diversity could be in the form of dependence upon multiple supply sources as well as exploitation of alternate energy resources.

## 2.4. OIL-DRIVEN FOREIGN POLICY AND GEO-STRATEGIC CONFLICTS IN THE TWENTIETH CENTURY

For almost a hundred years now, amongst other areas, global geo-politics has also been strongly influenced by pursuit for energy resources. Over this period fossil fuel resources in general and oil in particular have been amongst the most coveted commodities in the world. Not only have they played a crucial role in the architecture of foreign policies of the major economic and military powers but they have also led to geo-strategic conflicts in the world.

### 2.4.1 OIL'S INTRODUCTION INTO FOREIGN POLICY

With the advent of the twentieth century, as the economic benefits of the oil-era had been broadly realized, the desire to control oil resources also started to feature in Western politics. Of the two major oil hubs of the world—USA and Azerbaijan—the latter was in closer vicinity of Europe which was primarily the centre of global geo-political, technological and economic developments. There was an increased interest of European countries, particularly of Britain, in Azerbaijan's oil as nearly half of its total kerosene requirements were met from that source. Britain's oil interests in the region received a major boost when in 1901 a British subject was granted an exclusive 60-year concession to explore Iran's oil reserves.[10] By that time, Britain's industrial and economic primacy was being challenged by the dramatic rise of the German Reich, a new industrial great power on the European stage. With Africa and Asia long since claimed by some powerful nations, above all, Great Britain, Germany set out to develop a special economic sphere in the imperial provinces of the Ottoman Empire. Dynamically rising Germany was seen increasingly as the greatest threat to Britain's global dominance. The Berlin–Baghdad railway project initiated in 1903 was a move regarded by Britain as having long-term consequences not only for its political and economic interests in the region but also for the security of its oil supplies. Having already discovered oil in Mosul, Kirkuk, and Basra, the Germans also secured subsurface mineral rights, including for oil, along the path of the railway.[11,12]

One of the most important turning points in the history of modern energy was Britain's initiative in 1912 to convert its naval vessels to oil. It gave birth to a new geo-political age greatly influenced by oil. The idea was originally presented by Admiral Lord Fisher in 1882, the then Captain Jack Fisher, who urged that Britain should convert its naval fleet from bulky coal-fired propulsion to oil. Arguing that, 'in war, speed is everything', he strongly pushed for a switchover to oil that was a qualitatively far superior and efficient fuel.[11] In 1912, Fisher initiated the construction of the Queen Elizabeth, the first British battleship using only oil fuel. Shortly afterwards, Winston Churchill replaced Fisher as the First Lord of the Admiralty and saw the oil run-naval vessel programme home. The switchover from coal to oil, with the latter being a fuel that did not exist within British territorial borders unlike the former, was a strategic move that demanded a secure supply of oil to propel the new breed of naval vessels. The vigorous pursuit of oil thus became an important feature of the British campaign in several parts of the world. This was precisely the point where for the first time in history oil became an integral part of the foreign policy of a country. Churchill reacted to the situation saying: 'We must become the owners or at any rate the controllers at the source of at least a proportion of the oil which we require'.[11,13] With the First World War just round the corner, in 1912, in order to ensure supplies of oil for its naval vessels, Britain bought the controlling rights of the Anglo–Persian Oil Company (presently known as British Petroleum—BP). Having discovered oil in Iran in 1908, the company was formed in 1909 as a subsidiary by another British company namely the Burmah Oil Company.[14]

The multi-dimensional strategic power of oil became more evident during the First World War and the decades following it that experienced a significant change in the balance of power amongst the powerful states of the world—the terminal decline in the supremacy of some of the existing powers paralleled the equally amazing rise of some of the other powers. The conclusion of the Second World War presented the USA as arguably the most powerful nation on the global chessboard, a status that it has maintained thus far.

The fact that historically oil has not only influenced the foreign policies of nations but also led them to geo-strategic conflicts and wars can well be appreciated by reflecting upon the United State's stance towards the commodity. Its use as a weapon, as the USA imposed an embargo on Japan during the Japan–China war on 1 August 1941, is a typical paradigm. At that time Japan relied upon imports from USA for nearly 60 per cent of its total requirements. Shortly afterwards, Indonesia, contributing to almost 25 per cent of Japan's oil requirements also imposed an embargo on it. The embargos—imposed on Japan at a point when its economic growth, industrial revolution and war machinery relied on imports from the two countries to meet over 80 per cent of the requirements—created an oil crisis in the country. A large number of military historians, including R.A.C. Parker from Queens College Oxford, believe the oil embargo to be the key factor behind Japan's attack on Pearl Harbour that occurred four months later on 7 December 1941. Similarly, the Indonesian embargo is cited to be one of the main factors prompting Japan's invasion of the former in 1942.[15,16,17] During the course of the Second World War, like Japan, Germany also invaded Russia primarily for the sake of oil. In desperate need for oil for the German war machinery, in 1942, Adolf Hitler ordered his troops into the Caucasus as part of 'Operation Blue' to seize Baku's oil fields.[18]

## 2.4.2 POST-SECOND WORLD WAR ERA—US DOMINANCE ON OIL

At the eve of the Second World War the USA was quite self sufficient in its energy requirements as it produced over 60 per cent of the world's total oil. With the demand for oil on a rise across the world, US policy-makers were aware of the intense competition for it in the years ahead. The Middle East, where oil had recently been discovered, was of particular interest to the USA as can be seen from a 1944 US State Department memo that called oil 'a stupendous source of strategic power, and one of the greatest material prizes in world history.'[19] In August 1945, a top US State Department official wrote: 'A review of the diplomatic history of the past 35 years will show that petroleum has historically played a larger part in the external relations of the United States than any other commodity.'[19] The USA's aggressive approach is further substantiated by George Kennan, one of the main architects of the post-Second World War. US foreign policy, as he writes in a State Department Policy Planning Study in 1948: 'We have 50 per cent of the world's wealth, but only 6.3 per cent of its population. In this situation, our real job in the coming period is to devise a pattern of relationships which permit us to maintain this position of disparity. To do so, we have to dispense with all sentimentality. We should ease thinking about human rights, the raising of living standards and democratization'.[20]

Immediately after the end of the war the USA started manoeuvring to replace Britain and France, both greatly weakened by the war, as the predominant power in the Middle East region and principle beneficiary of its oil wealth. Control of the huge oil reserves of the Middle East was regarded as vital for US domination over the world in general and Europe in particular, as the then Secretary of Defence James Forrestal noted in his diary in 1947: 'Europe in the next ten years may shift from a coal to an oil economy, and therefore whoever sits on the valve of Middle East oil may control the destiny of Europe.'[21] Daniel Yergin in his famous book *The Prize: The Epic Quest for Oil, Money and Power* states: 'Petroleum would provide the way for Washington to punish and pressure its allies in Western Europe.'[21,22]

The 1956 Suez Canal crisis provided the vital leverage to the US to exert its hegemony over Middle Eastern oil. In response to Egyptian President Gamal Abdel Nasser's decision to nationalize the canal, the transport route for nearly two-thirds of Europe's oil, Britain, France and Israel rallied their troops to retake control. In the wake of a prolonged conflict, the allied forces approached the US for assistance as they feared an oil crisis in Europe due to a continuous supply disruption through the canal. The Eisenhower administration, however, made them withdraw their forces. Three years earlier there was another significant oil-motivated development in the region. In response to Iran's move to nationalize the Anglo–Iran Oil Company, previously known as Anglo–Persian Oil Company and presently as British Petroleum, the American Central Intelligence Agency (CIA) with the support of Britain's Secret Intelligence Service (SIS), orchestrated a coup, Operation Ajax, that overthrew a widely popular democratically elected government in 1953 to reinstall the Shah of Iran.[23,24,25] The American role in the coup and the subsequent inclusion of US oil companies in the Iranian consortium mark important milestones in the gradual process by which it replaced Britain as the main guardian of Western interests in the Middle East. By the 1960s, the US had displaced Britain from the region's oil resources to a great extent, as Harry Magdoff writes: 'In 1940, Britain controlled 72% of the Middle Eastern oil reserves while the US only held 10%. By 1967 their position was reversed: the US controlled nearly 60% while the British share had fallen below 30%.'[26,27]

Having attained primacy in the region, the US vowed not to compromise on secure supplies of oil it requires from the region. President Jimmy Carter's State of the Union address in 1980, also famously known as the 'Carter Doctrine' states: 'Let our position be absolutely clear. An attempt by any outside force to gain control of the Persian Gulf region will be regarded as an assault on the vital interests of the United States of America. And such an assault will be repelled by any means necessary, including military force.'[28,29] The creation of The United States Central Command (CENTCOM) further substantiates the American approach in the Middle East, as Michael Klare suggests: 'The original function of the Central Command, very clearly elaborated by the Reagan administration, was primarily to protect the flow of oil from the Persian Gulf to the United States and markets around the world. That's always been its primary focus.'[29] Control of oil has been intimately linked to broader political, military, and economic objectives of the US. These larger foreign policy concerns have shaped the issue of control and have, in turn, been shaped by it. Interestingly, all the major post-Second World War doctrines of US foreign policy—the Truman, Eisenhower, Nixon, Carter, and Reagan doctrines—relate, either directly or indirectly, to the Middle East and its oil.[30] Referring to numerous developments in the region including the secret oil-for-protection pact between US President Franklin Roosevelt and Saudi King Abdul Aziz Ibn Saud in 1945, Larry Everest suggests that US strategy to control Middle Eastern oil included: 'negotiations, legal actions, political arm-twisting, economic threats and covert coups against pro-British and French regimes'.[31]

## 2.4.3 OIL-DRIVEN EVENTS IN THE MIDDLE EAST

Apart from the USA's proactive involvement in a catalogue of oil oriented geo-political issues in the Middle East, other nations have also made significant contributions in this respect. The hallmark of examples is that of the 1973 Arab oil embargo. In response to Western support, particularly that of the USA, to Israel during the 1973 Arab–Israel War, members of the Organization of Arab Petroleum Exporting Countries (OAPEC) stopped supply of oil to the USA and several other Western countries. The 1973 embargo and its aftershocks led the US to adapt an aggressive policy about Middle Eastern oil reserves as depicted in the 'Carter Doctrine'.

The trend, 'War for Oil', set during the Second World War, still continues. The world over the last few decades has seen some tragic episodes. The quest for oil is cited to be one of the key reasons behind Iraq's invasion of Iran in 1980—Baghdad assumed that by capturing Iran's southwest Khuzestan province it could control the 20 per cent of world oil reserves also lifting production from 4 to 11 million barrels per day. Oil also played an important role in Iraq's invasion of Kuwait that led to the First Gulf War. One of the main driving factors that triggered the conflict was Iraq's ambition to seek compensation for the oil it alleged Kuwait had stolen through illegal slant-drilling from the Iraqi part of the Rumaila oilfield, commonly shared between the two countries. A consolidated occupation of Iraq over Kuwait would have not only provided it control over nearly one-fifth of the world's oil reserves but also posed a threat to neighbouring oil-rich countries, particularly Saudi Arabia. The development was not acceptable to the nations heavily relying on oil-imports from the region in general and to the USA in particular as it threatened the security of oil supplies from the region. The First Gulf War is, therefore, not only regarded as the operation of US and Allied forces to liberate Kuwait but also as a 'War for Oil'. Like many analysts, Sascha Muller-Kraenner also argues that American oil interests certainly played a role in the war. Alike is the wider public perception as seen in the manifesto of peace demonstrations, 'No Blood for Oil', across Europe.[32]

An account of geo-political developments in the world over the last century, as also highlighted above, reveals that oil has played a central role on numerous occasions. To the US, oil was an integral part of its foreign policy during the twentieth century, and is set to hold the status in the twenty-first century. The US Secretary of Energy with Bill Clinton, Bill Richardson substantiates the argument as he states:

> Oil has literally made foreign and security policy for decades. Just since the turn of this century, it has provoked the division of the Middle East after World War I; aroused Germany and Japan to extend their tentacles beyond their borders; the Arab Oil Embargo; Iran versus Iraq; the Gulf War. This is all clear.[33,34]

## 2.5. ROLE OF PETROLEUM IN THE GEO-POLITICS OF THE TWENTY-FIRST CENTURY

### 2.5.1 THE US–CHINA FRICTION

The unfolding geo-political landscape of the twenty-first century appears to have an even more prominent role for petroleum resources than that of the last century. Along with oil, gas is also set to become a coveted commodity. First and far most importantly, it is the localized nature of oil that is prone to trigger conflicts as the competition between nations over its resources intensifies. Of the top ten energy-intensive economies in the world only Russia and Canada are self-sufficient in their oil requirements as highlighted in Table 2.2.[35] Similarly, of the top ten energy-intensive economies only one sits in the list of ten countries in terms of largest oil reserves.

The dearth of oil reserves in energy-intensive economies is set to trigger a contest for a greater share of oil between states, a phenomenon of which the China–America rivalry is a typical paradigm. Historically, the US has been the leading consumer of oil, currently accounting for nearly a quarter of the world's total consumption. As of 2007, with a daily import of 11.8 million barrels, accounting for over half of its total needs, the US stands out from other nations. However in recent years, China has emerged as a strong competitor for oil. China's oil needs have doubled over the last decade and it has already surpassed Japan to become the second highest consumer of oil in the world. The EIA projects that China's demand for oil will more than double by 2025, reaching 14.2 million barrels per day, and more than 10.9 million barrels will be imported.[36] In order to satisfy its growing needs, China is proactively pursuing oil across the world. In doing so, in recent years, China has initiated new links while strengthening existing ones with petroleum rich countries. While busily signing contracts across the world, China's three largest oil companies, China National Petroleum Corporation (CNPC), China Petroleum and Chemical Corporation (Sinopec), and China National Offshore Oil Corporation (CNOOC) have substantially boosted spending on oil exploration and production worldwide. Considering Africa, the Chinese are latecomers here, yet their energy companies are increasingly active in the region and have established ties with fourteen countries including Nigeria, Libya, and Algeria, holders of the three largest oil reserves in the continent. These developments obviously are far from being appreciated by the United States. Similarly, a clash of interests between the two countries in other oil-rich regions including the Middle East and the Caspian Sea basin is leading to a growing degree of friction between them. Washington is watchfully monitoring China's manoeuvring in these regions. Already, there are voices in Washington that suggest stepping up American political, economic and military involvement in these regions so as to enhance America's competitive advantage in the struggle for access to the world's remaining untapped supplies of crude oil.[37]

**Table 2.2: Top 10 countries in the world in terms oil reserves, consumption and import**

| Reserves (billion barrels) | | Consumption (million barrels/day) | | Import (million barrels/day) | |
|---|---|---|---|---|---|
| Saudi | 267 | USA | 20.9 | USA | 11.8 |
| Iran | 132 | China | 7.0 | Japan | 5.3 |
| Iraq | 115 | Japan | 5.2 | China | 3.0 |
| Kuwait | 104 | Russia | 2.7 | Germany | 2.6 |
| UAE | 97.8 | India | 2.7 | S. Korea | 2.2 |
| Venezuela | 79.7 | Germany | 2.6 | France | 2.0 |
| Russia | 74.4 | S. Korea | 2.3 | Italy | 1.7 |
| Kazakhstan | 39.6 | Canada | 2.3 | Spain | 1.6 |
| Libya | 39.1 | Brazil | 2.2 | India | 1.5 |
| Nigeria | 35.9 | Mexico | 2.1 | Taiwan | 1.0 |

China's booming demand for petroleum resources is not the only concern for the international energy market in general and the US in particular. India is also a growing competitor for oil like a few other countries. With its continued dependence on imports, the growing competition for the limited resources is thus set to prompt the US to take measures it may assume appropriate to secure its desired level of supplies. Prominent American economist C. Fred Bergsten, who also served as the former Assistant Secretary for International Affairs at the US Treasury Department, is of a similar view as he notes in 2004:

> Energy is another area in which the United States is vulnerable, in both economic and foreign policy terms. The lack of an effective energy policy—highlighted once again by the recent failure of Congress to pass adequate legislation after three years of effort—keeps US foreign policy beholden to a few key producers and will probably force the United States to continue to launch periodic military interventions to satisfy its tremendous appetite for energy.[38]

## 2.5.2 The Russia–EU Affair

Alongside USA and China, the role of Russia as a proactive player on the chessboard of the energy world is going to be decisive in the decades ahead. Revived Russia, for instance, with its largest gas reserves and seventh largest oil reserves in the world, has emerged as an energy superpower of the world and is being deemed to play a key role in future energy supplies for Europe and Asia. Particularly, in Europe there is a growing degree of apprehension that the Kremlin would try to ride on its rich petroleum reserves to regain the status—of a superpower—it has held during the time of the former Union of Soviet Socialist Republics (USSR). There are concerns that Russian power politics in future may focus on the strength of Gazprom, Russia's largest energy company, rather on the weapons of the Red Army.

The European countries were reminded of Russia's strong position during the 2008 Russia–Georgia conflict over Georgia's breakaway regions of South Ossetia and Abkhazia. In the midst of the crisis, several EU states, including Britain and France, pushed for sanctions on Russia, as on August 2008 amid an emergency EU session, the French Foreign Minister Bernard Kouchner said that some EU states at the summit 'will propose sanctions.'[39] In the context of the fact that the EU depends upon Russia for almost half of its natural gas and 30 per cent of its oil requirements, the Russian ambassador to Britain, Yuri Fedotov, warned that 'any sanctions will hurt the European Union first of all much more than Russia.'[40] The EU summit ultimately dropped the idea of imposing sanctions and decided to resolve the issue through dialogue—a decision largely determined by the need to ensure security of energy supplies.[41] The proposal for sanctions could not get through, with energy being such an important factor. Most importantly, it was Germany that snubbed the proposal for sanctions, primarily for its energy requirements as it relies on Russia for 40 per cent of its gas and about 35 per cent of its oil imports. Energy, therefore, determined the course of EU's response to Russia. Russia generated another shockwave in January 2009 by switching off gas supplies to Ukraine, a move that affected a number of other EU countries as well, as shown in Figure 2.3.[42] Russia's rich oil and gas reserves are thus going to hugely favour it in determining the trajectory of its relationship with the rest of the world in general and the EU in particular.

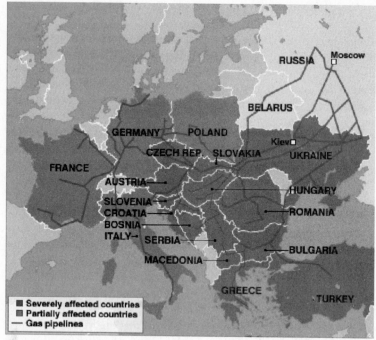

Figure 2.3: Russian gas supply disruptions caused in January 2009

### 2.5.3 The Mounting Role of the Middle East

The Middle East has been under the limelight for its vast oil reserves for nearly a century now. By the 1950s, it had established its standing as the largest oil-rich region of the world—its oil reserves were equal to the rest of the world's combined, and double the US reserves.[43] For the last six decades, the Middle East has been the source of abundant and cheap oil that propelled the economic growth of the world over this period. In 2006, it produced about 28 per cent of the world's total oil, while holding 65 per cent (728 billion barrels) of the world's oil reserves. During the same year, the region exported 18.2 million barrels per day. Besides oil, the Middle East region also has sizeable reserves (2,509 trillion cubic feet—Tcf) of natural gas, accounting for 41 per cent of the total proven world gas reserves.[44]

The importance of Middle East countries is several-fold. The oil and gas reserves in non-Middle East countries are being depleted more rapidly than those of Middle East producers. If production continues at the present rate, many of the largest, non-Middle Eastern producers in 2002, such as Russia, Mexico, US, Norway, China, and Brazil will cease to be relevant players in the oil market in less than two decades. At that point, the Middle East will be the only major reservoir of abundant crude oil—within twenty years or so about four-fifths of oil reserves could be in the hands of the Middle Eastern countries. Another dimension of the importance of the region is its excess production capacity as many circles including the EIA believe. The EIA suggests that the region represents essentially 100 per cent of excess capacity, all of which is located in Saudi Arabia, which becomes extremely important in the backdrop of surging oil prices and market volatility. Geologists also believe that a considerable proportion of future discoveries are likely to come from the region.

The role of the Middle East region in future oil supplies of the world is thus going to become even more prominent, as also highlighted in Figure 2.4.[45] The oil in the region also has qualitative advantages—its oil deposits are highly concentrated and located close to the surface, making them amongst the easiest in the world to tap.[46]

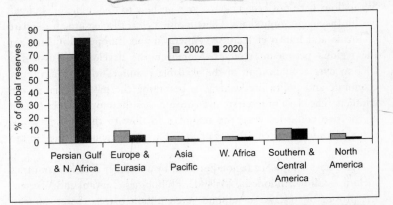

Figure 2.4: Growing share of Middle East (Persian Gulf) oil reserves in future

Since the birth of the oil-age in the early twentieth century the Middle East has been plagued by conflicts and geo-strategic unrest. The region has experienced wars of various magnitudes and for all possible reasons including imperialistic, economic, religious and ethnic motives. In the backdrop of a wide range of underlying disputes within the region, its vulnerability against similar challenges in future is ever more intense. It is especially critical when some of the vital issues behind the geo-strategic conflicts are still unresolved and the degree of religious and ethnic sentiments on them remains high.

## 2.5.4 ISSUES WITH THE CASPIAN SEA AND SOUTH CHINA SEA

Apart from the escalating intensity of competition for the petroleum reserves, another factor that is likely to prompt conflicts is disputes over their very existence. The Caspian Sea basin is a hallmark example in this regard. With billions of barrels of proven oil reserves and over 200 billion barrels of potential reserves in combination with up to 325 trillion cubic feet of natural gas, the region is the second richest in the world after the Middle East. The Caspian Sea basin is a 371,000 square kilometre land-locked body of water surrounded by Russia, Iran, Azerbaijan, Kazakhstan, and Turkmenistan. The contested boundaries and lively territorial disputes between these countries contribute to the volatility in the region especially when the issues have a history of violence amongst neighbouring countries. The status of the Caspian seabed reserves has been in limbo since the 1991 Soviet collapse and thus far there is no commonly acceptable legal framework covering their ownership. The five Caspian Sea nations have not been able to agree on how to divide the oil and gas wealth they commonly share. There is also a clear displeasure on the part of Russia and Iran over increased American and European influence on the region's petroleum reserves. Moreover, the developing Russia–US friction over capitalization of the available resources to gain maximum economic and political advantage is becoming the most crucial of the conflicts. The clash of interests also encompasses the supply routes as each of the two countries want the resources to flow to the outside world through routes of its choice to gain valuable geo-strategic leverage in the region.

The South China Sea region bordered by a number of Asian countries including China, Indonesia, Malaysia, Philippines, Taiwan, and Vietnam has proven oil reserves of around seven billion barrels. Some surveys, however, suggest that the total sum of discovered reserves and undiscovered resources in the offshore basins of the South China Sea could be as much as 28 billion barrels. With such a reasonable scale of reserves, the region, like many other energy-rich areas, also exhibits a catalogue of territorial disputes.

## 2.5.5 UNDERLYING ISSUES IN OIL-RICH REGIONS AND THEIR POTENTIAL IMPACTS ON GLOBAL ENERGY SCENARIO

The aforementioned analysis of the underlying contentious issues engulfing petroleum-rich regions of the world and the track record of pertinent confrontations over the last one hundred years provide compelling evidence to suggest that oil and gas resources are set to elicit conflicts and warfare in future. As to the nature, intensity and locations of the violence, however, only time will tell. The situation is further complicated when almost every country in the region, to the best of its capabilities, has accumulated piles of high-tech military hardware to protect its national interests in case of any incidents.

In this respect Sascha Muller-Kraenner reflects upon the challenges facing the energy world in the days ahead in the following terms:

> In the search of oil, money and power there seems to be no more room for noble principles of international law and the subtle instruments of international diplomacy. The gloves are off in the battle for last resources; securing national energy supplies has become the tough realpolitik for every country. Alliances are formed not with those that we like, but with those that we need. Russia, China, the European Union (EU) and naturally the US are the four main players up against each other in the Great Game of the 21st century. Unlike the 'Great Game' of the 19th century, when Russia and England competed with each other over the control of Central Asia, today's game is not only about wrestling for the political and economic influence zones, it is also about defining the rules of the game for the energy markets, in particular, and for the world of tomorrow in general.[47]

The destruction from any large-scale warfare would have severe ramifications not only for the countries/nations involved but also for the rest of the world—it would not only damage the energy infrastructure in the region but also disrupt supplies to the rest of the world. Iran and Iraq, for instance, have not yet fully recovered from the impact of their war (1980–1988). Two decades after the end of the war, neither of the two countries has been able to restore its pre-war oil production capacity. Considering the lethality of modern weaponry countries have in their armoury, in case of wars in oilrich regions, damage to the sustainability of the world in general, and to the energy base in particular, could be colossal.

## 2.6. DECISIVE ROLE OF OIL IN CONVENTIONAL WARFARE

Apart from leading the nations to military conflicts, oil, in the capacity of a vital logistical commodity, has also played a key role in determining the trajectory and outcome of wars. Logistic considerations have traditionally been at the heart of military planning. Effective logistics is an important element not only as part of wartime operations but also pre-war preparation. It is often the decisive element with regard to the timing and success of operations.

At the beginning of the twentieth century oil was not introduced to warfare. Wars were fought with foot soldiers, horse-mounted cavalry and horse-drawn artillery, while naval combats relied on coal-fired warships. The years leading to the First World War saw the development of a revolutionary breed of weaponry—the submarine, the airplane, the tank, and motorized transport—all powered by oil. A switchover of warships from coal to oil was also underway.

The outcome of the First World War, history's first mechanized war, was greatly determined by oil. It is the first war in world history where oil decided victory and defeat. Ultimately, the German Empire, for example, lost the war of attrition in the trenches of the Western front because its war machinery had run out of fuel.[48] Access to a secure supply of oil for weaponry was the factor that clearly favoured the Allied forces over their counterparts. The allied forces, particularly Britain and France, were able to get oil supplies from overseas sources including Iran, Mexico, and the United States. Germany, on the other hand, had access only to Romanian oil. When Germany was denied access to the Romanian oil fields by Allied forces, it gradually fell prey to chronic fuel shortages. The Allied forces were able to send urgent requests to the US for help, particularly during 1917 and 1918, when a shortage of oil supplies threatened to immobilize the Royal Navy and the French army. Towards the end of the war, the US was supplying the majority of the Allied oil requirements, and the American navy was playing a key role in supplying and protecting tanker transport of oil to Europe. The Allied blockade of German supply routes not only affected the mobility of war machinery but also industry's ability to support the war. By 1917, civilian trains were no longer able to function and airplanes were running poorly on substitute fuels. Being unable to even lubricate their tanks and trucks properly, the German army, having only a few days' fuel left, finally surrendered on 11 November 1918. Reflecting upon the vital role of oil in the First World War, the former Viceroy of India George Nathaniel Curzon, who also served as a member of the British War Cabinet and later Foreign Secretary, after the end of the War proclaimed that the 'Allied cause had floated to' victory upon a wave of oil'.[49]

Having fought in the First World War for four years, Adolf Hitler had learnt some lessons from it. He was determined to make sure that next time Germany had all the fuel it needed to fulfil its ambitions. Upon his accession to power in 1933, he immediately began a search for methods to increase oil exploration and production as he said: 'To fight, we must have oil for our machine.'[50] Under Hitler's orders, German engineers began working to produce synthetic fuels, mostly from coal and lignite, at an unprecedented pace. By 1941, synthetic fuel production had reached a level of 31 million barrels per year. Germany, however, needed more oil than it had to power its industries as well as the war machines at the front.

Hitler's decisive battlefield tactic 'Blitzkrieg' was all about speed, co-ordination and surprise, and thus imperatively required sustainable supplies of oil. Provision of a sufficient and continuous supply of oil was one of the top most priorities in the war planning on part of Hitler and his Nazi Generals. The intact capture of enemy oil fields became a primary task in all their invasions. One of the main motives behind Germany's invasion of Poland and the Soviet Union was also to control their oilfields. Germany's invasion of Russia ultimately turned out to be an ill-fated move. During their second major attack on Soviet soil in the summer of 1942, German troops, while heading to occupy the oil reserves of Baku, could not maintain their supply lines and literally ran out of oil, probably the last thing Germany wanted to see. The situation turned so disturbing for the German offence that often its vehicles were stranded for several days waiting for supplies. Having realized the gravity of the situation Hitler told Field Marshal Erich Von Manstein: 'It is a question of the possession of Baku. Unless we get the Baku oil, the war is lost.'[51] Finally, after having faced stubborn Soviet resistance and supply disruptions most importantly in the form of oil scarcity, German troops were ordered to retreat from the Baku campaign in January 1943. When the Allies eventually denied Germany access to those oil fields, the German war machinery ran out of oil.

By the second half of 1944, the German forces had become almost entirely dependent on synthetic fuel production as their main supply source, Romanian oil, was blocked by Allied forces. The synthetic fuel facilities then became the primary targets of Allied bombing. Between May and September 1944, Allied bombing reduced German synthetic fuel production by 85 per cent. Despite the fact that Germany produced record amounts of armaments during that year there was not enough fuel or lubricants to put into all those brand new machines. The production of aviation gasoline had also been reduced by 95 per cent, which created yet another oil paradox. Without fuel, the fighters could not fly to protect the oil facilities, which meant more destroyed refineries and therefore less fuel. In desperation, rather than waste fuel taxiing, aircraft were towed to runways by teams of cows and horses. Compared to Germany that mainly relied on the Romanian oilfield at Ploesti, the Allies were privileged to have control of the vast majority of the world's known oil reserves in America, Russia, and the Middle East. In contrast to the paralyzed German Air Force, the Royal Air Force of Britain had continuous access to superior 100-octane aviation oil from the US which improved engine performance, allowing faster takeoffs, quicker bursts of speed, and larger payloads.[50]

Like Germany, Japan also badly suffered from lack of oil. Facing an embargo from the US and the Dutch East Indies, Japan invaded the latter in 1942 to control its oilfields. Japan's plan, however, was thwarted by American submarine and air attacks. By 1944, Japan's forces started facing serious shortages of oil. In the last year of the war, the scarcity of oil grew to an extent that Japanese pilots could no longer be given navigational training and Japanese aircraft carriers could no longer afford to take evasive action—all for lack of fuel. Japan was thus unable to effectively resist the Allied offences and so was eventually forced to concede defeat. Many military historians believe that although the nuclear strikes on Hiroshima and Nagasaki ended the war, it was oil that fuelled the Allied armies to bring Germany and Japan to their knees. Oil powered the vast numbers of ships, tanks, and aircrafts that endowed the Allied forces with a decisive edge over their adversaries that lacked access to reliable sources of petroleum.

Being familiar with the importance of oil, both sides, the Allies and the Axis Powers, attempted not only to ensure security of their own supplies but also to disrupt supplies bound for the enemies. Like the Allied forces' campaign to blockade its supplies, Germany also attempted to damage their supplies. Like the attacks of the Allied forces on its supplies, early in the war, German U-boats sank US tankers in sight of the American East Coast in a campaign to interdict Britain's sea lanes to America. Similarly, once the Japanese occupied the oilfields in the Dutch East Indies, they eliminated all possible supplies in the Pacific between

America and the Middle East. It was the diversity in supplies that ultimately favoured the Allied forces over the Axis Powers.

The decisive role of oil in the Second World War has been appreciated not only by the countries that fought it but also by independent analysts. Highlighting the decisive factors in the outcome of the war, Winston Churchill stated: 'Above all, petrol governed every movement.'[52, 53] The Soviet leader Joseph Stalin expressed the importance of oil as: 'The war was decided by engines and octane.'[53] One of the most interesting comments were made during a post-war interrogation by Prof. Wakimura of Tokyo Imperial University as: 'God was on the side of the nation that had the oil'.[54]

After the Second World War the role of oil as a vital combat commodity became more prominent in military planning across the world. In a highly motorized-age, with mounted cavalry and horse-driven artillery being history now, oil is the key to modern warfare be it on the ground, in the air or at sea. Fossil fuel resources in general and oil in particular have thus strongly influenced strategic thinking. Powerful countries have placed a great deal of emphasis on security of their supplies.

## REFERENCES

1. Yashar Aliyev, Permanent Representative of Azerbaijan to the United Nations, remarked at the joint press conference on the inauguration of The Baku-Tbilisi-Ceyhan Oil Pipeline, New York, 13 July 2006.
2. Natural Gas, Energy Timeline, Energy Information Administration.
3. International Energy Agency Statistics 2009.
4. The History of Oil, Azerbaijan Section, Society of Petroleum Engineers.
5. Sascha Muller-Kraenner, *Energy Security*, Introduction, Earthscan Publications Ltd., UK, 2008, p. 19.
6. Issues and Instruments, G8 Summit 2006, St Petersburg, 15-17 July 2006.
7. A. Alhajji and J. Williams, Measures of Petroleum Dependence and Vulnerability in OECD Countries, *Middle East Economic Survey*, 46:16, 21 April 2003.
8. D. Yergin, Ensuring Energy Security, *Foreign Affairs* (2006) March/April.
9. Larry Hughes, The four 'R's of energy security, *Energy Policy*, Volume 37, Issue 6, June 2009.
10. Mohammad Malek, Oil in Iran between the Two World Wars, Iran Chamber Society, http://www.iranchamber.com/history/articles/oil_iran_between_world_wars.php
11. William Engdahl, *A Century of War: Anglo-American Oil Politics and the New World Order*, Pluto Press, 2004.
12. F. Engdahl, Oil and the Origins of the 'War to make the World Safe for Democracy', 22 June 2007.
13. Peter Sluglett, The Primacy of Oil in Britain's Iraq Policy, p. 103, http://www.globalpolicy.org/component/content/article/169-history/36381.html
14. History of British Petroleum, www.bo.com

15. R.A.C. Parker, *The Second World War: A Short History*, Oxford University Press, 2002.
16. Michael Klare, *Resources War*, Henry Holt and Company, New York, 2001, p. 31.
17. Richard Heinberg, *The Party's Over: Oil, War and the Fate of Industrial Societies*, Clairview Books, Sussex, 2003, p. 69.
18. Lutz Kleveman, *The New Great Game: Blood and Oil in Central Asia*, Grove/Atlantic, Inc., 2004, p. 18.
19. Larry Everest, *Oil Power and Empire*, Common Courage Press, Canada, 2004, p. 56.
20. Ibid., p. 229.
21. Ibid., p. 57.
22. Daniel Yergin, *The Prize: The Epic Quest for Oil, Money and Power*, Simon & Schuster Ltd, 1993, pp. 49, 480.
23. Dan De Luce, The Spectre of Operation Ajax, *The Guardian*, 20 August 2003.
24. Ibid., p. 60.
25. Ibid., p. 72.
26. Ibid., p. 59.
27. Harry Magdoff, *The Age of Imperialism*, New York: Monthly Review, 1969, 43.
28. Jimmy Carter, State of the Union Address, Jimmy Carter Library & Museum, 23 January 1980.
29. Michael Klare, *Blood and Oil*, Metropolitan Books, 2004.
30. David S. Painter, 'Oil,' entry in *Encyclopedia of American Foreign Policy: Studies of the Principal Movements and Ideas*, edited by Alexander DeConde, Fredrik Logevall, and Richard Dean Burns, Second Edition, New York: Charles Scribner's Sons, 2002.
31. Ibid., p. 59.
32. Ibid., p. 27.
33. Bill Richardson, 'Geopolitics of Energy into the 21st Century', Lecture at the Centre for Strategic and International Studies, Washington DC, 1999.
34. Ibid., p. 43.
35. EIA statistics 2008.
36. Editorial, *Washington Times*, http://washingtontimes.com/news/2006/apr/19/20060419-093142-9219r/(accessed on 4 January 2009).
37. Michael T. Klare, 'The US and China are over a barrel, In the costly competition for oil, cooperation is the wisest course', 28 April 2008, *Los Angeles Times*.
38. C. Fred Bergsten, 'Foreign Economic Policy for the Next President', Reprinted by permission of *Foreign Affairs*, March/April 2004, Copyright 2004 by the Council on Foreign Affairs, Inc.
39. Alan Crawford, Germany Split Over Russia May Hurt Unity at EU Summit, http://www.bloomberg.com/apps/news?pid=20601085&sid=a8RVWBfNsXIs&refer=europe (accessed on 4 January 2009).
40. UK Warns Over Russian Aggression, BBC, http://news.bbc.co.uk/1/hi/uk_politics/7590320.stm, (accessed on 4 January 2009).
41. EU Summit ends without sanctions against Russia, Peoples Daily Online, http://english.peopledaily.com.cn/90001/90777/90856/6491212.html, (accessed on 4 January 2009).
42. Russian Gas to Europe 'blocked', BBC, 13 January 2009, http://news.bbc.co.uk/1/hi/world/europe/7826142.stm
43. N. Chomsky, *The Fateful Triangle: The United States Israel and The Palestinians*, Boston South End Press, 1983.
44. Persian Gulf Region, Energy Information Administration, EIA, 2008 http://www.eia.doe.gov/emeu/cabs/Persian_Gulf/Background.html

45. M. Asif, T. Muneer, 'Energy supply, its demand and security issues for developed and emerging economies', *Renewable and Sustainable Energy Reviews*, 11 (2007) 1388–1413.

46. M. Klare, *Resources War: The New Landscape of Global Conflicts*, Henry Holt and Company, 2002, p. 54.

47. Ibid., 2008.

48. Lutz Kleveman, *The New Great Game: Blood and Oil in Central Asia*, Grove Press, New York, 2003, p. 18.

49. Michael Klare, *Resources War: The New Landscape of Global Conflict*, New York: Henry Holt & Company, 2001, p. 30.

50. Michael Antonucci, Blood for Oil: The Quest for Fuel in World War II, *Command*, January-February 1993.

51. Lutz Kleveman, *The New Great Game: Blood and Oil in Central Asia*, Grove Press, New York, 2003, p. 19.

52. Winston Churchill, *The Second World War: Triumph and Tragedy*, Houghton Mifflin Harcourt, 1953, p. 167.

53. Joel Modisette, A Model For The Propulsion Fuel Consumption Of An Aircraft Carrier, Naval Postgraduate School Monterey, California, 1990.

54. James, Rainy, Old Lessons New Thoughts, Air Force Logistics Management Agency, February 2004.

# 3

# The Energy Base of Pakistan and the Institutional Framework

## 3.1. DEVELOPMENT OF THE NATIONAL ENERGY BASE

Pakistan is situated in South Asia and lies between 23.8 and 36.7 degrees north latitude and 61.1 and 75.8 degrees east longitude. The country shares its borders with four countries, India in the East, Iran and Afghanistan in the West, and China in the North as shown in Figure 3.1. It has the Arabian Sea in the South with a coastline of 1064 km. The country has an overall area of 803,940 sq km and is divided into four provinces namely Punjab, Sindh, Balochistan, and North-West Frontier Province (NWFP), and also includes Federally Administered Tribal and Northern Areas.

The energy-supply-base of Pakistan constitutes two major segments, commercial and non-commercial. At the time of the country's independence in 1947, the proportion of energy coming through commercial channels was very small and is reported to be equivalent to around 1.2 million tonne oil equivalent (MTOE). For a total population of around 33 million, the installed electricity generation capacity, for example, was 50MW as indicated in Table 3.1.[1] Commercial energy had very little role to play in an average Pakistani's life. The major energy consuming sectors, i.e. industrial, transport, domestic, agriculture and commercial had very little reliance on the commodity. The industrial sector was almost non-existent and motorized travelling was not very common.[2] In the absence of a national grid, WAPDA sources suggest, out of over 200,000 towns and villages, only 640, making up 7 per cent of the population were connected to local grids.[3] The agriculture sector, on the other hand, was not introduced to machinery. Shortly after independence, the country being in need of a rapid infrastructural and economic growth, aimed to pursue new energy projects. It took almost a decade before the growth of the commercial energy base could truly takeoff.

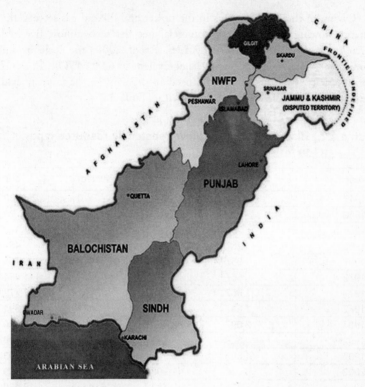

Figure 3.1: Map of Pakistan

## Table 3.1: Growth in primary energy consumption and installed power generation capacity[4]

| Year | Population (million) | Total Primary Energy (MTOE) | Installed Electricity Capacity (MW) |
|------|---------------------|------------------------------|--------------------------------------|
| 1947 | 33 | 1.2 | 50 |
| 1950 | 35 | 1.4 | 115 |
| 1960 | 45 | 3.0 | 425 |
| 1970 | 60 | 6.4 | 1,700 |
| 1980 | 81 | 12.5 | 3,500 |
| 1990 | 108 | 28.0 | 9,000 |
| 2000 | 140 | 42.0 | 17,000 |
| 2009 | 165 | 62.9 | 20,495 |

Owing to the developments in the power and oil and gas sectors, the energy flowing through the commercial net has seen almost five-fold increment over the last three decades. As of 2009, the scale of the commercial energy is reported to be equivalent to 62.9 MTOE. In terms of electricity, by 2007, the total installed capacity in the country had reached the 19,420MW mark, as shown in Table 3.2.

**Table 3.2: Historic growth of power sector by resource type in MW[5]**

| Year | Hydro | Thermal | Nuclear | Total |
|---|---|---|---|---|
| 1947 | 11 | 39 | 0 | 50 |
| 1952 | 13 | 60 | 0 | 73 |
| 1957 | 52 | 67 | 0 | 119 |
| 1962 | 267 | 190 | 0 | 457 |
| 1967 | 267 | 441 | 0 | 708 |
| 1972 | 667 | 650 | 137 | 1,454 |
| 1977 | 1,567 | 1,068 | 137 | 2,772 |
| 1982 | 1,847 | 1,407 | 137 | 3,391 |
| 1987 | 2,897 | 2,452 | 137 | 5,486 |
| 1992 | 3,329 | 4,134 | 137 | 7,600 |
| 1997 | 4,825 | 8,131 | 137 | 13,093 |
| 2002 | 5,039 | 12,298 | 462 | 17,799 |
| 2007 | 6,474 | 12,484 | 462 | 19,420 |

The fact that currently hardly 60 per cent and 20 per cent of the total number of households are connected respectively to the national electric grid and gas pipelines implies that the non-commercial base still makes up a considerably large proportion of the total supplies in the country. It mainly comes from the wide range of biomass resources. Firewood, for example, is vastly used for cooking and heating applications. Furthermore, the agricultural and livestock sectors produce abundant amounts of biomass in the form of crop residues and animal waste, such as bagasse, rice husk, and dung, much of which is currently collected and used outside the commercial base as unprocessed fuel for cooking and household heating. Estimates suggest that the biomass-based non-commercial form of energy makes up almost 35 per cent of the total consumption in the country.[6] There is no detailed data available on the non-commercial energy base to reflect upon its supply breakdown, generation and consumption trends, and pricing. The book henceforth focuses upon the commercial energy base of the country. Furthermore, the emphasis would be mainly on the power sector.

### 3.1.1 HYDROPOWER

Hydropower is one of the most important and reliable energy resources for Pakistan. It has traditionally played a pivotal role in meeting national electricity requirements in a secure and cost effective manner. In 1947, only two hydropower projects of a collective capacity of 10.7MW (9.6MW—Malakand Power Station and 1.1MW—Renala Power Station) existed in the territory of Pakistan. In the years immediately after independence, hydropower development remained sluggish owing to two major factors: firstly, the water-dispute between Pakistan and India and secondly, lack of financial resources required to orchestrate large-scale dam based hydropower projects. The situation allowed only the small-to-medium scale projects to be commissioned at certain sites. Consequently, in 1958 when the Water and Power Development Authority (WAPDA), the body that took over the task of hydropower development, was established, the installed hydropower capacity stood at only 52MW. By 1960, the installed capacity grew to as much as 253MW.[5]

The Indus Water Treaty between Pakistan and India, signed the same year under the aegis of the World Bank to resolve the underlying water conflicts between the two countries, proved to be a turning point in the development of hydropower in the former. The Treaty assigned the three Eastern Rivers (Ravi, Beas, and Sutlej) to India, and the three Western rivers (Indus, Jhelum, and Chenab) to Pakistan. It also provided construction of replacement works called Indus Basin Project (IBP) to compensate for the perpetual loss of Eastern Rivers' water. The works proposed under the Treaty included two multipurpose dams, i.e. Mangla Dam on the Jhelum River and Tarbela Dam on the Indus River with the provision for power generation. These were commissioned in 1967 and 1977 respectively. However, their capacities have been subsequently extended in different phases.

The planned growth of hydropower has been marred over the last three decades primarily due to the politicization and the consequent shelving of the Kalabagh Dam. Over this period, other than one major project, it is only the capacity extension of the existing projects that has been carried out. It is the 1,450MW run-off-river Ghazi Barotha project that was commissioned in 2003. With 111MW coming from IPPs, as of 2008, the total installed hydropower capacity stands at around 6,550MW. Details of WAPDA's hydropower project have been provided in Table 3.3.[7]

### Table 3.3: Overview of hydropower projects in Pakistan

| Project | Water Way (River/Canal) | Installed Capacity (MW) | Year(s) of Commissioning |
|---|---|---|---|
| Tarbela | Indus (Reservoir) | 3,478 | 1977–1992 |
| Barotha¤ | Indus (D/S Tarbela) | 1,450 | 2003–2004 |
| Mangla | Jhelum (Reservoir) | 1,000 | 1967–1994 |
| Warsak | Kabul (Reservoir) | 243 | 1960–1981 |
| Chashma | Chashma (Barrage) | 184 | 2000–2001 |
| Rasul¤ | UJC* | 22 | 1952 |
| Dargai¤ | Swat** | 20 | 1952 |
| Malakand¤ | Swat** | 19.6 | 1938–1952 |
| Nandipur¤ | UCC*** | 13.8 | 1963 |
| Shadiwal¤ | UJC* | 13.5 | 1961 |
| Chichoki¤ | UCC*** | 13.2 | 1959 |
| K/Garhi¤ | Kachkot***** | 4.0 | 1958 |
| Renala¤ | LBDC**** | 1.1 | 1925 |
| Chitral¤ | Ludko | 1 | 1975–1982 |
| ¤ | | | Run-of-River (Canal) Projects |
| * | UJC | | Upper Jhelum Canal from River Jhelum |
| ** | Swat | | Swat Canal from River Swat |
| *** | UCC | | Upper Chenab Canal from River Chenab |
| **** | LBDC | | Lower Bari Doab Canal from Balloki Headworks on River Ravi |
| ***** | Kachkot | | Kachkot Canal from River Kurram |

Hydropower currently makes around 32.7 per cent of the total installed power generation capacity in the country. During 2007–08, hydropower made up 28.3 per cent of the total generated electricity. The hydropower generation capacity is not uniform round the year but varies substantially between summer and winter due to seasonal variations of reservoir levels of the major projects such as Tarbela and Mangla. The maximum and minimum power generation capacity of Tarbela is reported to be 3,692MW and 1,350MW respectively. The respective figures for Mangla stand at 1,150MW and 500MW. The 2009 statistics suggest that, overall, WAPDA's hydropower generating capability varies between the two extremities of 2,414MW and 6,746.0MW over the cycle of a year.[7]

## 3.1.2 DEVELOPMENT OF THERMAL POWER

Parallel to the exploitation of hydropower resource, in 1960s, Pakistan also slowly developed its thermal power base. Thermal power plants were initially established as a backup to hydropower since the primary motive was to mitigate the impacts of seasonal fluctuation in hydropower generation capacity. Due to the typical nature of the hydropower resource, mostly the Northern Areas of the country improvise suitable sites of power generation. Transmission losses become an important issue over long distances. Thermal power was thus also intended to facilitate the areas difficult to be served by hydropower. The national thermal power base has been developed and is controlled by three major players: the Water and Power Development Authority (WAPDA); Independent Power Producers (IPPs); and the Karachi Electric Supply Company (KESC).

### 3.1.2.1 Thermal Power of WAPDA

At the time of WAPDA's inception in 1958, the installed thermal power generation capacity was equivalent to 67MW. Thermal power grew at a handsome pace during the 1960s as the total capacity hit the 650MW mark by 1970. During the 1970s, 1980s and the first half of the 1990s, WAPDA experienced gradual growth in its thermal power, hitting the 6,238MW mark in 1996, accounting for 56 per cent of the total installed power generation capacity in the country. The healthy progress being made by WAPDA, however, was brought to a sudden halt by the Government of Pakistan's decision in the early 1990s to bar the department from setting up thermal power plants anymore. The move had wide ranging detrimental impacts not only upon WAPDA but also on the whole power sector. In terms of installed capacity of WAPDA, the decision could only lead to gradual erosion due to the ageing power plants. Consequently in 2008, WAPDA's thermal power stations, detailed in Table 3.4, were worth 4,899MW contributing only 24.4 per cent to the gross power generation capacity of the country.[5]

**Table 3.4: WAPDA's installed thermal power plants**[7]

| Project | Current Capacity (MW) | Fuel used | Date of commissioning |
|---|---|---|---|
| Multan | 195 | Gas/FO | 1960–1963 |
| Faisalabad | 132 | Gas/FO | 1967 |
| Shahdara | 59 | Gas/HSD | 1966–1969 |
| Guddu | 640 | Gas/FO/HSD | 1974–1986 |
| Faisalabad | 244 | Gas turbine | 1975 |
| Guddu | 1,015 | Gas/FO/HSD | 1985–1993 |
| Jamshoro | 850 | Gas/FO/HSD | 1990–1991 |
| Pasni | 17 | HSD | 1991 |
| Muzaffargarh | 1,350 | Gas/FO | 1993–1995 |
| Kotri | 174 | Gas/HSD | 1994 |
| Lakhra | 150 | Coal | 1995–1996 |
| Punjgoor | 38 | Gas turbine | 1999–2000 |
| Quetta | 35 | Gas/HSD | 2004 |

### 3.1.2.2 The Independent Power Producers

Owing to negligence in timely reaction to growing demands, Pakistan faced a serious shortfall of electricity during 1980s and 1990s. To address the crisis at hand, in 1994, the Government of Pakistan created a new organization, the Private Power Infrastructure Board (PPIB) that aimed to facilitate private sector's participation in power generation. In March 1994, a new power policy was introduced to attract private investment. It was not the first attempt of its kind. Earlier in 1985, the first private power policy was introduced by the Government of Pakistan which, however, failed to serve the purpose due to the rather tedious mechanism involved and stringent terms and conditions.[8] The 1994 Power Policy aimed at expediting the process by providing 'one-window' service. The previous government also claimed that the 1994 power policy had many similarities with the Medium Term Energy Plan approved by the Cabinet Committee in February 1993.[9]

Some of the important features of the 1994 power policy were as under:[10]

- The Independent Power Producers (IPPs) were free in the choice of site, plant size, technology and fuel. The fuel range included residual furnace oil, diesel oil, natural gas, LAPG etc.
- GOP was to ensure transmission access and guaranteed fuel supply

- IPPs were exempted from most taxes and were allowed free repatriation of equity/dividends
- Sovereign guarantees were made for power purchase payments and fuel supply
- Mechanism was developed for indexation of certain components of tariff based upon Rupee/Dollar exchange rate, fuel price variations, interest rates and inflation

Under the energy policies of 1994 and 2000, eighteen projects with a total capacity of 6,296.5MW achieved financial closures (including Tavanir from Iran and Rental Power Project). The major lenders include IFC, EXIM Bank of Japan, US EXIM Bank, Asian Development Bank, and commercial banks. The existing IPPs, as of August 2009, are highlighted in Table 3.5.

**Table 3.5: Overview of the operational IPPs[7]**

| Name of Project | Gross Capacity (MW) | Technology | Date of commissioning |
|---|---|---|---|
| KAPCO | 1,638 | Combined cycle, steam turbine on LSFO/Gas/Diesel | 27.06.1996 |
| HUBCO | 1,292 | Steam turbine on fuel oil | 31.03.1997 |
| Kohinoor Energy Ltd | 131 | Diesel engines on fuel oil | 20.06.1997 |
| AES Lalpir | 362 | Steam turbines on fuel oil | 06.11.1997 |
| AES Pakgen | 365 | Steam turbines on fuel oil | 01.02.1998 |
| Southern Electric Power | 117 | Diesel engines on fuel oil | 10.03.1999 |
| Habibullah Coastal Power | 140 | Combined cycle on natural gas | 11.09.1999 |
| Fauji Kabirwala Power | 157 | Combined cycle on gas | 21.10.1999 |
| Rousch (Pakistan) Power | 450 | Combined cycle on fuel oil | 11.12.1999 |
| Saba Power | 134 | Steam turbine on fuel oil | 31.12.1999 |
| Japan Power Generation | 135 | Diesel engines on fuel oil | 14.03.2000 |
| Uch Power | 586 | Combined cycle gas | 18.10.2000 |
| Altern Energy | 10.5 | Flared gas/Gas engine | 06.06.2001 |
| Liberty Power | 235 | Combined cycle on natural gas | 10.09.2001 |
| Tavanir, IRAN | 39 | Import from Iran | -09. 2003 |
| Rental Power Station | 150 | Gas turbine | 22.02.2007 |

In the wake of the prevalent electricity crisis in the country, 6,233MW of new IPPs are being promised to be streamlined by 2011. Of these, 2,700MW are to come from rental power projects. In terms of the employed fuel, 3,959MW, 910MW and 1,364MW are to be respectively run by oil, dual fuel (gas and oil), and gas.

### 3.1.2.3 Karachi Electric Supply Company

The Karachi Electric Supply Company (KESC) generates all its electricity from thermal power plants. According to the 2008 statistics the company has total installed capacity of 1,756MW as detailed in Table 3.6.[4]

**Table 3.6: Thermal power stations operated by KESC**

| Power Station | Installed Capacity (MW) | Fuel |
|---|---|---|
| Korangi | 316 | Gas/Furnace oil |
| Korangi Town | 80 | Gas |
| Site | 100 | Gas |
| Bin Qasim | 1,260 | Gas/Furnace oil |

In order to compensate the ageing plants and to meet growing demands, the new management of the KESC claims to be planning to set up over 700MW of new projects by 2011.

### 3.1.3 NUCLEAR POWER

Nuclear power accounts for around 2.3 per cent of the total installed capacity in the country. It is controlled by the state owned department Pakistan Atomic Energy Commission (PAEC). Pakistan started its limited programme for research and development in atomic energy in 1954 and it took more than a decade to sign the deal for its first nuclear plant with the Canadian government. In May 1965, PAEC asked the Canadian firm General Electric to design and build a 137MW nuclear reactor named KANUPP (Karachi Nuclear Power Plant) to be located at Karachi. Subsequently, Pakistan's first nuclear power plant, KANUPP, was commissioned in 1972. The plant operated safely for thirty years and generated 10.7 billion kWh before retiring in December 2002. It was reconditioned in 2004 to extend its life by fifteen years though at a reduced capacity. A second nuclear power plant CHASNUPP-1, located at Chashma, with a gross capacity of 325MW, was commissioned in

September 2000 as indicated in Table 3.7. Currently, only these two nuclear power stations (KANUPP and CHASNUPP-1) are operating in the country with an overall installed capacity of 462MW. Efforts are being made for the construction of a third nuclear power plant of 325MW named as CHASNUPP-2 again at Chashma and to be completed by 2011.[11]

**Table 3.7: Nuclear power projects**

| Project | Capacity (MW) | Year of Installation |
|---------|--------------:|---------------------:|
| KANNUPP | 125 | 1972 |
| CHASNUPP | 325 | 2000 |

### 3.1.4 RENEWABLE ENERGY

Renewable energy is not new to Pakistan as such. Several initiatives were taken in Pakistan as early as almost three decades ago. Several hundred Photovoltaic systems were installed in different parts of the country. Similarly, small-scale wind turbines were installed on a pilot project basis. The most significant of renewable energy developments was made in the area of biomass as over 4,000 biogas units were setup during the 1970s and 1980s.[12] None of these initiatives, however, could proliferate due to the dearth of intent on the part of pertinent authorities and departments. Over the years a number of departments such as Appropriate Technology Development Corporation (ATDC); National Institute of Silicon Technology (NIST); Pakistan Council for Appropriate Technologies (PCAT); and Pakistan Council of Renewable Energy Technologies (PCRET) were set up to promote the cause of renewable energy. These departments, however, could not deliver as they largely remained constrained to demonstration projects. Another effort was made in 2002 when the Alternate Energy Development Board (AEDB) was set up. The AEDB vowed to pursue vigorous targets particularly with regard to wind power. It promised to deliver 100MW and 700MW of wind power by 2005 and 2007 respectively. The long-term tasks ahead of AEDB was to contribute 5 per cent of the total national power generation capacity, estimated to be around 9,700MW, through renewable energy technologies by the year 2030. Another major target was the accomplishment of the village electrification programme under which 7,874 remote villages in Sindh and Balochistan were to be electrified through renewable energy technologies. AEDB was also to develop a comprehensive plan for the development of solar products, like, solar lights, solar fans, solar cookers and solar geysers through the participation of the private sector. Under the village electrification programme AEDB has, as of mid-2009, achieved the following:[13]

- 6MW 'wind farm' installed in Jhimpir
- 2 wind turbines each of 10kW capacity installed at Kallar Kahar
- 100 micro wind turbines each of 500W capacity installed in Sindh and Balochistan as part of the village electrification programme
- Solar home systems each of 80W capacity installed in 1,000 homes

AEDB is still far from being able to play a noteworthy role in the energy scenario of the country. Its above mentioned achievements do not complement its defined targets in any respect and are too humble to make any positive impact on the power sector.

### 3.1.5 Oil and Gas

Pakistan does not have rich oil and gas reserves. The oil reserves in particular are very limited. The history of oil and gas exploration, in this part of world, dates back to the latter half of the nineteenth century.[14] Oil production is reported to have started in 1886 from the wells drilled in Khattan. In 1915, the first of a series of commercial oil discoveries was made at the Attock oil field. After Independence, the first major exploratory success was the discovery of the Sui gas field in 1952. There were no considerable oil discoveries during the 1950s. To provide an extra impetus to the exploratory efforts that had slowed down towards the latter half of the 1950s, the Government of Pakistan established the Oil and Gas Development Corporation (OGDC) in 1961. Between 1947 and 1977, only 160 exploration wells were drilled by foreign companies while OGDC drilled an extra 30 wells.[15] New discoveries and the development of new oil fields triggered a sharp increment in the production of oil in the 1980s—from almost 4.3 million barrels in 1982 to 22.4 million barrels in 1992. The production from domestic oil refineries also rose in the 1980s, reaching 42 million barrels annually in the early 1990s.[16] There have been considerable developments over the last two decades as a result of which annual production neared 24 million barrels in 2007. However, despite this growth in the production of domestic oil, the contribution it makes is only about 16 per cent of the total national requirement. According to the EIA, Pakistan's total recoverable oil reserves at the end of 2007 stand at around 300 million barrels.[17] According to the Ministry of Petroleum and Natural Resources, however, the country has over 326 million barrels of oil.[18]

Pakistan is among the most gas dependent economies of the world. Natural gas was first discovered by Pakistan Petroleum Ltd. in 1952 at Sui in Balochistan. After successful exploration and extraction, it was brought into service in 1955. Shortly afterwards another major gas field, Mari, was discovered in 1957 by ESSO Eastern. Over the years a number of other gas fields have been discovered in various parts of the country. Gradually, the share of natural gas in the energy supply mix rose to such an extent that presently it has become the backbone of the national energy base—gas contributes to nearly 48 per cent of the total primary energy supplies. The country has integrated infrastructure for transporting, distributing and utilizing natural gas with more than 8,200 km transmission and 59,183 km of distribution and service lines network developed progressively over the last five decades. Pakistan's discovered recoverable gas reserves todate are around 52,900 billion cubic feet of which nearly 23,200 billion cubic feet have been consumed. During 2007–08 the countrywide production of natural gas stood at 1,418 billion cubic feet.[18] Table 3.8 presents annual production from the major gas fields.

**Table 3.8: Overview of the major gas fields in Pakistan 2007–2008**[18]

| Gas field | Annual production (million cubic feet) | Original reserves (million cubic feet) |
|---|---|---|
| Sui | 231,381 | 12,625,000 |
| Qadirpur | 193,174 | 5,056,850 |
| Mari | 171,418 | 6,800,000 |
| Sawan | 152,889 | 15,00,000 |
| Zamzama | 138,872 | 2,324,000 |
| Bhit | 121,683 | 1,605,000 |
| Uch | 70,812 | 5,098,900 |
| Kandhkot | 52,646 | 1,680,000 |

## 3.2. PRESENT GENERATION AND CONSUMPTION TRENDS

### 3.2.1 PRIMARY ENERGY

Pakistan has traditionally been unable to meet its energy requirements from local resources. Currently, indigenous resources—mainly natural gas, hydropower, coal, and oil—contribute to nearly 70 per cent of the total demand. Of the total primary energy consumption, around 87 per cent is met from fossil fuels. Natural gas alone provides around 48 per cent of the total requirements. Other significant contributions come from oil, coal, and hydropower that respectively make up 30.5 per cent, 9.2 per cent, and 10.9 per cent of the supplies. Liquefied Petroleum Gas (LPG) and nuclear power respectively add 0.7 per cent and 1.2 per cent to the supplies as indicated in Figure 3.2. In recent years, Pakistan has started to import electricity from Iran that presently accounts for 0.1 per cent of the total supply mix.[18]

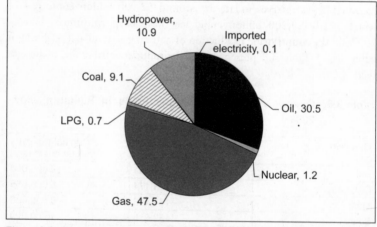

Figure 3.2: Primary commercial energy mix of Pakistan in percentage, 2008

In terms of consumption, the industry, transports and domestic sectors are the major shareholders. Excluding the energy consumed in power generation, the three sectors respectively account for 42.6 per cent, 29.3 per cent, and 20.4 per cent of the total consumption as shown in Figure 3.3.

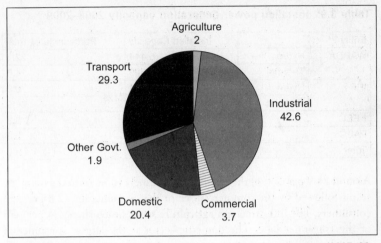

Figure 3.3: Consumption of primary energy by sector in percentage, 2007–08

## 3.2.2 ELECTRICITY

In terms of electricity, the installed capacity can be distributed amongst four major stakeholders. The first and the largest shareholder is the Water and Power Development Authority (WAPDA) that contributes 11,343MW accounting for 56.6 per cent of the total capacity as highlighted in Table 3.9. Around 56.8 per cent of WAPDA's installed capacity comes from hydropower while the remaining 43.2 per cent is made by thermal power. The second most significant contribution is made by the group of Independent Power Producers (IPPs) that have a total installed capacity of 6,391MW making up around 31.9 per cent of the total capacity. Around 98.3 per cent of the IPPs installed capacity comes from thermal power while the rest consists of hydropower. Next comes the Karachi Electric Supply Corporation (KESC) that with its 1,756MW of installed capacity contributes to around 8.8 per cent of the total. Lastly, it is the Pakistan Atomic Energy Commission (PAEC) that, with its 462MW of installed capacity, contributes to around 2.3 per cent of the total capacity.[7,18]

**Table 3.9: Installed power generation capacity 2008–2009**

| Entity | | Installed Capacity | Percentage of Total |
|---|---|---|---|
| WAPDA | Hydro | 6,444 | 32.1 |
| | Thermal | 4,899 | 24.4 |
| IPPs | Hydro | 111 | 0.6 |
| | Thermal | 6,391 | 31.9 |
| KESC | | 1,756 | 8.8 |
| PAEC | | 462 | 2.3 |
| Total | | 20,063 | 100 |

Around 84.9 per cent of the electricity consumers come from the domestic sector followed by the commercial sector that accounts for 12.3 per cent consumers. The industrial and agriculture sectors each share 1.4 per cent of the consumer base. The domestic sector is the largest consumer of electricity in the country accounting for 46 per cent of the total consumption. It is followed by the industry, agriculture, and commercial sectors respectively consuming 27 per cent, 14 per cent, and 7 per cent of the total consumption as suggested in Figure 3.4.

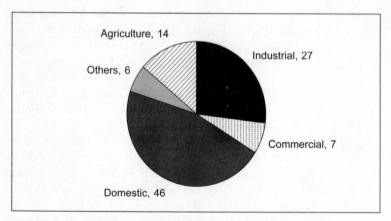

Figure 3.4: Electricity consumption by sector in percentage, 2008-09

### 3.2.3 PETROLEUM PRODUCTS

The transport sector is the largest user of petroleum products accounting for 51.9 per cent of the consumption, followed by the power sector, industry, agriculture, and household respectively accounting for 39.4 per cent, 6.5 per cent, 0.7 per cent, and 0.6 per cent of the total as presented in Figure 3.5.[18]

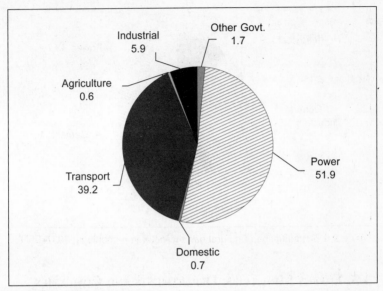

Figure 3.5: Consumption of petroleum products by sector in percentage, 2007–08

## 3.2.4 NATURAL GAS

Pakistan depends heavily on its natural gas reserves for different sectors of the economy. Because of its importance as an alternative and relatively cheaper fuel, the share of gas in total energy mix is on the rise. The power sector is the largest consumer of gas in the country. The share of the power sector in total consumption has grown from 28.9 per cent in 1997–98 to 33.7 per cent in 2007–08. The share of the domestic sector over the same period has dropped from 20.6 per cent to 16.0 per cent. Another notable trend over this period has been rapid growth in consumption of gas in the transport sector—over the same period, the use of Compressed Natural Gas (CNG) has grown from 0.1 per cent to a staggering 5.6 per cent. The number of CNG-run vehicles jumped from 60,000 in December 1999 to 1,700,000 in February 2008. The industrial and domestic sectors respectively consume 23.8 per cent and 18.1 per cent of the total gas. The fertilizer industry is a major consumer of gas and it alone stands for 15.6 per cent of the total consumption as shown in Figure 3.6.

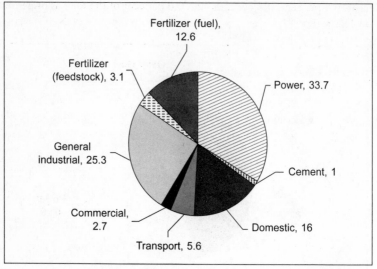

Figure 3.6: Consumption of natural gas by sector in percentage, 2007–2008

## 3.3. ENERGY MINISTRIES, DEPARTMENTS AND COMPANIES

In the early years of Pakistan, the limited commercial-energy-circle of the country was taken care of by a few energy departments and companies. The growth of national energy requirements coupled with new generation- and consumption-trends, saw a gradual development with regard to energy entities both in terms of size and number. In particular, over the last two decades a great number of energy departments and companies have emerged on the scene. The energy departments and companies can be broadly classified under two sectors: power sector, and oil and gas sector. The power sector includes those departments that directly deal with generation and/or transmission and distribution of electricity. The oil and gas sector includes those departments that deal with petroleum products. They are involved in a wide range of activities such as exploration, production, transportation and distribution of these fuels.

Most of the energy departments are governed/coordinated by two ministries: Ministry of Water and Power, and Ministry of Petroleum and Natural Resources. The scope and functions of the important energy departments has been briefly discussed in the following sections.

### 3.3.1 POWER SECTOR DEPARTMENTS AND COMPANIES

#### 3.3.1.1 Ministry of Water and Power

The Ministry of Water and Power is the Government of Pakistan's executive arm dealing with the two vital resources, water and electricity. The ministry, in addition to all policy matters relating to the development of these two resources, performs certain specific functions such as carrying out strategic and financial planning for the long-term master plans in the public and private sectors. The long-term power sector projects submitted by WAPDA and its allied corporations are scrutinized in the ministry through its attached departments keeping in view the technical and financial viability of such projects. Similarly, private sector projects in the power sector are being processed by PPIB in close supervision by the ministry which sets the policy guidelines for approval of private projects.[19]

The five-year plans and the annual development programme (ADP) in the water and power sector are all overseen by the ministry. The Ministry of Water and Power deals with issues relating to power/electricity generation, transmission and distribution, pricing, regulation, and consumption in the country, and exercises this function through its various line agencies as well as relevant autonomous bodies. It also serves to coordinate and plan the nation's power sector, formulate policy and specific incentives, and liaise with provincial governments on all related issues. Table 3.10 provides an overview of the prominent power sector departments.

**Table 3.10: Public power sector players—role and responsibilities**

| Department | Role |
|---|---|
| Water and Power Development Authority (WAPDA) | After restructuring, its role has been confined to development of new projects, and operation and maintenance of existing hydro-power stations. |
| Pakistan Electric Power Company (PEPCO) | Has an oversight role over operation and development activities of thermal GENCOs for generation, of NTDC and DISCOs for transmission and distribution systems. For new IPPs, NTDC liaisons with PPIB and provides interconnection points. NTDC also procures power from existing IPPs. |

| | |
|---|---|
| Private Power and Infrastructure Board (PPIB) | It arranges for required capacity addition through private investments and to provide one-window facility to eliminate unnecessary delays in finalization and approval of IPPs. |
| Pakistan Atomic Energy Commission (PAEC) | It is responsible for the promotion of, and research work on the peaceful uses of atomic energy involving nuclear power stations and the generation of electricity, and to perform other functions relating to the civil applications of atomic energy. |
| AEDB | Aims to generate power from renewables such as wind, solar and biomass. |
| National Electric Power Regulatory Authority (NEPRA) | Regulates the power sector by issuing licenses for generation, transmission and distribution, by tariff determination and by establishing and enforcing performance standards and codes. |
| National Energy Conservation Centre (ENERCON) | Aims to promote energy conservation and management practices across all sectors. |
| Pakistan Council of Renewable Energy Technologies (PCRET) | Aims to coordinate Research and Development (R&D) in the field of renewable energy technologies. |

### 3.3.1.2 Water and Power Development Authority

The Water and Power Development Authority (WAPDA) of Pakistan has traditionally been the focal point of power generation in the country. The department was established in 1958 as a semi-autonomous body for the development of Pakistan's water resources and for construction, operation and maintenance of power generation, transmission and distribution facilities throughout the country, except in the Karachi area. Until very recently it was the largest power producer in the country—in 2007, of the total installed capacity in the country (19.4GW), around 58 per cent (11.3GW) was controlled by WAPDA. In 2007, WAPDA was restructured into two broader entities, i.e. WAPDA and Pakistan Electric Power Company (PEPCO). WAPDA now governs water and hydropower development, whereas, PEPCO manages thermal power generation, transmission, distribution and billing. PEPCO is responsible for the management of all the affairs of the fourteen corporatized companies that include nine distribution companies (DISCOs); four generation companies (GENCOs); and the National Transmission and Despatch Company (NTDC).[7]

Media reports in March 2010 suggested that the government has decided to merge PEPCO into WAPDA. The decision has apparently been taken to improve coordination between various power sector entities.

In order to avoid confusion for the reader, the traditional functions of WAPDA which are presently being looked after by PEPCO have also been described under the umbrella of the former, the parent body.

### 3.3.1.3 Pakistan Electric Power Company

The Pakistan Electric Power Company Limited (PEPCO) is a subsidiary body of WAPDA that aims to enable the reformation and restructuring of the power sector and to transform the fourteen corporate entities into autonomous and commercially viable enterprises, through induction of effective corporate management and utility practices, and to bridge the growing supply-demand gap, so as to meet the customer's electricity requirement in a sustainable fashion.[20] The key objectives of PEPCO are to:

- Control load-shedding
- Construct new grid stations
- Reduce line losses; minimizing tripping and theft control
- Revamp generation units and improve customer services, and
- Develop an integrated automated power planning system for generation, transmission and distribution to ensure system stability, fault isolation and upgrade relying, metering and tripping system at the NTDC as well as DISCOS level

### 3.3.1.4 Karachi Electric Supply Company

The Karachi Electric Supply Company Limited (KESC), initially established in 1913 is the oldest power company of Pakistan. In 1952 the Government of Pakistan took control of the company by acquiring majority shareholding. KESC is principally engaged in generation, transmission and distribution of electricity. The licensed area of KESC is spread over the entire city of Karachi and its suburbs up to Dhabeji and Gharo in Sindh and over Hub, Uthal, Vindhar, and Bela in Balochistan. The total area covered is around 6,000 sq km.[21] KESC was privatised in November 2005 with the transfer of 73 per cent shares of the Government of Pakistan along with management control to the new owners. KESC is estimated to have a customer base of around 2 million.

### 3.3.1.5 Private Power and Infrastructure Board

The Private Power and Infrastructure Board (PPIB) was created in 1994 to facilitate the private sector in the participation of power generation in Pakistan. PPIB aims to provide a one-window facility to private sector investors in matters concerning establishing power projects and related infrastructure. These matters include negotiation of the Implementation Agreement (IA). PPIB also provides support to the power purchasers and fuel suppliers while negotiating the Power Purchase Agreement (PPA); Fuel Supply Agreement (FSA)/Gas Supply Agreement (GSA); other related agreements; and liaison with the concerned local and international agencies for facilitating and expediting progress of private sector power projects.[22]

### 3.3.1.6 National Electric Power Regulatory Authority

The National Electric Power Regulatory Authority (NEPRA) is the regulatory authority established to regulate the power sector in order to promote a competitive structure for the industry and to ensure the coordinated, reliable and adequate supply of electricity in future. NEPRA was established in 1995 and is independent in its functions without any administrative control of the government. However, for the sake of interaction with the federal and provincial governments it was originally attached to the Ministry of Water and Power. Subsequently, it was required to route its correspondence with the government through the Ministry of Law and Justice. In 2000, it was attached to the Cabinet Division. The authority comprises of a chairman to be appointed by the federal government, and four members also to be appointed by the federal government on the recommendations of the four provincial governments. NEPRA's main responsibilities are to:[23]

- Issue licenses for generation, transmission, and distribution of electric power
- Establish and enforce standards to ensure quality and safety of operation and supply of electric power to consumers
- Approve investment and power acquisition programmes of the utility companies; and
- Determine tariffs for generation, transmission and distribution of electric power

### 3.3.1.7 National Transmission & Despatch Company

The National Transmission & Despatch Company Limited (NTDC) was incorporated in 1998. It was organized to take over all the properties, rights and assets obligations and liabilities of 220KV and 500KV grid stations and transmission lines/network owned by WAPDA. The NTDC operates and maintains nine 500KV grid stations, 4,160 km of 500KV transmission lines and 4,000 km of 220KV transmission lines in Pakistan. NTDC was granted a transmission license in 2002 by the National Electric Power Regularity Authority (NEPRA) to engage in the exclusive transmission business for a term of thirty years.[24] Under the regime set out in the license, the NTDC is entrusted to act as: central power purchasing agency; system operator; transmission network operator; and contract registrar and power exchange administrator.

### 3.3.1.8 Pakistan Atomic Energy Commission

The Pakistan Atomic Energy Commission (PAEC) looks after nuclear power in Pakistan. It was originally established in 1956 as the Atomic Energy Research Council. In 1972, the Commission was transferred from the Science and Technology Research Division to the President's Secretariat. PAEC is charged with the promotion of, and research work on the peaceful uses of atomic energy in the fields of agriculture, medicine and industry, as well as the execution of development projects involving nuclear power stations and the generation of electricity, and to perform other functions relating to the civil applications of atomic energy as  mandated by the government. In principle, the commission is engaged in:[25]

- Development of nuclear power and fuel-cycle facilities
- Promotion of use of radiation and radio-isotopes in agriculture, medicine and industry
- Research, development and training of manpower to support the programmes of nuclear power and radio-isotope applications

### 3.3.1.9 Alternative Energy Development Board

 The Alternative Energy Development Board (AEDB) is responsible for the advancement of renewable energy. It was formally established in 2003 with a clear mandate to exploit renewable resources of the country in order to contribute to the national energy supply mix. The board initially worked as an autonomous body under the Cabinet Division. In 2006, however, it became a subsidiary of the Ministry of Water and Power. Its prominent functions as described in the Presidential Ordinance under which the board was established are to:[26]

- Develop national strategy, policies and plans for utilization of alternative and renewable energy resources to achieve the targets approved by the Federal Government in consultation with the Board
- Act as a forum for evaluating, monitoring and certification of alternative or renewable energy projects and products
- Act as a coordinating agency for commercial application of alternative or renewable technology
- Facilitate power generation through renewable energy resources by providing wide-ranging services

### 3.3.1.10 National Energy Conservation Centre

The National Energy Conservation Centre (ENERCON) is the department responsible for promoting energy conservation and management. Having been originally set up in 1986 under the Ministry of Planning and Development, it became a subsidiary of the Ministry of Water and Power in 1993. The department was transferred to the Ministry of Environment in 1996. ENERCON is to serve as the national focal point for energy conservation/energy efficiency activities in all sectors of the economy, such as industry, agriculture, transport, building and domestic. The department aims to encompass a broad range of activities, starting from identification of energy conservation opportunities and including technology demonstration, undertaking pilot projects, information and outreach, training and education, and development of plans and policies for promoting energy efficiency.[27]

### 3.3.1.11 Pakistan Council of Renewable Energy Technologies

The Pakistan Council of Renewable Energy Technologies (PCRET) was set up in 2001 to coordinate research and development (R&D) in the field of renewable energy technologies. It was created by merging the National Institute of Silicon Technology (NIST) and the Pakistan Council for Appropriate Technologies (PCAT). Before the establishment of the Alternate Energy Development Board (AEDB), PCRET was the main department in the country to promote renewable energy. PCRET is a subsidiary of the Ministry of Science and Technology and operates through its head office in Islamabad and the four provincial offices based at Karachi, Lahore, Peshawar and Quetta. PCRET mainly deals with biomass, hydropower, solar and wind power technologies.[28] It, however, also covers geothermal and wave and tidal technologies though there have not been any initiatives on these fronts.

### 3.3.2 OIL AND GAS-SECTOR—DEPARTMENTS AND COMPANIES

#### 3.3.2.1 Ministry of Petroleum and Natural Resources

The Ministry of Petroleum and Natural Resources was created in 1977. Prior to that, it was part of the Ministry of Fuel, Power, and Natural Resources. The ministry is responsible for dealing with all matters relating to petroleum, gas, and mineral affairs. It aims to ensure availability and security of a sustainable supply of oil and gas for economic development and strategic requirements of Pakistan and to coordinate development of natural resources of energy and minerals. Some of the prominent functions of the ministry are as follows:[29]

- Policy, legislation, planning regarding exploration, development and productions. Policy guidelines to regulatory bodies in oil and gas sectors
- Policy guidelines and facilitation of import, export, refining, distribution, marketing, transportation and pricing of all kinds of petroleum and petroleum products
- Federal agencies and institutions for promotion of special studies and development programmes
- Facilitate the development of petroleum and mineral sectors
- Attract private investment
- Petroleum concessions agreements for land, off-shore and deep-sea areas
- Facilitation of import of machinery equipment etc. for exploration and development of petroleum and minerals
- Coordination of energy and mineral policies
- Research, development, deployment and demonstration of hydrocarbon energy resources

### 3.3.2.2 Oil and Gas Development Company Limited

The Oil and Gas Development Company Limited (OGDCL) was set up in 1961 to facilitate the oil and gas sector. The mandate of the Company, initially called Oil and Gas Development Company (OGDC), was to explore and develop oil and gas resources of the country. Prior to the emergence of the Company, these functions were carried out by Pakistan Petroleum Ltd. (PPL) and Pakistan Oilfields Ltd. (POL). It was the agreement between USSR and Pakistan in 1961, under which the former facilitated the latter with financial and technical assistance, which led to the establishment of OGDCL. The Company adopted the status of a Public Limited Company in 1997. Important functions of the Company include: exploration, drilling, production, reservoir management and provision of engineering support. OGDCL's daily production of oil and gas has been highlighted in Table 3.11.

**Table 3.11: Average daily production from OGDCL during February 2009[30]**

| Product | Quantity |
|---------|----------|
| Oil | 40,640 Barrel/day |
| Gas | 968 MMcf/day |
| LPG | 120 M Ton/day |
| Sulphur | 66 M ton/day |

### 3.3.2.3 Pakistan Petroleum Limited

Pakistan Petroleum Ltd (PPL), one of the leading petroleum exploration and production companies in the country, was incorporated in 1950 in order to coordinate exploration, development and production of Pakistan's oil and natural gas resources. PPL inherited all the assets and liabilities of the Burmah Oil Company (Pakistan Concessions) Limited and commenced business on 1 July 1952. The four operational strands of PPL are:

- Exploration
- Drilling
- Production
- Mining

Starting out concurrently with the first major gas discovery at Sui in 1952, PPL now operates four production fields at Sui, Kandhkot, Adhi, and Mazarani and holds a working interest in seven partner-operated production fields. Presently, PPL contributes around 26 per cent of the country's total natural gas production besides producing crude oil/natural gas liquids (NGL) and liquefied petroleum gas (LPG). PPL's exploration portfolio comprises twenty-four exploration blocks, including four that are offshore. On 30 June 2008, the company's hydrocarbon reserves stood at approximately 3.71 trillion cubic feet of natural gas, 23.3 million barrels of oil/NGL and 321,000 tonnes of LPG.[31]

### 3.3.2.4 Pakistan State Oil

Pakistan State Oil (PSO) is the largest distributor of petroleum products in the country. The origin of PSO dates back to January 1974 when the government took over the company and merged Pakistan National Oil (PNO) and Dawood Petroleum Limited (DPL) as Premier Oil Company Limited (POCL). Shortly afterwards, in June 1974, Petroleum Storage Development Corporation (PSDC) came into existence. PSDC was then renamed as State Oil Company Limited (SOCL) in August 1976. Following that, the ESSO undertakings were purchased in September 1976 and control was vested in SOCL. The end of the same year saw the merger of the Premier Oil Company Limited and State Oil Company Limited, giving way to Pakistan State Oil.

Pakistan State Oil is mainly engaged in marketing and distribution of various Pakistan Oilfields Limited (POL) products, including motor gasoline, high-speed diesel, furnace oil, jet fuel, kerosene, LPG, CNG, petrochemicals and lubricants. PSO possesses huge infrastructure facilities throughout the country. This entails nine installations and twenty-six depots with a storage capacity exceeding 850,000 metric tones, representing over 80 per cent of the total storage capacity owned by all oil marketing companies.[32] To make the most of its storage facilities, PSO also provides hospitality to refineries and other oil marketing companies that include Chevron, Total PARCO and Hascombe. PSO caters to POL requirements of a wide spectrum of customers comprising the retail consumer, various industrial units, government departments, power projects, aviation and marine sectors of Pakistan.

### 3.3.2.5 Oil and Gas Regulatory Authority

The Natural Gas Regulatory Authority (NGRA) was established subsequent to the NGRA Ordinance of government in 2000 to regulate the transmission, distribution and sale of natural gas, and to determine gas tariffs. In 2002, it was decided to broaden the scope of NGRA as the Oil and Gas Regulatory Authority (OGRA) so as to also cover the technical regulations of refineries, oil storages, oil pipelines and oil marketing companies. In 2003, OGRA was further assigned the functions for the regulation of activities relating to liquefied petroleum gas (LPG) and compressed natural gas (CNG) sectors. Some of the key functions of the Authority are to foster competition; increase private investment and ownership in the midstream and downstream petroleum industry; protect the public interest while respecting individual rights; and provide effective and efficient regulations. The Authority is associated with the Cabinet Division and comprises of one Chairman and three members.[33]

### 3.3.2.6 Sui Northern Gas Pipelines Limited

Sui Northern Gas Pipelines Limited (SNGPL) is the largest integrated gas company serving more than three million consumers in Central and the Northern Pakistan through an extensive network in Punjab and NWFP. Having been incorporated in 1963, SNGPL has over forty-five years of experience in the operation and maintenance of high-pressure gas transmission and distribution systems. It has also expanded its activities to undertake the planning, designing and construction of pipelines, both for itself and other organizations. The SNGPL transmission system extends from Sui in Balochistan to Peshawar in North-West Frontier Province (NWFP) comprising over 7,016 km (as on June 2008) of the transmission system (main lines and loop lines). Its distribution activities covering 1,224 towns along with adjoining villages in Punjab and NWFP are organized through eight regional offices. SNGPL's distribution system consists of 59,951 km (as on June 2008) of pipeline.[34]

### 3.3.2.7. Sui Southern Gas Company

The Sui Southern Gas Company (SSGC) mainly deals with the transmission and distribution of natural gas besides construction of high-pressure transmission and low-pressure distribution systems. The SSGC transmission system extends from Sui in Balochistan to Karachi in Sindh comprising over 3,200 km of high-pressure pipelines. The distribution activities covering over 1,200 towns in Sindh and Balochistan are organized through its regional offices. Company statistics suggest the an average of about 357,129 million cubic feet (MMCFD) gas was sold in 2006–2007 to over 1.9 million industrial, commercial and domestic consumers in these regions through a distribution network of over 29,832 km.[35] The Company also owns and operates the only gas meter manufacturing plant in the country, having an annual production capacity of over 550,150 meters. SSGC is primarily a state-owned company with over 70 per cent of the shares belonging to the Government of Pakistan. The company is managed by an autonomous board of directors for policy guidelines and overall control. Presently, SSGC's board comprises of fourteen members. The managing director/chief executive is a nominee of the Government of Pakistan and has been delegated with such powers by the board of directors as are necessary to ensure the effective conduct of business by the Company.

### 3.3.2.8 Pakistan Oilfields Limited

Pakistan Oilfields Limited (POL) deals with exploration and production of oil and gas. POL, a subsidiary of the Attock Oil Company Limited (AOC), was incorporated in 1950. In 1978, POL took over the exploration and production business of AOC that was established in 1913. Since then, POL has been investing independently and in joint ventures with other exploration and production companies to search for oil and gas both within the country and abroad. In addition to exploration and production of oil and gas, POL plants also manufacture LPG, solvent oil and sulphur. POL markets LPG under its own brand name of POLGAS as well as through its subsidiary CAPGAS (Private) Limited. POL has a 25 per cent shareholding in National Refinery Limited, which is Pakistan's only local refinery producing lube base oils and is the single largest producer of high quality asphalts. POL also operates a network of pipelines for transportation of its own as well as other companies' crude oil to Attock Refinery Limited.[36]

### 3.3.2.9 Pak-Arab Refinery Limited

Pak-Arab Refinery Limited (PARCO) is one of the most important energy companies in the country dealing with refining, storage and transportation of oil. Established in May 1974, as a public limited company, PARCO is a joint venture between the Government of Pakistan and Abu Dhabi Petroleum Investment (ADPI) respectively holding 60 per cent and 40 per cent shares in it. It owns and operates the country's largest refinery and crude-cum-products pipeline system. PARCO's major activities are: oil refining and allied facilities; oil pipeline systems, storage and allied facilities; and marketing of petroleum products.

Over the years, PARCO has implemented a number of infrastructure enhancement projects which have substantially contributed towards complementing oil logistics with the overall national development plans. Pak-Arab Pipeline Company Limited (PAPCO), a joint venture between PARCO, Shell, PSO, and Chevron with respective shares of 51 per cent, 26 per cent, 12 per cent and 11 per cent makes a significant contribution to the High Speed Diesel (HSD) supply chain in Pakistan. It provides the strategic infrastructure to transport HSD from Karachi to Shikarpur and Mahmoodkot. It is interconnected with both Port Qasim and Keamari Ports as well as with Pakistan Refinery Limited (PRL), National Refinery Limited (NRL) and Pak-Arab Refinery Limited (PARCO). It has the flexibility to receive imported and locally produced petroleum products from multiple sources and to deliver them at different demand centres. PARCO looks after the operations and management of PAPCO.[37]

### 3.3.2.10 Oil Companies Advisory Committee

The Oil Companies Advisory Committee (OCAC) is a representative body of oil companies operating in the country. It coordinates the Downstream Oil Sector (DOS) activities such as refining, marketing and distribution that are vital to ensure uninterrupted supply of petroleum products in the country. The members of OCAC include refineries, marketing companies and a pipeline transportation company. The OCAC is governed by a committee comprising of the chief executives of each of the member companies. The committee chairman is elected from within the member companies for a working term of one calendar year.[38]

### 3.3.2.11 Lakhar Coal Development Company

The Lakhar Coal Development Company (LCDC) operates coal mines in Lakhar and supplies it for the coal fired power-plant of WAPDA in Dadu. It was established in 1990 as a joint venture of Pakistan Mineral Development Corporation (PMDC); Water and Power Development

Authority (WAPDA); and Government of Sindh (GOS). The LCDC possesses a leased area of 7,943 acres. It has been availing expertise of a Chinese firm for geo-technical studies and the development of mechanized coal mines.[29]

### 3.3.2.12 Hydrocarbon Development Institute of Pakistan

The Hydrocarbon Development Institute of Pakistan (HDIP) is responsible for research and development in the area of fossil fuels. It is an autonomous body of the Ministry of Petroleum and Natural Resources originally established in 1975. It carries out applied research; provides consultancy and laboratory services to the petroleum industry; and renders technical advice to the government on matters referred to it.[39]

## REFERENCES

1. Hydel Power Policy 1995, WAPDA.
2. Charles Ebinger, *Pakistan: Energy Planning in a Strategic Vortex*, Indiana University Press, 1981.
3. Former Member WAPDA, Telephonic Interview, 20 January 2008.
4. Z. Mahmood, Energy Security of Pakistan, MSc thesis, Glasgow Caledonian University, UK, 2008.
5. Electricity Marketing Data, NTDC, 2008.
6. M. Asif, Sustainable Energy Options for Pakistan, Renewable and Sustainable energy Reviews, 13, 4, 2009.
7. WAPDA website, www.wapda.gov.pk (accessed on 11 December 2009).
8. Commercialization of Wind Power Potential in Pakistan, Financial and Economic Evaluation, PAK/97/G42, Hagler Bailly Pakistan, July 2003.
9. 'The Perils of High Cost Imported Energy', Sartaj Aziz, *The Nation*, 28–29 November 1994.
10. Policy Framework and Package of Incentives for Private Sector Power Generation Projects in Pakistan, GOP, 1994.
11. Pakistan Atomic Energy Commission website, Islamabad, Pakistan.
12. Karen Dunn, 'Pakistan's Energy Positions: Problems and Prospects', *Asian Survey* Vol. 31, No. 12, 1991.
13. AEDB officials, data provided through email, 20 May 2009.
14. Pakistan: Oil & Gas Sector Review, Document of the World Bank, Report No. 26072-PK, 2003.
15. Charles Ebinger, Pakistan: Energy Planning in a Strategic Vortex, Indiana University Press, 1981.
16. Peter Blood, ed. *Pakistan: A Country Study*. Washington: GPO for the Library of Congress, 1994.
17. Energy Information Administration Statistics 2007.
18. Pakistan Energy Year Book, 2008.

19. Ministry of Water and Power website, http://202.83.164.26/wps/portal/Mowp (accessed on 11 December 2009).
20. PEPCO website, http://www.pepco.gov.pk/ (accessed on 11 December 2009).
21. KESC website, http://www.kesc.com.pk/en (accessed on 11 December 2009).
22. PPIB website, http://www.ppib.gov.pk/ (accessed on 11 December 2009).
23. NEPRA website, http://www.nepra.org.pk/ (accessed on 11 December 2009).
24. NTDC website, http://www.ntdc.com.pk/ (accessed on 11 December 2009).
25. PAEC website, http://www.paec.gov.pk/ (accessed on 11 December 2009).
26. AEDB website, http://www.aedb.org/ (accessed on 11 December 2009).
27. ENERCON website, http://www.enercon.gov.pk/ (accessed on 11 December 2009).
28. PCRET website, http://www.pcret.gov.pk/ (accessed on 11 December 2009).
29. Ministry of Petroleum and Natural Resources website, http://www.mpnr.gov.pk/
30. OGDC website, http://www.ogdcl.com/ (accessed on 11 December 2009).
31. PPL website, http://www.ppl.com.pk/Pages/index.aspx (accessed on 11 December 2009).
32. PSO website, http://www.psopk.com/ (accessed on 11 December 2009).
33. OGRA website, http://www.ogra.org.pk/ (accessed on 11 December 2009).
34. SNGPL website, http://www.sngpl.com.pk/ (accessed on 11 December 2009).
35. SSGC website, http://www.ssgc.com.pk/ssgc/index.php (accessed on 11 December 2009).
36. POL website, http://www.pakoil.com.pk/ (accessed on 11 December 2009).
37. PARCO website, http://www.parco.com.pk/ (accessed on 11 December 2009).
38. OCAC website, http://www.ocac.org.pk/aboutus.html (accessed on 11 December 2009).
39. HDIP website, http://www.hdip.com.pk/ (accessed on 11 December 2009).

# 4

# The Energy Crisis 2006–2007:
# Origin, Dimensions and Implications

From the outset, Pakistan has struggled to have a stable energy scenario. Especially, when it comes to electricity, the equation has been quite roller coaster like—in terms of demand and supply there have been regular spells of intense shortfall. The most recent trough the national electricity system has experienced was triggered in 2006–07 with a gradual buildup of a gap between demand and supply. Very quickly it turned into the worst energy crisis in the country's history. Three years on, rather than having any relief, helpless Pakistanis are finding the intensity of the problem on the rise as in March 2010, they were enduring up to eighteen hours of load-shedding even in the metropolitan cities. The make-up of the prevailing energy crisis has been highlighted in Figure 4.1.

The present crisis is also a self-inflicted problem resulting from years of poor policies and reckless attitude on the part of concerned authorities. The scale of the problem has now almost grown beyond any instant solution. It has happened at a time when energy is considered to be the backbone of human activities and also a vital commodity for the survival of modern economies. Alike global trend, energy has become a lot more important in the life of an average Pakistani. At the time of independance in 1947, for a total population of 33.7 million people, the installed capacity of electricity generation in the country was 50MW.[1] In 2007, for a population of about 160 million, the installed capacity had grown to 19,500MW. It simply means that in a matter of six decades the per capita electricity consumption has increased by 82-fold. The staggering rise in its per capita consumption implies that electricity, the most refined form of energy, has become an integral part of present day life in Pakistan. However, the near bankrupt national electricity portfolio suggests that the trend of electricity proliferation is likely to be hampered for at least the next few years.

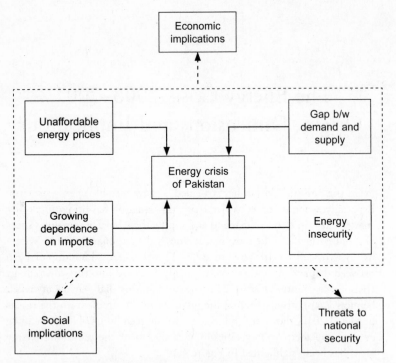

Figure 4.1: Composition of the energy crisis and its key implications

Energy crisis is not new to Pakistan. Load-shedding, for instance, has frequently plagued the country, particularly over the last three decades. Nevertheless, the present ordeal is far too complex and profound. The current crisis, from its early days, has inflicted enormous economic, socio-political and strategic damage. This chapter investigates the origin of the present crisis, its major dimensions and its wide-ranging implications for the country.

## 4.1. GAP BETWEEN ENERGY DEMAND AND SUPPLY

### 4.1.1 PRIMARY ENERGY AND ELECTRICITY SHORTFALL

Pakistan has experienced a rapid growth in primary energy demand in recent decades—figures indicate around 150 per cent increment in primary energy consumption over the last twenty years.[2] Here it is noteworthy that primary energy is a much broader commodity and it takes into account all forms of energy such as electricity, gas and fuel for transportation and other industrial and commercial applications. The demand far exceeds supplies making the country energy deficient in totality. The gap between demand and supply is on a gradual rise. Statistics suggest that over the last thirty-six years, the gap between commercial energy demand and supply in Pakistan has grown by a factor of nearly six—the gap rose from nearly three million tons of oil equivalent (MTOE) in 1971–72 to around 18 million MTOE in 2007–08.[2,3] The demand for electricity is also on a steep rise due to urbanization, and extension of electricity grid supply to un-electrified areas and village electrification. The number of electricity consumers has jumped from 7.9 million in 1992–93 to 19.9 million in 2008, showing a growth of more than 150 per cent over the last eighteen years. Despite such a sharp rise in the consumer base, still only around 60 per cent of the total population in Pakistan is connected to the national grid.

The most obvious indicator of the scarcity of energy is the shortfall of electricity. Pakistan has faced a deficit of electricity from the outset. Senior WAPDA officials report that in 1947 only 7 per cent of the population was connected to local grids while no national grid was in place. Over the years, while a major proportion of the population still remains deprived of the national grid, those who are connected to it have hardly enjoyed a secure supply of electricity. One of the few exceptional periods—when the country had an adequate supply of electricity—constituted the latter half of the 1990s and the earlier half of the 2000s as shown in Figure 4.2. However, over the last ten years the generation capacity has not been enhanced in response to swallowing electricity requirements. Failure to react to the situation not only eroded the surplus generation capacity but also drove the country into a massive deficit of electricity. WAPDA's daily report on 3 January 2008, for example, recorded a supply of 7,237MW against a demand of 11,509MW, recording an astounding shortage of over 37 per cent. During the summer, the same year, the electricity shortfall grew as much as 5,454MW as shown in Table 4.1. The intensity of electricity shortfall is on a consistent rise. WAPDA sources suggest that on 22 March 2010, as the weather was in transition from winter to summer, the country faced a deficit of over 5,300MW. From this figure it can well be imagined that the shortfall could easily jump over 6,000MW during the peak summer months of the year.

**Table 4.1: Electricity demand and supply during 2008[5]**

| Month | Date | Peak Demand (MW) | Corresponding supply (MW) | Gap (MW) |
|---|---|---|---|---|
| January | 23 | 12,255 | 9,104 | 3,151 |
| February | 16 | 12,123 | 10,122 | 2,001 |
| March | 29 | 13,682 | 9,845 | 3,837 |
| April | 29 | 15,124 | 11,568 | 3,556 |
| May | 31 | 16,649 | 11,195 | 5,454 |
| June | 25 | 17,398 | 12,442 | 4,956 |
| July | 29 | 17,715 | 12,822 | 4,893 |
| August | 7 | 17,272 | 12,751 | 4,521 |
| September | 4 | 17,852 | 13,637 | 4,215 |
| October | 5 | 15,766 | 12,982 | 2,784 |
| November | 1 | 13,000 | 11,243 | 1,757 |
| December | 16 | 11,358 | 7,945 | 2,162 |

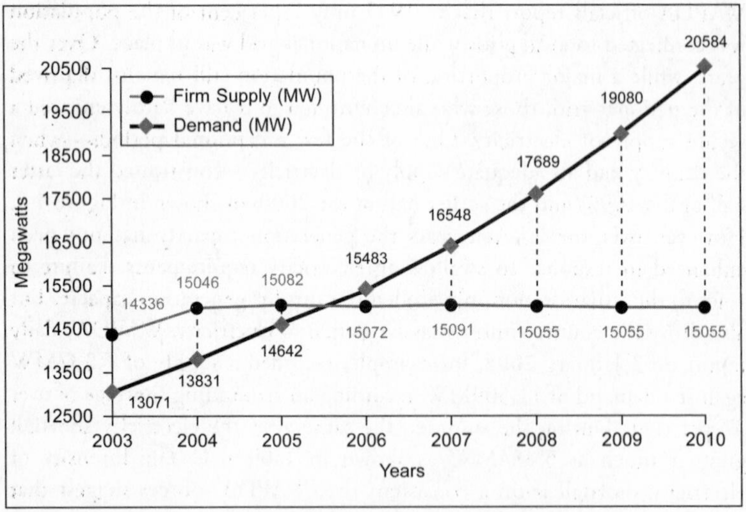

Figure 4.2: Growing gap between electricity demand and supply

The average annual economic growth in the country during the first half of the 2000s was about 7 per cent. The national target is to attain an average economic growth of a similar order, 7 to 8 per cent per year, over the next twenty-five years as highlighted in the Medium Term Development Framework (2005–10). To achieve this economic growth, it is forecasted that the primary energy demand will increase by more than six times, from 55 MTOE (Million Tonnes of Oil Equivalent) in 2005 to 361 MTOE in 2030. Similarly, electricity demand will increase by a factor of 8, from 19,540MW in 2005 to 163,000MW by 2030.[6]

### 4.1.2 GAS SHORTFALL

The electricity crisis is not the only headache for Pakistan but a severe gas crisis is also fast approaching. For the last five decades the country has enjoyed a supply of gas from indigenous resources healthy enough to match the demands of the national gas pipeline network that reaches around 20 per cent of households and a considerable degree of industrial and commercial consumers. The indigenous supply of cheap gas has greatly helped industrial and economic activities to flourish. The demand and supply situation, however, is quickly changing from affluence to deficiency. Reports suggest that demand and supply were at par in 2006 and since then the country has entered into the deficiency phase.[7]

According to the Ministry of Petroleum and Natural Resources, during 2007–08, the production of gas jumped from 3,873 to 3,973 million cubic feet per day recording a 2.6 per cent increment. The growth in consumption outpaced the growth in production as the former increased by 4.4 per cent over the same period.[8] The consequences of the shortfall such as gas load-shedding and supply cuts have been quite common during the winter months of recent years affecting all sectors including domestic, industrial, and commercial. The problem touched new heights in 2009 as even during the summer months a large number of textile mills and other industries faced supply disconnections. The severity of the issue can be gauged from the government's decision in November 2009 to impose a two days a week gas load-shedding on industry and CNG stations from November 2009 to March 2010.[9] If this trend continues and the government fails to respond to the crisis urgently and effectively, by 2030 the demand is likely to outpace supplies by eight times as indicated in Table 4.2.

**Table 4.2: Demand and supply projection (Millions of cubic feet per day)[10]** .

| Years | Demand | Supply | Net Difference |
|-------|--------|--------|----------------|
| 2004-05 | 3,173 | 4,033 | 860 |
| 2009-10 | 4,,565 | 4,424 | -141 |
| 2019-20 | 9114 | 3,001 | -6113 |
| 2029-30 | 19,035 | 2,299 | -16736 |

According to the Energy Information Administration, in 2007, Pakistan's natural gas reserves were around 28,000 billion cubic feet.[2] At the same year's consumption level, the reserves are said to last for twenty-one years.[10] However, with a consistent growth at the demand end, the reserves are bound to be exhausted more quickly.

The local natural gas reserves were of strategic importance for the country but have been used relatively irresponsibly, particularly over the last decade or so. In 2008, 34,742 GWh of electricity was produced from gas, accounting for 35 per cent of the total electricity generated in the country.[11] Using gas for such a large proportion of power generation when other more sustainable options like hydropower and coal were available has been a reckless move. The mushroom growth of CNG stations over the last few years has also added to the burden on the gas production and supply network.

In the backdrop of the imminent gas crisis, Pakistan has been exploring options for gas import. In this regard, the three different options that have surfaced over the years are as follows and as shown in Figure 4.3.[12]

• Natural gas pipeline from Turkmenistan to Pakistan through Afghanistan
• Natural gas pipeline from Qatar to Pakistan through Oman
• Natural gas pipeline from Iran to Pakistan

There have not been any developments over the first two options. The greatest hurdle to the pipeline from Turkmenistan is the volatile geopolitical situation in Afghanistan. There are also issues with regard to the price of gas. There has not been much development on the Qatar pipeline either for various reasons. A considerable section of this pipeline would have to be under the sea which makes it a more costly and complicated affair. The Iran pipeline proposal has matured the most thus far.

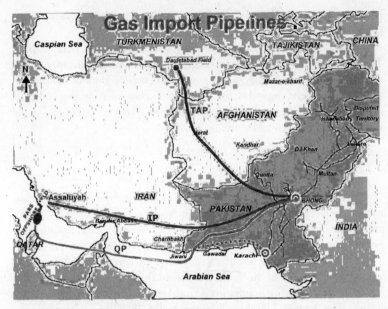

Figure 4.3: Proposed gas import pipelines

The idea for the Iran–Pakistan pipeline project was originally conceived in 1995 as a Iran-Pakistan-India (IPI) pipeline. It was to be 2,700km in total length with 1,100km, 1,000km and 600km long sections in Iran, Pakistan, and India respectively. However, after almost thirteen years, India finally decided to quit the project in 2008. In May 2009, Pakistan and Iran have finally signed the initial agreement to start working on the project by 2010 that would take around five years to completion.[13] Pakistan aims to capitalize the gas imported through this pipeline mainly for usage in power generation and heavy industries. A number of issues including the price of gas are yet to be finalized. This is a healthy development but it does not guarantee the successful completion of the project for a number of reasons such as: still unresolved project details, volatile geo-political situation in the region, pressure on Pakistan from Western countries in general and the US in particular to refrain from economic and strategic ties with Iran, and doubts on the consistency of policies on both sides particularly at the Pakistani end. Sources suggest that the gas pipeline project 'continues to be a victim of missed opportunities, delayed decision-making, flawed strategy and incorrect planning, and project development.'[14] It is, however, hoped that policy-makers make the best of the Iran–Pakistan pipeline project as it is in Pakistan's national interest.

The dependence upon imported gas would have serious implications. The switchover of the base gas load from the indigenous to foreign resources is going to be very tough not only on socio-economic conditions at the micro level but also on the macro-economics of the country. Official sources suggest that by 2025 the annual import bill of gas alone would stand at around $18 billion.[10]

### 4.1.3 WATER SHORTFALL

Owing to its versatile and vital uses, water is arguably the most important natural resource, in fact the source of life. Water resources across the world are under intense pressure for a number of reasons including growing populations, urbanization, industrialization and changes in the ecosystem. There are numerous calls for increased water conservation and cooperation amongst the nations of the world. Parallel to this, there are also warnings in place about growing international confrontations on water resources in future. The former UN Secretary General Kofi Annan, for example, warned in 2001: 'Fierce competition for fresh water may well become a source of conflicts and wars in the future.'[15] Similarly, in 1995, the World Bank Vice President Ismail Serageldin suggested that, 'the wars of the next century will be about water,' an outlook echoed regularly ever since.[16]

Pakistan cannot remain isolated from these developments as its own fresh water resources are also under increasing stress. If the government does not act on an urgent footing the country will face a desperate water scarcity situation in a few years.[17] Estimates suggest that the annual per capita availability of water has dropped from 5,260m$^3$ in 1951 to 1,100m$^3$ in 2006.[18] A country is said to experience water stress when the annual per capita water supplies drop below 1,700m.$^3$ When the annual per capita supplies drop below 1,000m,$^3$ the country faces water scarcity for all or part of the year.[19] Under these circumstances, when Pakistan needs to save every drop of the available water, it could only be said to be a national misfortune that every year over 30 million acre feet of water that could have been usefully capitalised is thrown into the sea. Also, bearing in mind the energy crisis the country is facing, it becomes almost imperative to capture this water for various applications including electricity generation, irrigation, and drinking.

At a time when a large number of medium to large-scale dams are being constructed in India and China, Pakistan is showing little respect for this precious source of energy. In recent years there have been many reports in the Pakistani media that accuse India of having developed a number of illegal dams on the rivers that it has no right to interfere with under the Indus Water Treaty. The ongoing construction of Baglihar and Ganga Kishan dams—projects that Pakistan firmly believes is an Indian attempt to steal the former's water—has been making headlines for several years now.[20,21] Concerns over the developments in India are escalating on this side of the border. Pakistan has also invited international mediators to look into the matter but the problem remains unresolved as India, despite having violated the water rights of Pakistan, as determined under the Indus Basin Treaty, shows little flexibility in its stance.[22]

As a matter of fact the issue of the distribution of river-waters between the two countries—that was first triggered by India in the form of closure of water to Pakistan in 1948—remains a bone of contention between them. The initial confrontation of 1948 ultimately led to the Indus Water Treaty in 1960 under the auspices of the World Bank. This treaty defined the use of the Indus System of Rivers between India and Pakistan. Under the treaty, the water from the three Eastern Rivers of this System—Sutlej, Beas and Ravi—was assigned to India. Similarly, the three Western Rivers of this Indus System of Rivers—Indus, Jhelum and Chenab—were retained by Pakistan. While in recent years, India is tampering with the water of the Jhelum and Chenab rivers in clear violation of the Indus Water Treaty, there have been numerous calls on the Pakistani administration from various corners of the country to adopt a tougher stance in ensuring the security of its water supplies from India.

The water of rivers flowing from India is a lifeline for the energy and agriculture sectors of Pakistan. Concerned energy circles believe that in future India may resort to the sabotage of Pakistan's water supply for various reasons. Shams-ul-Mulk a retired chairman of WAPDA, in the backdrop of the country's passive attitude towards exploitation of its hydropower resource, even fears that: 'India may seek to renegotiate Indus Water Treaty and snatch Pakistan's water if the latter does not capitalise its resource.'[23]

A recent study published in the journal *Nature* has also raised alarm bells that the issue of water resources could make India's already fraught relationship with Pakistan even worse. According to the study NASA has identified that aquifers in north-western India, also known as the country's breadbasket and bordering Pakistan, are being depleted at a much greater rate than they're being replenished. Matt Rodell, a hydrologist at NASA's Goddard Space Flight Centre in the United States, perceives: 'Potentially if India's using a lot of water and drawing down the water table and it affects Pakistan that could irritate the tensions that are already there.'[24] Pakistan would, therefore, inevitably have to adopt a definite and bold stance, unlike the current one, to safeguard its vital strategic interests that depend upon the uninterrupted supply of its share of water from the three western rivers of the Indus system: Indus, Jhelum and Chenab. If Pakistan does not change its attitude towards meaningful exploitation of its water resources for various applications in general and for electricity generation in particular, the days ahead are going to be extremely difficult so far as socio-economic conditions and national sovereignty are concerned.

## 4.2. DEPENDENCE ON ENERGY IMPORTS

Another alarming dimension of the national energy scenario is import dependency as the energy demand far exceeds indigenous supplies. Statistics indicate that in 2008 Pakistan met almost 31 per cent of its energy requirements through imports. The indigenous gas and oil reserves are quite limited—at the end of 2008, they were respectively reported to be 29.8 trillion cubic feet (TCF) and 326.7 million barrels.[8] The Energy Information Administration (EIA), however, quotes relatively lower reserves. In terms of reserve to production ratio, oil and gas reserves are sufficient only for fourteen and twenty-one years respectively.[10] The oil resources only contribute to a small fraction of the total requirement. In 2008, for example, almost 86 per cent of the total oil requirements were met through imports as also shown in Figure 4.4.[8] Gas reserves which, until a couple of years ago, were meeting requirements satisfactorily are on a decline as discussed earlier.

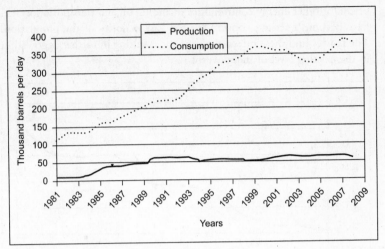

Figure 4.4: Gap between demand and supply of oil

The dependency on foreign supplies of oil has imposed massive financial stresses on the country. The petroleum import bill between 2003–04 and 2007–08 increased by nearly four-fold, from around $3 billion to $11.46 billion respectively.[25,26] In 2008–09 the import bill for petroleum fell by 17 per cent to $9.51 billion due to a drop in oil prices in the international market. Traditionally, petroleum products have been on top of the import list every year accounting for around 25 per cent of the total import bill. Keeping in mind the volatility in oil prices and forecasts of a surge in oil prices in the years ahead, the petroleum import bill is expected to swallow in future. Within the next few years the addition of natural gas to the list of import commodities, as anticipated, is going to raise the import bill further.

## 4.3. RISING ENERGY PRICES

The commercial energy and electricity generation mix of Pakistan relies heavily on fossil fuels. The price of major forms of commercial energy, i.e. electricity, gas and transportation fuels (i.e. petrol and diesel) has steadily grown over the years. Between 1990 and 2008, the price for electricity, for example, has grown by over 500 per cent as shown in Figure 4.5. The prices for natural gas have also experienced an identical trend—recording over 500 per cent increment over this period.[11] The soaring prices for other energy commodities including oil and transportation fuel have become a serious concern for the vast majority of the population. The masses find these prices unaffordable resulting in further aggravation in the existing level of fuel poverty.

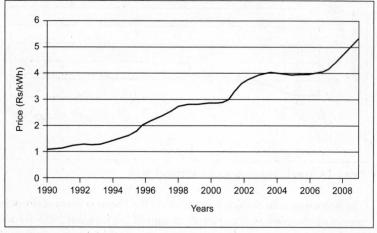

Figure 4.5: Countrywide growth in electricity prices. As of December 2009, 1 Rupee = $ cent 1.25 and € cent 0.91

Given the fact that energy is at the heart of all modern-age activities, the high-energy prices are having an adverse impact on the socio-economic conditions of the country both at the micro- and macro-level. Volatile oil prices and continuously surging electricity and gas prices are having a knock-on effect on all other living expenses making life harder for the majority of the population. For a substantial proportion of the population, utility bills account for a significant chunk in the household budget. After paying for utilities, there is less than sufficient left with them to spend on other basic needs such as food, shelter, education, and health.

The numerous challenges facing the global energy scene are pushing energy prices up across the world. The situation in Pakistan, however, is a lot more severe. Unfortunately, some decisions taken by the government have actually led to a promotion of these problems. The expensive and unnecessary rental power programme is a perfect example here. On the one hand, the controversial tariff of the 1990s, offered to IPPs, is still haunting the country, and on the other hand the rental projects are being signed at even higher tariffs, as discussed in detail in Chapter 6.

In the backdrop of Pakistan's financial agreements with foreign donors, earlier in 2009, electricity prices were to be increased by up to 30 per cent by the year's summer. The growing degree of financial loss it has to absorb to provide subsidy on electricity prices in conjunction with the mounting pressure by the International Monetary Fund (IMF) is becoming unbearable for the government. Media reports during July/August 2009 suggest that in order to comply with IMF commitments the government has once again decided to increase electricity tariff by 26 per cent. It will be carried out in two to four phases between October 2009 and April 2010. A more alarming dimension of the electricity tariff rise is the complete removal of subsidy by 2011 as has been reported in the media.[27,28]

The removal of subsidy would simply bring havoc to the already wretched Pakistanis. The first step in this direction was taken as electricity prices were increased by 6 per cent on 1 of October 2009.[29] Again, as the second episode, electricity prices were increased by a staggering 13.6 per cent on the first of January 2010. In addition to that, on 31 of December 2009, the government dropped another bombshell on the hapless masses by raising gas prices by up to 18 per cent.

As a matter of fact, it is an utterly reckless strategy to keep on surging electricity and gas prices without looking at the broader picture. A number of factors including energy crisis, and unstable political and internal security conditions have already exacerbated the across the board financial circumstances in the country. The masses, and industrial and commercial bodies are thus absolutely unable to absorb a further increment of even 1 per cent in electricity or gas tariff. The consequent wave of enormous economic implications as a result of these tariff hikes would thus force a considerable proportion of industrial and commercial organizations out of businesses and would drive millions more below the poverty line. The aggravating economic problems are going to adversely impact the social conditions and lead to growth in crime-rate. The situation would inevitably also lead to even a higher level of electricity- and gas-thefts.

## 4.4. Fuel Poverty

Energy-conscious societies are committed to eliminating the problem of fuel poverty. The concept of fuel poverty is considered as a yardstick to gauge the energy sustainability levels of a society or country. Any house that cannot afford to maintain comfortable temperature conditions is said to be fuel poor. More precisely, fuel poverty is said to occur when a household needs to spend more than 10 per cent of its income on fuel to heat or cool the home environment to a stipulated standard of temperature.[30] The temperature range that is considered to be ideal for living is between 21–24°C. The desired temperature range, however, may vary from place to place. For example, in colder climes, the adequate temperature is generally defined as 21°C in the main living room and 18°C in other occupied rooms, as recommended by the World Health Organization (WHO).[31] Fuel poverty results from a combination of low household income, unaffordable energy prices, inadequate thermal insulation, and inefficient and uneconomic heating/cooling systems.

Fuel poverty is a major issue even in some of the richest and energy-affluent societies. In the UK, for example, back in 1991 there were 7.3 million households that were either fuel poor or considered vulnerable. By 2002, this figure had fallen to just over 2 million.[30] With nearly a two-fold increment in electricity and gas prices between 2004 and 2008, the figure has once again substantially increased.

The degree of fuel poverty in Pakistan can be judged from the per capita energy consumption, an index to measure socio-economic prosperity in any country. The per capita primary energy consumption in Pakistan stands at 4,391kWh. The same figures for the UK and the USA are 44,245kWh and 108,424kWh respectively. The world average is 21,286kWh, almost five times higher than Pakistan.[2] The status of the country in terms of electricity consumption is not very enviable either. The annual per capita electricity consumption is only 430kWh against 5,774kWh in UK and 12,924kWh in the USA. The world average annual per capita electricity consumption is 3,240kWh, more than seven times greater than that of Pakistan as shown in Figure 4.6.[32]

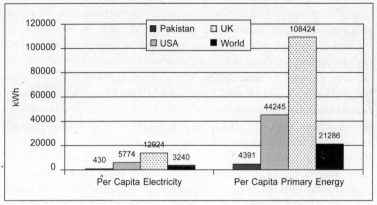

Figure 4.6: Comparison of per capita electricity and primary energy consumption

The challenge of tackling fuel poverty in Pakistan is far more complicated than it is for developed countries such as the UK. Realistically, the status of fuel poverty in Pakistan is at the opposite end compared to developed countries—only a wee fraction of the population lives in fuel prosperity. A number of factors have contributed to this unhealthy situation. Firstly, the amount of per capita availability of energy is very small in comparison to the developed countries. The lesser amount of available energy adversely dictates the prices thus affecting its affordability. The odd state of affairs can be explained by a simple comparison of affordability of petrol which is one of the most important energy commodities. An average Pakistani worker on daily wages makes around Rs300/day. His daily income can only get him 4.6 litres of petrol as per August 2009 prices. A UK worker even at the bottom of the daily wages scale would be able to purchase over 40 litres of petrol from a single day's income. This implies that the energy-purchasing capacity for a typical Pakistani is much lower, almost one-ninth that of a British citizen.

Secondly, owing to certain features of its cultural values and lifestyle, Pakistan has a consumption pattern that is quite different to that in the UK. For example, in the latter case, the majority of homes on average remain unoccupied for nearly 8 to 10 hours of the day since every family member is out for work/study or similar commitments. In Pakistan, on the other hand, houses remain occupied round the clock, thus generating a continuous demand for energy. Thirdly, just like the UK, Pakistan does not sit in a temperate climatic location. However, when looking at climate

from the energy consumption perspective, there turns out to be an
enormous difference between the two countries. Most of the regions in
Pakistan experience weather of both extremes. For nearly half of the year
(April–September), one has to cope with extreme heat. Air conditioning
becomes essential to maintain the temperature within the comfort zone
(defined by the World Health Organization). From December to February,
heating becomes a necessity. Air conditioners are amongst the most energy
intensive home appliances. Keeping in mind the current electricity prices,
an average Pakistani cannot afford to use an air conditioner throughout
the summer months even for a few hours a day. Those attempting to live
in WHO's suggested temperature range, round the clock, would end up
paying utility bills that would far exceed their total annual income. Lastly,
unlike enveloped housing in UK, people in Pakistan live in airy and open
houses or claustrophobic, tennement-like apartments in the larger cities.
Thus, the poor home-insulation would demand a lot more energy to
achieve thermal comfort.

As a matter of fact for the overwhelming majority of the population
in Pakistan, energy has become an unaffordable commodity even to meet
the basic necessities of life. It is only the ruling and economic elite,
making up one or two per cent of the population, that cherish a life of
fuel prosperity. In the wake of the planned steep rise in the price of
electricity, gas and petroleum products—in the last quarter of 2009 and
first quarter of 2010—the elite may continue to do so whereas the
common man is bound to be pushed into deeper layers of fuel poverty.
Unless radical changes are made in the generation, marketing, and
consumption of energy, the problem cannot be addressed.

## 4.5. The Modern Stone Age

Half naked, half covered with leaves, barefooted, with shoulder-long hair
and a spear in hand, hiding behind a stone or atop a tree ready to ambush
his prey—this is a scene that normally portrays stone age life. Fortunately,
this age is gone, but the people of Pakistan are experiencing a new version
of it as highlighted in Figures 4.7 to 4.13—the modern stone age—thanks
to the rampant energy crisis in the country.

The ingredients of modern stone age life are slightly different, however.
Now the hapless people still spend their days and nights in darkness,
though not of caves, but of well-built, spacious and modern homes and
villas fitted with precious chandeliers and florescent lights. They have

## Public suffering at the hands of the energy crisis

Figure 4.7: The future generation of Pakistan struggles for some of the basic necessities of life (light and water) thanks to electricity load-shedding. Courtesy *Daily Express*

Figure 4.8: An absurd media campaign by a leading utility company in the country asking people to stop using gas heaters if they want to have gas for cooking. Courtesy *Daily Express*

Figure 4.9: Relentless load-shedding during the summer months forces people to spend the night on the streets, Karachi, 12 May 2008. Courtesy *Daily Jang*

Figure 4.10: People facing scarcity of fuel at fuel stations, Lahore, 2 February 2009. Courtesy *Daily Express*

Figure 4.11: Car being pushed, due to the shortage of CNG/petrol in Islamabad, 5 January 2009. Courtesy *Daily Express*

Figure 4.12: A victim of load-shedding uses his rickshaw to highlight his sufferings while making a mockery of the customary false promises by the concerned authorities. Courtesy *Daily Express*

Figure 4.13: People protesting at overbilling, while in the inset is a person who died because of a heart attack he had at receiving an excessively high electricity bill, 23 October 2008. Courtesy *Daily Express*

modern ovens in their kitchens but are unable to prepare food. Digital televisions, computers and hi-fi electronics sit in drawing rooms and lounges, but are silent. Air-conditioners and refrigerators are in place but non-functional. The credit goes to lengthy planned and unplanned disruptions of electricity and gas. Luxury cars and motorbikes are out there but can't run, thanks to often observed unavailability of fuel. The equation is simple and straightforward—the luxuries of life mankind cherishes today are totally dependent on supply of sufficient, consistent and affordable energy. No matter how many luxurious and high-tech gadgets one may have, they are of no use unless supplied with the due amount of energy.

Man has become slave to energy. In the backdrop of the industrial revolution, the trend started to emerge in the West during the late nineteenth and early twentieth century. The change in the developing world, however, appeared a few decades later. In a matter of decades, lifestyles were transformed to become hugely dependant on energy. So was the case in Pakistan. For example, the energy requirement of an average Pakistani at the time of the country's independence was minimal. Simply a little oil and some wood/biomass respectively required for a lantern and cooking. His limited traveling if not by foot would be on animal driven carts or bicycles. Electricity, gas and engine-driven transportation played no role in his life. Compared to that time, with the advent of the twenty-first century, he, in his everyday life heavily relies on numerous energy-run gadgets such as bulbs and tube lights, fans and air conditioners, irons, fridges, heaters, ovens, televisions, computers, automobiles, pumps and motors. His life thus has become immensely dependant on exponentially greater amount of energy that is also a lot more refined.

Despite its crucial role, energy is becoming increasingly rare in Pakistan. It is not just the scarcity of electricity that is troubling people, but that of gas as well. Collectively, shortage of these two sources of energy has driven the nation to distraction. The crisis is so severe that people are not able to carry on with their daily routine. With the beginning of 2010, the majority of the cities and towns across the country were experiencing up to 18 hours of electricity and gas disruptions. During the summer months the load-shedding-driven sleepless nights have been no less than mental and physical torture to hardworking people. Daytime hours do not offer any relief either as electricity is still a rarely seen commodity when the temperature consistently stays over 40°C, occasionally also rising above 50°C.

In many cases, some very peculiar trends such as hour-long load-shedding on alternate hours have been experienced round the clock. While this is the treatment dealt out to cities, the miserable state of the remote areas and smaller towns and villages can well be imagined. Those who can afford it are resorting to Uninterrupted Power Supply (UPS) systems and generators as backup to have their basic electricity needs met during the load-shedding hours. Many, however, despite after having spent handsome amounts on these are still struggling, thanks to the sub-standard equipment being sold in the market. Since 2007, the national media has reported many tragic incidents of people dying due to heat exhaustion during lengthy spells of load-shedding. Under such unfavourable circumstances, living life in a normal manner has become all but a dream.

In winter, people have to endure the cold when gas becomes a rarely seen commodity. During the 2008–09 winter months, as temperatures were near freezing in many areas, the largest gas company in the country, Sui Northern Gas Pipelines Limited (SNGPL) launched a media campaign to warn people that they have to stop using gas heaters if they want to have gas for their kitchens as shown in Figure 4.8. The slogan of the campaign sums up the whole situation as it says: 'Use either heater or oven—choice is yours'. The irony is that people do not have enough gas supply even for their cooking requirements. It is not just the scarcity of electricity and gas that tests people's patience but also that of water. Water vanishes just after the electricity disruptions leaving people puzzled as how to get fundamental household and kitchen needs going.

During the course of 2009, the turmoil continued and households struggled to have access to enough electricity and gas to meet their most basic needs satisfactorily. Children and breadwinners find it hard to get ready for schools and work commitments respectively. Lengthy and irritating spells of relentless electricity load-shedding have forced people to rediscover candles and lanterns that were discarded decades ago by their grandparents. Students are actually studying in candle light, but finding it very difficult to concentrate.

Industry is also amongst the major victims of the crisis and is not being provided with the due level of electricity and gas, thus more and more factories are closing down. It is virtually impossible for industry to run cost effectively in an environment when frequent power and gas breakdowns keep on interrupting its operations. Not only that, but the quality and even the development of products are also sabotaged by these breakdowns. Mid-process disruptions in textile and tannery industry, for example, can be particularly disastrous. As a matter of fact, a large number of factories that totally rely on gas are refused its supply from time to time. There are cases where gas supply to factories has been completely disconnected for weeks at a time, leading to severe losses. Consequently, a considerable number of factories have been forced to lock their gates, making their employees jobless. Government estimates suggest that over 400,000 workers have lost their jobs due to load-shedding. The closure of industry is also inflicting huge economic losses to the country. Government statistics suggest that the loss the industrial sector alone is suffering amounts to over Rs240 billion per annum.

The export sector is also paying a huge price. Exporters are missing their deadlines, several of them have been blacklisted for that very reason. Textile exporters in particular have been seriously affected and the national export targets are hardly being met. Here it is noteworthy that the textile sector is the backbone of Pakistan's economy as it contributes more than 60 per cent to the total export earnings of the country and provides employment to 38 per cent of the manufacturing labor force. The turmoil is set to intensify with the government's decision of November 2009 to impose a two days a week gas load-shedding on industry from November 2009 to March 2010. It is an unfortunate situation that the prevalent energy crisis has forced a number of large textile groups to start shifting their manufacturing base to other courtiers while many more are considering following the suit.

Fruit and vegetable exporters are also at the losing end as their processing units i.e. polishing, waxing and grading systems, are unable to function at the desirable level. The situation with the business and trade and commercial enterprises is not much different either. The agriculture sector has also been badly hit by the electricity shortfall. Farmers heavily rely on tube wells to manage water for their crops because the irrigation system in place lacks quantity as well as quality—the canal infrastructure neither reaches out to all concerned areas nor does it provide sufficient amount of water on a consistent basis. The inability of farmers to run tube wells as and when required is causing adverse implications on crops. All other important sectors including academic institutes, research centres, hospitals and medical stores are also facing the heat of the crisis. In hospitals, deaths due to delays in crucial surgery because of sudden and lengthy disruptions of electricity are also occurring.

A new addition in the catalogue of problems facing the people is the disruption in the supply of transportation fuel which occurs for two reasons. Firstly, electricity failures prevent petrol/gas stations from providing service despite the fact that they hold sufficient fuel. Secondly, since 2007, there has been a considerable scarcity of CNG during the winter months, resulting in lengthy automobile queues outside CNG stations. Unavailability of petrol/diesel for a day or two has also become a monthly event if not weekly. People are made to desperately search for it from one station to another. Those who are already running low on it are to face another torture—after having used the last drop of petrol, they have to end up pushing their cars and motor-bikes. In many cases they are made to purchase petrol/diesel at a price nearly double to that of the official rate. Ironically, they are being ripped off in every possible way and they have no recourse to justice. Both the petrol pumps and oil cartels are shifting the blame on each other for creating the chaos. The common man is concerned not about who is right and who is wrong but about getting some relief from ever compounding problems.

The aforementioned economic, social, and psychological implications of the ruthless crisis are persecuting the people. On top of that, issues like tariff hikes and over billing prove too much for many to take. So much so, there are cases when some have lost their lives at the hands of unexpectedly high bills while some others in an attempt to find relief from the whole set of sufferings have committed suicide.[33,34] Nevertheless, credit goes to brave Pakistanis who despite such unfavourable circumstances are surviving in this modern stone age.

## 4.6. Environmental Concerns

Pakistan, like the rest of the world, is facing serious environmental challenges posed by global warming. Little, however, is being done to protect the environment and to mitigate the impacts of climate change. The release of toxic industrial emission into air and water is unchecked. Poor conditions of vehicles and engines in conjunction with largely used substandard lubricants and fuels are aggravating transport emissions. Factors like untreated industrial waste water and use of fertilizers and chemicals are having detrimental impacts upon the quality of ground  water. Increased levels of air and water pollution are having numerous implications upon health conditions. The inhabitants of the large cities and towns in particular are suffering from respiratory and water-borne diseases. Growing use of fossil fuels is playing a catalytic role in exacerbating the environmental problems.

Forests are vital for the environmental and economic sustainability of a country. Deforestation is another major environmental issue facing Pakistan—currently less than 2.5 per cent of the country's land area is left covered by forest. In terms of forest cover, Pakistan has a ranking of 177th in the world.[35] Forests are being eradicated at a rapid pace to meet energy requirements of people who are not connected to national gas network and electric grids. The powerful timber and land mafias are also aggressively involved in the deforestation process.

Ironically, the masses in Pakistan have a long list of problems on hand. To mention a few, for example, they have been made to suffer from the scarcity of fundamental needs including access to electricity and gas, clean drinking water, education and health services. Environmental concerns are somewhere very down in the list of issues for them especially when socioeconomic injustice has pushed a large proportion of the population below the poverty line. The existence of these problems, however, does not lessen the gravity of the environmental problems facing them. Damage is continuously being done to the environment. Sooner or later, attention will have to be paid to address environmental concerns in Pakistan. The earlier they are reacted to the easier it would be to handle them.

The issue requires a collective national effort on the part of institutions as well as individuals. As a matter of principle, everyone has to offer respect to the environment. Extravagant use of water, almost a national culture, must be addressed. Domestic waste and industrial and transport emissions need to be curtailed and where required processed before being disposed off. An appropriate switchover to environmentally friendly forms of energy should also be pursued to reduce greenhouse gas emissions. Deforestation must be curbed and effective forest management programmes should be launched. The concerned departments and initiatives are failing to deliver—the annual *Shajar Kari Muhim* (tree plantation campaign), for example, has never yielded any tangible output. The environmental departments and authorities, who presently are ineffective either due to their inherent passiveness or corruption and thus indeed are part of the problem, need to be overhauled.

## 4.7. Energy Security and National Sovereignty

The national sovereignty of Pakistan requires that the country should look after the interests of its people first and foremost and manage resources within its territorial borders any way they see fit. In the present age energy security is of paramount importance in ensuring national sovereignty. By its very nature, energy security of a country demands provision of adequate, affordable, and consistent energy to its people.

Threats to energy security have become a reality for Pakistan owing to a number of factors such as lack of sufficient energy, inconsistent supplies, unaffordable prices and a significant degree of dependence upon imports to meet national energy requirements, as highlighted in earlier sections. Furthermore, frequent incidents of sabotage which disrupt the supply of gas make things worse from the energy security perspective. The situation thus places serious question marks on national sovereignty and the decision-making autonomy of the country, especially when the energy rich regions of the world are by and large geo-politically unstable. Other crucial energy concerns important in terms of national energy security and sovereignty are discussed below.

An important issue here is that of the frequent incidents of sabotage of gas installation. The Sui field producing 28 million cubic meters of gas per day, about 45 per cent of the total national production, is historically prone to security challenges. The recent wave of problems started on 11 January 2005, when the production of gas from Sui was completely suspended due to attacks by tribal militants on the gas supply installations. Following this event the gas supply was suspended to the southern and northern regions of Pakistan. The damage inflicted was of such magnitude that despite it being treated as a national emergency it took over a week for repairs to be completed. It was not an event of sabotage in isolation— the main gas supply pipeline for Lahore, the second largest conurbation within Pakistan, was also damaged. These incidents resulted in a daily loss of almost US$0.3 million for the country's power generation system. The cost of repairing the damage caused to gas infrastructure was also in millions of US dollars.[36] It has now been more than four years and hardly a month goes by without sabotage incidents, though on a smaller scale.

One of the fundamental dimensions of national sovereignty—decision-making autonomy—is not guaranteed any more. A major blow has been dealt to national sovereignty as various international agencies such as the IMF dictate terms with regard to tariff structure and energy subsidies. In recent months media reports repeatedly suggest that the IMF has demanded that the Government of Pakistan should increase electricity prices by removing the government subsidy on it. According to senior WAPDA officials the tariff setting is not the independent domain of utility companies and the Ministry of Water and Power any more. Pakistan, having borrowed power sector development loans from international donors, has to accommodate their demands in some crucial policy issues including determination of tariff.

Deep social unrest over the energy crisis being expressed in the form of peaceful as well as violent protests and civil disobedience-like activities, as shown in Figures 4.14 to 4.21, is another critical matter. The profound energy crisis is not only barring people from carrying on with their essential daily routines but is also depriving many of their livelihoods. To conscious citizens, it is simply beyond their comprehension that having duly paid all bills, taxes, and revenues this is the return they are offered from the government. They find such treatment a violation of their fundamental civic rights. Thus, people are coming out onto the streets to record their protest, which often turn violent. Protests have continued since 2006 in various parts of the country. The violent protest in Multan on 14 April 2008, however, provided the first real glimpse of the underlying unrest in the society. A mob of hundreds of textile sector workers protesting against persistent electricity and gas disruptions rioted, ransacking several buildings including the offices of WAPDA, torching a bank and leaving at least thirteen people injured. There were also scenes of firing as some of the protestors were carrying arms that they had

## Public Expression of Frustration

Figure 4.14: Mass load-shedding protest that shortly afterwards turned violent, Multan, 14 April 2008. Courtesy *Daily Express*

Figure 4.15: WAPDA vehicle set on fire during a violent protest, Multan, 14 April 2008. Courtesy *Daily Express*

Figure 4.16: WAPDA properties under attack during protests against load-shedding, Multan, 14 April, 2008. Courtesy *Daily Express*

Figure 4.17: Exchange of fire between violent demonstrators and WAPDA officials, Multan, 14 April 2008. Courtesy *Daily Express*

Figure 4.18: WAPDA offices attacked during protests in Lahore on 20 October 2008. Courtesy *Daily Express*

Figure 4.19: Train set on fire after having been looted by violent protestors demonstrating against load-shedding, Jhang, 22 July 2009. Courtesy *Express News*

Figure 4.20: Electricity bills being set on fire by protestors, Lahore, 20 October 2008. Courtesy *Express*

Figure 4.21: Electricity bills are being burnt in protest against heavy load-shedding and increased tariff—a deplorable and blatant sign of civil disobedience, Karachi, 22 October 2008. Courtesy *Daily Express*

snatched from the security guards of the attacked offices. A WAPDA official was also seen retaliating in similar fashion in order to disperse the attacking mob.[37]

Over time, the electricity and gas crisis driven rioting has become increasingly intense and frequent. The year 2008 experienced frequent waves of demonstrations orchestrated by enraged ordinary citizens as well as trade bodies. People from all major cities including Karachi, Quetta, Lahore, Peshawar, Rawalpindi, Faisalabad, Gujranwala, Sialkot, and Sahiwal recorded their protests. At many places, these protests resulted in attacks on utility infrastructure, shutter-down strikes and blockade of roads. The catalogue of protests kept on building throughout 2008, the last episode of which was a series of demonstrations in various cities on 31 December with reports of clashes with police at various places. The most important event of the day was the protest by women and children in Rawalpindi against the prolonged disruptions of natural gas supplies. It was dealt with by baton weilding police. The first day of the new year, 2009, saw even uglier incidents as violent protests erupted across the country. The tragic highlights of the day included blockade of roads, gun shot injuries, destruction of public and private properties, looting, and clashes with police. WAPDA offices, and offices and residences of political leader were also attacked.

Throughout the summer of 2009, violent protests were waged across the country on an almost daily basis as people found their daily routines pounded by up to 18-hours of load-shedding. On many occasions there were clashes with police also resulting in large scale casualties and even killings as a result of shooting.[38] Incidents like attacks on WAPDA infrastructure and beating of its staff members have been reported in the national media almost on a daily basis. There have also been incidents of attacks on the homes of WAPDA staff.[39] July 2009, in particular, experienced violent protests on a daily basis that also saw a passenger train set a fire after having been looted by people who had gathered to protest against load-shedding.[40] During 2008 and 2009, in response to sudden tariff increments, people have even resorted to civil disobedience measures such as withholding payments of bills till the announced tariff hike was withdrawn and burning of utility bills.[41,42] The year 2010 also started with ugly scenes of violent protests across the country. On 18 March, the situation took a new turn as the federal capital, Islamabad, was hit by intensely violent protests against increased transport fare. The protests that continued the next day, until the decision of a jump in transport fare was repealed, resulted in clashes between police and demonstrators causing injuries to many on both sides, destruction of public and private property, and over 300 arrests. Even paramilitary forces were needed to help restore peace.

Another noteworthy consequential development was an attempt on part of certain groups to portray the load-shedding driven protests as inter-provincial confrontations. Allegations were levelled at the province of Punjab—badly hit by load-shedding leading to closure of industries and also resulting in large-scale unemployment—of an attempt to destabilize the political system. There were also attempts to raise the political temperature as the protests were alleged to be sponsored to meet certain agendas. In the wake of attacks on trains in Punjab, the federal minister for railways also threatened to stop train services in the province.[43] However, in the end, the political leadership behaved sensibly to dispel all such attempts.

These alarming developments suggest that the frustration level of the sufferers has hit the saturation level. Pakistan, with an already volatile internal situation on a number of fronts, cannot afford to add to its problems with energy-related unrest amongst the masses. Similar fears have been echoed in recent studies conducted by the Massachusetts

Institute of Technology (MIT) and the International Energy Agency (IEA), concluding that in the emerging energy scenarios in the world, those at the top of the economic ladder would be able to procure the basic necessities of life. On the other hand, those at the lower end would find themselves increasingly barred from access to such vital commodities as food, land, and shelter. Analysts also warn that the supply shortages could lead to disturbing scenes of mass unrest and the situation could spin out of control and turn into a complete meltdown of societies.[44,45,46] It is therefore important for the relevant authorities to comprehend the intensity of the underlying unrest in Pakistani society over the energy crisis. Measures need to be taken to stop the occurrence of agitated protests and any other developments that pose a threat to national sovereignty. Obviously, the first step in this regard would be to make meaningful efforts to arrest the prevailing energy crisis and to take the public into confidence over the measures being taken. In this regard the policy-makers ought to show their commitment to the people of Pakistan.

## REFERENCES

1. Hydel Power Policy—1995, Pakistan WAPDA.
2. Pakistan, Country Statistics, Energy Information Administration, 2008.
3. Karen Turner Dunn, Pakistan's Energy Position: Problems and Prospects, *Asian Survey*, Vol. 31, No. 12, 1991.
4. Aftab Sherpao, Presentation by the Minister for Water and Power, Pakistan Development Forum, 18 March 2004.
5. Data provided by PEPCO officials, Lahore, May 2009.
6. Medium-Term Development Framework (2005-2010), Planning Commission, Govt. of Pakistan, May 2005.
7. Pakistan heading towards serious gas crisis, *Business Recorder*, 24 July 2007.
8. Pakistan Energy Year Book 2008.
9. *Business Recorder*, 5 November 2009.
10. Robert Hathaway and Michael Kugelman (eds.), *Powering Pakistan*, Oxford University Press, 2009, p. 32.
11. Electricity Marketing Data, 33rd issue, NTDC, 2008.
12. Energy Sector Assessment for USAID/Pakistan, June 2007.
13. Pakistan, Iran finally sign gas pipeline accord, *Dawn*, 24 May 2009.
14. Munawar Ahmed, Pakistan's Energy Crisis, *Nation*, 10 February 2009.
15. *Bridges over Water: Understanding Transboundary Water Conflict, Negotiation and Cooperation*, Ariel Dinar, World Scientific Publishing Co. Ltd, Singapore, 2007.
16. Peace in the pipeline BBC, 13 February 2009.
17. Pakistan Council for Research in Water Resources, http://www.pcrwr.gov.pk/water_quality.htm (accessed on 5 December 2009).
18. WAPDA web site, www.wapda.org.pk (accessed on 5 December 2009).

19. People and the Planet 2000-2009, http://www.peopleandplanet.net/doc.php?id=671&section=14 (accessed on 5 December 2009).
20. 'Kishan Ganga Dam to be discussed again in India', *Daily Times*, 4 June 2008.
21. 'Pak questions construction of Kishan Ganga Dam by India', *Thaindian News*, 13 April 2009.
22. 'First Baglihar, then Kishanganga', *Newsline*, June 2005.
23. Former Chairman WAPDA, Interview, Islamabad, May 2009.
24. Carly Laird, Potential for water conflict between India and Pakistan, *ABC News*, Australia, 15 August 2009.
25. M. Asif, 'Sustainable Energy Options for Pakistan', *Renewable & Sustainable Energy Reviews*, 13, 4, 2009.
26. Drop in global crude prices: Country's oil import bill tumbles 17.04 per cent, *Daily Times*, 25 July 2009.
27. Phased increase in power tariff from October, *Daily Times*, 16 July 2009.
28. *Daily Express*, 27 August 2009.
29. *Dawn*, 1 October 2009.
30. Meeting the Energy Challenge: A White Paper on Energy, Department of Trade and Industry, UK, May 2007.
31. M. Asif, Fuel Poverty in Pakistan, *Dawn*, 18 January 2008.
32. Electricity Data, Nation Master.com.
33. *Express*, 23 October 2008.
34. A. Khayal, PK on Web, 10 July 2009, http://pkonweb.com/tag/load-shedding/(accessed on 5 December 2009).
35. Environmental statistics, nationamaster.com, http://www.nationmaster.com/graph/env_for_are_of_lan_are-environment-forest-area-of-land (accessed on 5 December 2009).
36. T. Muneer and M. Asif, Prospects for Secure and Sustainable Electricity Supply for Pakistan, *Renewable & Sustainable Energy Reviews*, Volume 11, Issue 4, May 2007, Pages 654-67.
37. *Daily Express*, 15 April 2008.
38. *Express*, 6 August.
39. *Daily Express*, 28 August 2009.
40. *Express*, 22 July 2009.
41. KESC consumers protest against load-shedding, *Dawn*, 19 March 2008.
42. Protests across Punjab as outage hours multiply, *The Nation*, 5 September 2009.
43. *Express*, 23 July 2009.
44. M. Asif and M.T. Khan, Possible US-Iran Military Conflict and its Implications Upon Global Sustainable Development, *Journal of Sustainable Development*, Vol. 2, No. 1, March 2009.
45. Ashley Seager, *The Guardian*, 22 October 2007.
46. M. Klare, *Resources War: The New Landscape of Global Conflict*, Henry Holt and Company, New York, 2002, p. 24.

# 5

# The Energy Crisis and the Role of the Relevant Stakeholders

In order to have a better understanding of the energy challenges facing Pakistan it is important to look into not only the composition of the prevailing crisis but also the underlying issues that have contributed to it. In this regard, it is vital to evaluate the role of the departments and authorities responsible for the development of the energy sector. This chapter duly examines the performance of a number of crucial stakeholders including the policy and decision-makers, academia, industry and the key energy departments. This novel scholarship unfolds the characteristic weaknesses of these stakeholders who have gradually undermined the national energy scene. It encompasses not only an account of the author's experiences and assessment of the core issues but also views of a number of prominent energy officials and experts that were interviewed as part of this work. The names and/or departmental identities of some of the interviewees, particularly of those who are currently holding office, have been kept anonymous at their own request.

## 5.1. POLICY AND DECISION-MAKERS

One of the fundamental reasons for Pakistan still being a developing country that relies heavily on foreign aid and resources in nearly every sector after sixty-two years of independence is the weakness of its institutions. Institutions in Pakistan are far from being firmly established and have largely disappointed the nation in their performance. Public sector departments, with the exception of a few, are perfect examples in this regard. Thus, the wider impression is that of failure on the part of the entire system.

The greatest responsibility to safeguard national energy interests and to determine the directions and development of its departments and infrastructure rests with the ruling regimes. Here, bureaucracy is part and parcel of the policy and decision-making process along with the political/ administrative arm of any regime. In Pakistan's typical context, some political parties, particularly with ethnic manifestos, who may or may not have formally enjoyed public office within the system, have also influenced the directions of the energy sector. These three stakeholders hereunder are discussed as the 'policy and decision-makers'. They may occasionally be also referred to as the 'ruling elite' as they are commonly referred in Pakistan.

Although Pakistan has never enjoyed a prosperous energy scene, after having overcome the immediate post-independence challenges, it made some very healthy developments, under the Ayub Khan and Zulfikar Ali Bhutto regimes, during the 1960s and 1970s. The oil and gas sector took off at a reasonable pace. Towards the development of the water and power resource base in particular, these regimes exhibited sound vision and political will. The power sector made remarkable progress as some state of the art hydropower power projects were orchestrated during this period. Nuclear power was also brought on board. Experts believe that in terms of the development of the power sector, Pakistan was well ahead of comparative countries. The momentum however could not be sustained in the years to come. Over the last three decades, the performance of the successive regimes has been by and large below par. The current disastrous state of affairs reflects upon their disconcerting role in the energy sector and asks gripping questions on their commitment and competence.

The energy problems facing the country are largely a consequence of poor management on the part of pertinent authorities. Irrespective of where problems exist in the chain of command, as a matter of principle the bucket stops at the highest possible policy and decision-making levels. Concerned energy circles reveal a catalogue of compelling evidence that suggests that the root cause of the downfall of the energy sector is the wrong attitude—a combination of a lack of vision, bad governance and pursuance of vested interests on the part of a section of policy and decision-makers and departmental authorities has created this quagmire. Without attempting to generalise them, this book acknowledges that there are some extremely dedicated and proficient people within the ranks of all concerned stakeholders who are doing their utmost to help their respective departments and forums progress in a positive mode. These brave souls, however, are marginalised when it comes to the stage of vital policy and decision-making. Some of the major shortcomings of the policy and decision-makers which have fostered the energy crisis are discussed as following.

### 5.1.1 LACK OF VISION

One of the major weaknesses regimes have exhibited is lack of vision. They have either failed to foresee the gathering storms or have deliberately given them a blind eye. The current energy crises primarily seen in the form of electricity shortfall, as emerged in 2006–07, for example, could easily have been avoided had they exhibited due resolve during the preceding few years. Over the last decade, Pakistan has experienced a steep rise in electricity demand as the average annual economic growth rate for most of the years had been noted to be around 7 per cent. This rapid growth in electricity demand has been principally triggered by an exponential rise in the number of energy intensive home appliances such as air conditioners, refrigerators, televisions and microwave ovens. Air conditioning alone is the single most important factor in the overall surge in electricity demand. Estimates suggest that it almost makes up a staggering one-third of the total demand in the country—in July 2008, due to sudden change in weather the peak demand was noted to slide down from over 17,600MW to below 12,000MW.[1]

The sustainability of economic activities requires adequate, consistent and affordable supply of energy. No rocket science is required to understand the fact that with the growing population coupled with the trends of increasing modernization and urbanization, energy demands are bound to rise. Over the last few years, a proportionate and timely increment on the supply end was therefore essential in order to maintain the momentum of economic, industrial, and social development. Increment at the supply end was, however, completely neglected. Statistics suggest that between 2000 and 2007, the national electricity consumer base jumped by 55 per cent, from 11.58 million to 17.96 million, however, no arrangements were made to boost the supply base to a corresponding magnitude.[2] The last government came up with a fancy slogan of bringing electricity to every village of the country by 2007 under the 'Khushal (prosperous) Pakistan Programme', however, without setting up new power plants that were essential to make sure there is enough generation capacity. The attitude of the concerned regime indicates that it could not care less for energy. Consequently, the gradually growing gap between demand and supply has driven the country right into the eye of the storm.

It is clear that the prevalent energy crisis has not appeared overnight. The signs were obvious for a good number of years but the authorities failed to react in time. How well the relevant authorities were prepared to anticipate any challenges can be observed from the fact that on 18 March 2004, in one of his policy setting presentations at the Pakistan Development Forum, the Minster for Water and Power Aftab Ahmed Sherpao predicted an electricity deficit of less than 1,500MW by 2007.[3] Contrary to that, by December 2007, the shortfall actually grew to as much as 4,500MW, more than three times that of the forecasted figure.

Senior WAPDA officials claim that as early as 2002 it was categorically told to the then government that a severe energy crisis was set to hit the country within a few years unless effective measures were taken to enhance the electricity generation capacity. The timely warning, however, failed to receive any appreciation. Rather going a step further, such warnings were snubbed and the outspoken officials were penalized in various fashions. A former member WAPDA claims that between 2003 and 2006 alone, on at least 13 occasions, WAPDA had categorically requested the successive prime ministers and the president of Pakistan to set up new power plants to match the growing demand. The department is said to have begged for new projects clearly warning them that in case of a power crisis it was WAPDA that would be blamed and would have to take most of the heat in the form of hostile public reaction. The officials who were personally part of the process are extremely dejected that their fears have become a reality, also because their time and again warnings were not given any attention.[4]

Repeated earlier, in 2002, an ex-acting chairman of WAPDA wrote to the Government of Pakistan to give serious consideration to the approaching crisis but was told to 'stop raising false alarms.'[5] The price for this blunder is being paid by people that in turn are expressing their anger at the WAPDA offices—in the wake of the ongoing electricity shortfall WAPDA in particular has become a target for the public's frustration as discussed in detail in Chapter 4. Unfortunately, the masses do not comprehend that the responsibility for their suffering does not lie with the department but with those who held the policy and decision-making offices and who repeatedly neglected WAPDA's opportune warnings. The authority to make decisions and get them implemented is not in WAPDA's domain but of the regime's.

The short-sightedness of successive regimes, a customary phenomenon in Pakistan, has had a detrimental impact on the energy sector. What they usually exhibit is a 'project-oriented' approach rather than a 'goal-oriented' one. Almost every regime over the last three decades has dealt with energy on an ad-hock basis. There are no trends of long-term and sustainable planning. Concepts like value engineering and life cycle costing are words unheard of in the corridors of power. Energy projects require rigorous planning and huge investments for which reasons they become undesirable to regimes. The delay in implementing effective energy projects has been one of the most important driving factors behind the energy crises in the country. In trying to catch up, when things start getting out of control haphazard measures are sought. A typical example is the Independent Power Producers (IPPs) programme of the 1990s. The hurried IPPs programme, apart from the financial controversies, has shown a number of ramifications as discussed in the later sections of this chapter.

The over-reliance upon oil-based power generation—an evidence of bad policies and poor management—is hurting the country in numerous ways. A relatively new phenomenon in this respect has been the inability of oil-based power plants to operate at optimum performance due to the liquidity crunch which in turn is a consequence of the vicious circular debt.

The problem of circular debt started in 2006 when electricity prices were frozen for political reasons. The Musharraf–Aziz regime decided not to increase oil prices as their government was heading for election the next year.[6] Incidentally, the policy paralleled the steep rise in oil prices in the international market. At the same time the government did not duly compensate power companies against the provision of increasingly subsidized electricity at the consumer end. The power companies therefore were not in a position to make payments to the oil companies. Consequently it reduced the oil companies' capacity to import the oil needed for thermal power plants. Finally, most of the thermal power plants were forced to operate at a very low capacity factor thus resulting in increased shortfall of electricity. The roots of the debt circle are quite deep and would take some serious efforts on the part of various bodies to get resolved. As of March 2009, for example, WAPDA's payables to various entities stood at Rs283.3 billion while its total receivables were Rs265.1 billion as indicated in Table 5.1 and Table 5.2. Apparently, it may not appear such a bad position for WAPDA in terms of the balance of its net payables and receivables. In reality, however, the situation is quite adverse. Senior officials believe that WAPDA would hardly get 10 to 20 per cent of the total receivables while its payables would have to be honoured in totality.[1]

The prevalent energy crisis, thus, should not be of any surprise when this is the level of respect the ruling elite has offered to this important field. It is all but obvious that the failure on the part of policy and decision-makers to respond to the emerging energy challenges in a timely and pragmatic fashion has actually fostered the dire crisis. Once the crisis is underway, they are still far from pursuing coherent and sustainable solutions. The common man has little access to electricity, gas, petrol, and water—the basic necessities of life—as discussed in detail in Chapter 4. The ruling elite, however, do not appear to be concerned.

**Table 5.1: WAPDA's receivables as of 31 March 2009**

| Entities/Department | Amount (Billion Rupees) |
|---|---|
| KESC (As per NEPRA determination) | 80.1 |
| FATA | 81.8 |
| Provincial Governments | 33.9 |
| Federal Government Departments | 1.8 |
| AJK | 2.8 |
| GOP share @ 40 per cent (for agriculture tube wells in Balochistan) | 0.6 |
| GOB share @ 30 per cent (for agriculture tube wells in Balochistan) | 4.1 |
| Private | |
| Non-controllable: a) Spill-over | 12.0 |
| b) Deferred amount (litigation cases) | 2.7 |
| c) Permanently disconnected | 19.3 |
| Controllable d) Running Defaulters | 39.4 |
| Others (Autonomous bodies) | 1.3 |
| Total | 265.1 |

**Table 5.2: WAPDA's payables as of 31 March 2009**

| Entities/Department | Amount (Billion Rupees) |
|---|---|
| IPPs | 54.3 |
| Gas suppliers | 19.5 |
| Oil suppliers | 6.7 |
| WAPDA hydro | 39.5 |
| Other (NTDC, GENCOs, Rental Power etc) | 7.3 |
| Bank Borrowing (2006–2009) | 75.8 |
| TFCs | 80.2 |
| Total (2009–10) | 283.3 |

## 5.1.2 Lack of Respect for the Common Man

The endless sequence of the energy problems suggests that the policy and decision-makers in Pakistan have traditionally shown little concern for the welfare of the common man. A tragic trend that started in 2007–08—on the one hand the country faces a serious shortfall of electricity and on the other hand the installed thermal power plants are underperforming due to the liquidity crunch—is an example of bad management and carelessness on the part of pertinent authorities. The poor functioning of a number of thermal power plants due to lack of liquidity has significantly intensified the shortfall of electricity. Similarly, there are cases of plants being closed for maintenance or due to breakdowns at odd times, again adding to the intensity of the electricity shortfall. The ultimate sufferer in this whole fiasco is the common man. Another recent development to cite here is that of regular disruptions in transportation fuel supplies. Once again the common man is either denied supply of fuel altogether or is made to purchase it at exhorbitant prices as discussed in Section 4.5. One often wonders if there is any existence of the writ of the government. It is certainly possible to avoid such situations as long as the concerned authorities exhibit a sense of responsibility.

Insensitivity is the usual mode of operation of policy and decision-makers as the author also observed at a high profile forum in May 2009. There, a senior PPIB official spoke in favour of rental power plants and the new wave of IPPs by presenting a very rosy picture of their performance. He further declared that the concerned stakeholders namely the Government of Pakistan, investors and power companies were all satisfied at the new deals being signed. Interestingly enough, the common man—the ultimate customer in the whole affair—was not in the list of 'pertinent' stakeholders. Representatives of the so-called stakeholders including a federal minister attending the forum were satisfied to have the discussed deals signed. They were not troubled by the fact that the masses, who were already struggling with the existing tariff would find the electricity produced by these rental power plants and IPPs extremely expensive and unaffordable. When this fundamental weakness—the un-affordability of the common man—was pointed out to the minister and other officials, they were all speechless.[7]

Another example of reckless moves on the part of policy and decision-makers while bulldozing public opinion is the untimely tariff-hike—prices for electricity and gas are increased even in the very midst of intense shortfalls of the respective commodities. For instance, in August 2008, as the country braced to endure a wave of up to 18 hours of load-shedding, the government decided to raise the electricity tariff by 31 per cent.[8] The decision exploded like a bombshell on the already tormented people. A number of trade and commercial bodies and representatives of civil society having categorically rejected the tariff hike, decided to withhold payment of bills unless the decision was withdrawn. In subsequent protests utility bills were also burnt across the country.[9] The embarrassing situation forced the government to repeal the decision.[10] Similarly, in the first week of January 2009, as the country was once again engulfed by violent protests against electricity and gas disruptions, the gas-tariff was increased by up to 17 per cent. Tariff-hikes despite the fact that people's patience is already being tested to the limit by the relentless crisis were not helpful in terms of winning public confidence, particularly, when oil prices in the international market had slumped from US$147/barrel to less than US$34/barrel, the lowest in four years.

The policy and decision-makers, and the general public, in terms of lifestyle and available privileges, are poles apart. Irrespective of the crises and difficulties the country and the public face respectively, the ruling elite remain immune from all stresses. The case with the ongoing energy crisis is not any different. No matter how critical the energy crisis gets in the country the ruling elite continue to enjoy energy-lavish lifestyles. Usage of energy departments' machinery and infrastructure for personal benefits is a norm. Blatant usage of official transport for personal use is not considered to be an issue at all. Special plane- and helicopter-flights, to transport friends, clothing and even favourite food—or for recreational activities—have all been reported in the national press over the years. While the common man experiences up to twenty hours of load-shedding

Figure 5.1: A reflection of the rampant status differentiation between the ruling elite and the common man—a staff member comforts federal minister Ijaz Jakhrani with a hand-fan while the latter enjoys lunch—reminding one of the colonial age. Courtesy *Daily Express*, 18 April 2009

they remain immune, thanks to their centrally air-conditioned offices, transport and residences all being maintained by public money. If, for instance, they have to spend a few moments without air-conditioning, the poor common man is there to look after them, as seen in Figure 5.1 in which a federal minister is being fanned by a typical common man in a load-shedding-ridden-gathering.

### 5.1.3 NEPOTISM

Nepotism is another malpractice that has been patronised by regimes leaving an extremely adverse impact on the energy sector. Appointments of irrelevant and incompetent personnel in energy offices have been quite a common phenomenon. The problem not only exists at every level within the energy departments but also at the ministerial level. Energy is one of the most technical and vital ministerial portfolios yet ironically it is almost always handed over to people who are ill-qualified. Not very long ago, a Minister for Water and Power had only passed high school. The 'educated' ones who happen to hold these offices are graduates in irrelevant subjects who come without any experience of energy during their academic and professional life. Having appointed 'non-technical' persons to run offices, no extra support in the form of visionary and qualified advisers is ensured in order to run the business with some degree of satisfaction.

As a matter of fact, energy offices are amongst the most coveted positions in any cabinet, simply because they are considered to be the most lucrative. Paradoxically, there are cases when energy offices have been used as a 'bargaining tool' in political deals. Concerned officials within the energy sector believe that even in the midst of the prevailing crisis, the worst in the country's history, several people with unconvincing and even in some cases ineligible credentials have been picked for some of the highest possible energy offices.

One of the hallmark examples in this regard that make a mockery of the system is that of an appointment at an extremely sensitive and crucial position—Chairman NEPRA—in 2008. Sources closely related to the saga and reports in the national media suggest that the appointment of Khalid Saeed to this position has been a daylight robbery. It tells of the moral and professional bankruptcy of the system. In 2007, for the vacant position of Chairman NEPRA, seventy-two candidates applied. Having shortlisted five of them in order of priority after a rigorous screening process, the selection committee sent the file to the prime minister's secretariat for formal approval. Rather than appoint one of the five shortlisted candidates the position was handed over to the personal secretary to the prime minister.[11] Interestingly, the appointee had to re-arrange the job criteria in order to get the position because he did not  possess the required expertise. Also, he never appeared before the committee constituted to interview all prospective candidates.[12] Details of such unethical activity at the hands of the top officials of the country have also been provided to the author by two of the five shortlisted candidates. The energy circles in particular and the civil society in general were appalled at such a reckless paradigm of governance. It became such a major issue that having passed a resolution against the appointment, the Senate of Pakistan, formally asked the prime minister to nullify the illegal appointment and fill the post on merit from amongst the shortlisted professionals. In a letter, the Deputy Chairman of the Senate Jan Muhammad Jamali wrote to the caretaker Prime Minister Muhammad Mian Soomro requesting that the appointee be replaced in the light of the unanimous resolution of the Senate. The letter states: 'It is imperative that the notification appointing Khalid Saeed as chairman NEPRA, in blatant violation of NEPRA Act, selection procedure and merit be withdrawn forthwith and the appointment of the most appropriate candidate, who fully meets the criteria be made, among the panel of five professionals as recommended to the Prime Minister through a summary.'[13] The calls for justice proved too weak to get the illegitimate decision rectified....Khalid Saeed continues to cherish the vital and prestigious position.

Another appointment that is worth highlighting here is that of the prime minister's adviser for petroleum and natural resources. In an era when even minor ministries were being looked after by up to two full time ministers, the Ministry of Petroleum and Natural Resources did not have even a single minister. Strangely, from November 2008 to August 2009, as the energy crisis was in full swing, such a crucial portfolio was run by an adviser to the prime minister. Much to the surprise of the energy circles, the adviser, Dr Asim Hussain, was a medical doctor by profession who had nothing to do with energy prior to holding this vital office. Experts find it hard to comprehend the wisdom behind appointing a medical practitioner to run the crucial energy ministry when the country has a considerable pool of energy professionals equipped with appropriate qualifications and rich expertise. It is not unusual in Pakistan to appoint advisers in areas that are not pertinent to their specialities but are lucrative. In this particular case, energy circles and media reports cite Dr Asim's friendship with President Asif Ali Zardari as the only credential to win such a coveted office. *The Wall Street Journal* states:

> Among the members of Mr Zardari's inner circle: his former physician, Dr Asim Hussain, who in addition to running a hospital in Karachi, is the government's adviser on petroleum affairs and runs the oil ministry, despite having no background in the industry.[14]

The said adviser has also been reported to be involved in hefty corruption.[15]

The story with WAPDA is not very different. The Chairman WAPDA, Shakeel Durrani, is a retired civil servant who is reported not to have worked in the energy sector before cherishing the Chairmanship of WAPDA.[16]

Concerned circles express great regret that one of the most delicate and crucial departments, Planning Commission of Pakistan, has also been infected by political interference. The office of the operational head of the Commission, Deputy Chairman, traditionally used to be run by well-qualified and competent senior officials. However, since the 1990s, on several occasions, this vital position has been handed over to politicians, irrespective of their deservedness or capability.[17] Like all other sectors, proliferation of energy would also greatly depend upon the degree of support it receives from the Planning Commission. Reckless decision-making at this level thus can have severe bearing on the energy sector.

### 5.1.4 CORRUPTION AND VESTED INTERESTS

Corruption is a real problem in Pakistan. The wider understanding amongst concerned circles is that though corruption exists at all levels, it mainly stems from and is patronized by the policy and decision-making circles. This tragic phenomenon has been reflected upon in the Global Corruption Report 2009 by the global anti-corruption watchdog, Transparency International (TI) as it declares about Pakistan that: 'there exist no law against corruption.'[18] The report further states: 'Corruption in privatization in Pakistan is endemic: manipulation of the process can be found at all stages, from the evaluation of profits and assets of a company to the provision of kick-backs on completion of a settlement.'[19] The aforementioned observation of TI is all about the policy and decision-makers. Interestingly, for example, it was the former Prime Minister Shaukat Aziz and his team of ministers and friends who are almost consensually considered to have masterminded a number of privatization scandals in recent years, also mentioned in the TI report. He is also said to have played an instrumental role in orchestrating the ongoing energy crisis in the country as discussed later in this section.

Concerned circles believe that the policy and decision-makers have inflicted colossal damage to the energy sector by buying inappropriate projects or by jeopardizing extremely crucial projects for their vested interests be it financial corruption, political leverage or other hidden agendas. Patronization of corruption of various types on their part has seriously dented the progress of this sector as a whole. Here it is noteworthy that when it comes to financial corruption and financial kickbacks, the energy sector is the second to none.

Sources, including Pakistani officials and representatives of foreign energy/investment groups, have informed the author of their first hand experiences with the issues of kickbacks and corruption at extremely high levels in the Government of Pakistan. The 1990s IPPs programme is a classic case in this regard, as discussed in detail later in this chapter. An adviser to a large international energy group who was closely involved in negotiations for setting up power plants in Pakistan during the 1990s claims that unofficial payment of 10 million dollars was demanded for a single project.[20] Similarly, ex-Member WAPDA Syed Tanzeem Hussain

Naqvi provides an interesting account of a high level meeting between Pakistan's senior energy officials and their Indian counterparts. During the informal discussion at the post-meeting dinner, a member of the Indian delegation asked the Pakistani officials why did Pakistan decide to go for over 20,000MW IPPs (the initial target) when it was having a shortfall of over 1,500MW, quoting the example of India that had a deficit of around 20,000MW and yet was reluctant to go for IPPs. The frank one-word answer given by Pakistani officials was 'kickbacks'.[21] Another ex-Member of WAPDA, Javed Nizam, shares his experience as he was invited by an upcoming IPP to join it at a lucrative position in 2004–05. Before accepting the position, he was tempted to look into the project details. He was taken aback when he came across serious irregularities—'criminal' in his own words—as he studied the financial details of the project. He refused the offer because he did not want to be a part of corruption.[22]

Serious corruption is also said to have played a role in the privatization of KESC in 2005. The Corporation was reportedly privatised and sold for just Rs22 billion while its assets and receivables at the time were estimated to be worth around Rs200 billion. According to Syed Tanzeem Naqvi, who is also ex-Chairman KESC, the Corporation's shares, which actually stood as Rs9/share were disposed of in a criminal fashion at Rs1.65/share.[23] Transparency International wanted to look into the allegations of corruption over the privatization deal but has not been helped with the required documentation by the pertinent authorities—despite repeated calls the Privatization Commission is not providing the deal agreements while the Ministry for Water and Power is also reluctant to play a role in this regard.[24]

Another example of the noxious attitude of the policy and decision-makers at the highest possible level is that of a 1,000MW thermal power project that WAPDA wanted to orchestrate to help tackle the approaching power crisis but was hurdled, as revealed by another top WAPDA official who was closely involved in the whole process. Having done all the necessary homework in 2005, the department was looking forward to get the project operational by April 2007. The project summary, after having been approved through various layers of the planning process, was rejected by the Prime Minister's Office considering it contradictory to the Government of Pakistan's policy of barring WAPDA from new thermal power projects. With the initial shockwaves of the current crisis in August 2006, in an emergency meeting called to look into the issue, chaired by President Pervez Musharraf and Prime Minister Shaukat Aziz, the dumping of that particular project was recognized as a mistake. A few days later, WAPDA officials were invited to get the project formally approved by the prime minister. They visited his office only to be stunned by orders from Prime Minister Shaukat Aziz in the presence of Ex-Senator Saifur Rehman to hand over the project to a Middle Eastern business group introduced to him by the latter. The WAPDA officials reportedly begged the prime minister to let WAPDA complete this project as the Authorities had already diligently done all the necessary homework. They also offered the prime minister to allow WAPDA to hand over any other appropriate project as an alternative to the foreign group, but their pleas were rejected. The said senator, actively involved in the hijacking of this valuable project, was the person who had been in hibernation for the previous few years after having earned a nationwide villainous reputation as Chairman of the Accountability Bureau during Mian Nawaz Sharif's second tenure as prime minister during the late 1990s. The project was thus taken away from WAPDA only to be jeopardised. Towards the end of 2007, after more than a year since the project was snatched from WAPDA, the department was once again asked to implement it as the foreign group had pulled out. Now, WAPDA had to redo a considerable amount of homework and could only get things settled with foreign partners at a much higher overall project cost. And only half of the original project capacity is going to be installed by 2010–11. The let down by Prime Minister Shaukat Aziz resulted in a loss of project capacity by 50 per cent, wasted three to four precious years and cost WAPDA an extra tens of millions of US dollars.[25] In this particular case, the partnership of Shaukat Aziz and Saifur Rehman is a reflection of how coordinated and ruthless the ruling elite are in their efforts to secure illegitimate benefits at any cost to the nation.

### 5.1.4.1 State Engineering Corporation's Indigenization Plan for Achieving Lower Cost of Power Generation

One of the most scandalous and destructive, yet unheard of, affairs the energy sector has seen in recent decades is the dumping of an impressive power indigenization plan, 'Indigenization Plan for Achieving Lower Cost of Power Generation' prepared by the State Engineering Corporation (SEC) in 1994–95. It was not a mere proposal but an extremely visionary and rigorously worked out project plan that could have significantly helped the country achieve energy sustainability. The SEC had arranged foreign investment to produce 2,000MW of turnkey thermal projects to satisfactorily meet the growing demand at the time. The real magnificence of the project lay in the technology transfer it encompassed and provision of electricity at a price far cheaper compared to what was shortly afterwards agreed to be paid to the IPPs. Had this extremely viable plan not been sabotaged for the sake of vested interests, experts believe, not only could it have revolutionized the national power sector but it could also have brought a multitude of financial, technological, and social benefits to the country. It arguably is the biggest setback to the national energy sector that also cost tens of billions of dollars to the country. Sources believe that this remarkably prosperous project was sabotaged to foster the 1990s IPPs programme. The elements behind this havoc are said to be once again in action to launch the controversial and ineffectual rental power programme and another wave of IPPs.

Details reveal that, in 1991–92 as Pakistan was experiencing a shortfall of electricity, the SEC, with the support of the Ministry of Industries and Production and Ministry of Water and Power took a timely and pragmatic initiative by developing General Cooperation Agreements with several American, European, and Chinese firms for co-financing and co-manufacturing of complete power plants in Pakistan as highlighted in Table 5.3. The SEC channelled partners of international repute and prepared short-term as well as long-term programmes to achieve indigenization of power plants. It envisaged the best utilization of national resources of engineering, manufacturing and technical services available in the public and private sector. Under the arrangement, local participation in all areas, i.e. development of project proposals and feasibility studies, design and engineering, manufacturing, erection, commissioning and trial runs would have been increased from project to project with complete technical backing and support of foreign consortium partners.

The SEC offered WAPDA 2,000MW of power projects backed with a complete financial package.[26] Through technology transfer, initially the projects were to be locally manufactured to the extent of 26 per cent by value (60–65 per cent by weight). Gradually, the local manufacturing share was to be extended to 55 per cent (80 per cent by weight). The offer covered financing, local as well as foreign, to be provided by SEC and its foreign partners, without seeking government sovereign guarantees.

**Table 5.3:** **Types of turnkey projects and their consortium collaborators as offered by the SEC**

| Project | Consortium collaborator |
|---|---|
| Conventional steam power plants based on oil/gas and coal | GEC Alsthom (France & UK) and Babcock (Germany), China Machine Building International Corporation, Ministry of Machine and Electronic Industry |
| Combined cycle power plants | GE (USA) and Cockerill Mechanical Industries (Belgium) |
| Small to medium-scale hydropower projects | Sulzer Escher Wyss (Switzerland), Biwater (UK), GE Hydro (Canada), NEYRPIC (Canada) and other Chinese partners |

Official documents reveal that despite an in-principle agreement on the part of WAPDA, the government refused to entertain the SEC indigenization plan in 1995 saying that it was already in negotiation for 17,000MW of IPPs. Interestingly, the SEC plan was on the table long before the IPPs negotiations were initiated—having taken the initiative of indigenization of power plants in 1991, the SEC had offered six projects of a total capacity of 2,000MW backed with a complete financial package in March 1994.[27] Also, WAPDA had already sent recommendations for some of the projects to the government while others were under serious consideration as can be seen in the official correspondence between SEC and WAPDA during 1993–94.[28,29] Ironically, in May 1995, the PPIB arranged the SEC project to be dumped despite the fact that the Ministry of Industries and Production had recommended it to the Economic Coordination Committee (ECC) of the Cabinet citing its comparative strong financial and technological advantages against the IPPs.[30,31] The project summary was not allowed to be put up in an ECC meeting chaired by Prime Minister Benazir Bhutto. Sources suggest that all efforts were successfully made to hide the facts from the nation and possibly even from the prime minister. The responsibility is said to rest with a group of bureaucrats and politicians led by the then Secretary Water and Power Salman Farooqi—the long time close ally and the current principal secretary of President Asif Ali Zardari. It is noteworthy that Mr Farooqi is also facing charges of wide-ranging and large-scale corruption.[32,33]

An ex-Deputy Chairman of the Planning Commission, who observed the developments on the SEC project very closely, recalls with great regret:

The public and the country are still suffering from the expensive power purchased from IPPs. Only a few people benefitted at huge perpetual cost which is a continuous damage to energy sector, industry, agriculture and in fact the entire national economy. Colossal damage has been inflicted on this poor nation by a few individuals.[33]

Some of the key implications of binning the project are as follows:

- WAPDA could have saved tens of billions of dollars over the next twenty-five years by producing comparatively much cheaper electricity from its own resources rather than purchasing it from the IPPs. Through the SEC proposed project WAPDA could have generated electricity at under 4 cents/kWh along with added benefits of technology transfer, job creation and human resource development. Rejecting this brilliant offer, WAPDA was made to purchase electricity from IPPs at 6.1 cents/kWh while a few years down the line at over 13 cents/kWh.
- It could have led the country to technology self sufficiency in the area of power plants while also providing huge saving in foreign exchange that could have been multiplied in future.
- The timely availability of spares and maintenance facilities could have resulted in a much better maintenance level of the national power infrastructure thus bringing substantial financial benefits—by ensuring better levels of system maintenance and timely repairs billions of rupees, for example, could have been saved in the case of the recent breakdown of the Mangla power project alone.
- Future power-plants could have been designed and orchestrated at a much lower cost and with greater ease.
- It could have helped the country to considerably reduce the trade deficit by curtailing the import of power-plant equipment.
- It could have delivered massive socio-economic benefits through the creation of thousands of jobs.
- Through development of a rich skilled human resource base it could have helped the wider engineering expertise excel in many directions.
- Had the aforementioned American and European companies developed manufacturing facilities in Pakistan and the project got underway, it would have been one of the greatest confidence building measures for investors and industrialists from across the world.
- Sabotage of this project badly dented the credibility of Pakistan in the eyes of foreign investors and industrialists.

### 5.1.4.2 Kalabagh Dam

The energy outlook of Pakistan cannot be complete without an account of the Kalabagh Dam. The project was a natural progression of the Indus Basin Development Programme. Apart from its massive importance as a storage medium for a large amount of vital irrigation water and a cushion for flood control, it was also to serve as a large resource of cheap and sustainable electricity. The project was originally to be completed by the early 1990s, however due to its politicization every government over the last three decades kept on shelving it. The current government went a step further to declare that the dam is being scrapped.[34] Interestingly, this decision came when the country was facing the worst crisis of its history and energy deals were being made that were disastrously expensive and unsustainable compared to what the Kalabagh Dam could have offered. Moreover, the decision was made without any concrete discussion on the subject in parliament.

A quick review of the electricity generation potential of the project reflects upon its importance for the power sector. The installed capacity of the Kalabagh dam would be 3,600MW. The dam is estimated to be capable of annually generating 11,400GWh of electricity. Furthermore, the conjunctive operation of Kalabagh and Tarbela would enable the latter to generate 336GWh of electricity in addition to its existing power production, thus taking the tally to 11,736GWh. This much electricity from IPPs is being purchased in 2009 at a price of around Rs131.5 billion. Generating it from Kalabagh Dam would have cost below Rs6.5 billion. Simply the energy price Pakistan is paying for neglecting the Kalabagh Dam during 2009 stands at over Rs125 billion. It has been nearly twenty years now that WAPDA and Pakistan are experiencing huge economical damage for delaying the project. Ironically, the magnitude of the damage would grow year upon year. Considering the economics of the power projects in pipeline, the annual price of delaying the Kalabagh Dam in 2010 would easily rise up to a staggering figure of Rs150 billion. Including the agricultural benefits the dam would bring, the total cost of neglecting it becomes considerably higher.

There have been some provincial objections on the viability of the Kalabagh Dam particularly from NWFP and Sindh in terms of possible reduced quota of water and threats of flooding. WAPDA officials, including those belonging to NWFP and Sindh, however, who have been involved with the project in different capacities over the years, think otherwise. On the basis of its own assessments and the independent studies undertaken by foreign companies, WAPDA dismisses the apprehensions from these provinces. According to WAPDA, the independent reviews have completely dismissed the fears of flooding. While the issues of mangrove forests and fisheries have also been adequately addressed in these studies, WAPDA, in conjunction with the Government of Pakistan and other relevant departments, also pledges to ensure the sufficient supply of irrigation water for all provinces. Commitments have also been made to resettle the displaced people.

Obviously, the project like all other reservoir based hydropower projects in the world is bound to have certain implications on the local ecosystem and displace several thousand people. Rather than taking the issue to the streets, political parties and other concerned stakeholders should have come to the drawing board to evaluate and try to address genuine concerns. Over the years there have been numerous occasions when Kalabagh Dam could have been pursued but the respective governments neither exhibited a true understanding of the importance of the project nor the political will to get a national consensus over its development. If, for the sake of their political compromises they were unable to build Kalabagh at least they should had developed Bhasha Dam or any other project of similar significance. Over the last three decades, in the wake of the Kalabagh controversy, depriving the country of cheap, secure and sustainable hydroelectricity and subsequent agricultural benefits by not exploring other potential projects has shown the utter failure on the part of respective governments.

The ex-Chairman WAPDA Shamsul Mulk who interestingly belongs to Nowshehra—the same town that is said to be prone to flooding—is probably the biggest and most outspoken supporter of the Kalabagh Dam in the country. He strongly supports this project and categorically rejects the technical objections brought forward by the NWFP and Sindh provinces on it. He believes:

> The greatest beneficiaries of the Kalabagh Dam project will be NWFP and denying the project is denying the fruits of the Indus Basin. Kalabagh is also going to benefit Sindh by supporting its agriculture with increased level of water.[35]

Moreover, he believes that: 'some segments of society in the two concerned provinces have fallen in the trap of politicians; they don't believe in the truth of WAPDA but the lies of politicians.'[35]

The explanations furnished by some political figures including the Awami National Party (ANP) leadership in denouncing the Kalabagh Dam sum up the whole story. As part of its initiative to get political consensus on the project, in 2001 WAPDA arranged a series of meetings with concerned political parties. One of these meetings was held in Shahi Bagh (Charsadda) on 15 August 2001 between WAPDA's top management led by the Chairman Lt. General (retd.) Zulfiqar and the main leadership of ANP. The ex-Member WAPDA, Javed Nizam, who was also present in the meeting describes that the ANP leadership including its late president Khan Abdul Wali Khan, current president Asfandyar Wali Khan, Begum Naseem Wali, Ajmal Khattak and Azam Hoti were given a detailed briefing by one of the members of WAPDA, Sardar Tariq, who interestingly also belonged to the NWFP. He addressed all controversial issues including flooding and waterlogging of the catchment area of the Kalabagh Dam. At the end of the briefing and after a sumptuous lunch the Chairman WAPDA asked about the decision of the ANP. Abdul Wali Khan straightforwardly said, 'although technically I don't have any problem with the Kalabagh Dam, but my politics is based on this issue, so how can I let this issue die. I will also be dead if I don't oppose it'.[36] Similarly, another source suggests that the ex-Prime Minister Benazir Bhutto expressed her interest in Kalabagh Dam during her second tenure but was advised otherwise by some of the party leaders from Sindh. Again the argument brought forward to her was the same—a go ahead to the project would damage the political interests of the party in the province.[37]

The disastrous floods of July/August 2010 are a wake-up call for the policy and decision-makers, especially the political leadership, to change their impeding attitude towards the large-scale hydropower projects in general and the Kalabagh Dam in particular. The natural catastrophe, reportedly the worst of its type in the history of the country, has, as per initial estimates, resulted in over 1,600 deaths, while affecting more than 15 million people and inflicting hundreds of billion of Rupees worth of damage to the infrastructure, private properties and agriculture. Kalabagh Dam and other major dams could have considerably helped avoid this devastation by providing a significant cushion against the rampant flood-water. Also, until two weeks prior to the flood, the provinces were seriously at odds with each other, at the Indus River System Authority (IRSA) meetings, over getting their desired share of irrigation-water from the country's limited reservoirs. Now, when they have affluent water that can be capitalized to help meet their irrigation needs satisfactorily, they don't have enough storage capacity to capture this vital resource. Furthermore, on 6 August 2010, four people were killed and ten were injured in police crossfire on a demonstration against electricity load-shedding in the Khyber Pakhtunkhwa province (previously known as NWFP). Absurdly, just the day before this killing the ANP government in the province had strongly denounced the Kalabagh Dam that could have actually provided cheap and secure electricity not only to the people of Khyber Pakhtunkhwa but also to those living elsewhere in the country.

As a matter of fact, people from all the four provinces are paying a hefty price for the delay in the development of the Kalabagh Dam. The sufferings of people are more than likely to continue unless the politicians from all the provinces bridge their differences and orchestrate this project. The goodwill gesture recently shown by some of prominent politicians from Punjab, as they have offered the other three provinces to take full charge of the distribution of water from the proposed Kalabagh Dam, is a very positive sign. It can be made a good starting point towards getting a broader national reconciliation over the development of the Kalabagh Dam. It is time for politicians to rise above their petty political interests in order to think for the wider national interests and for the future of the coming generations.

### 5.1.5 DEARTH OF COMPETENCE

The aforementioned issues inevitably imply that successive regimes have fallen short of showing the due level of competence and commitment required to propel the energy sector forward in a healthy fashion. Not only have they failed to anticipate the dimensions and scale of the emerging challenges but also to react to them in a timely and pragmatic manner. It also suggests that there is a certain degree of the scarcity of the right type of skills and committed professionals amongst the ranks of the policy and decision-makers. Even the policy documents prepared at the highest possible level, as provided to the author by pertinent officials, have fundamental mistakes in them which shows a lack of understanding on the subject of energy. One of the most senior of the current policy making officials when asked about this particular issue replied: 'Government of Pakistan's policy and decision-making forums do lack qualified experts.'[38] An ex-Chairman Planning Commission also reflected upon the issue as: 'Owing to nepotism the system in general lacks expertise and capabilities.'[39]

Here it is worth highlighting that energy sustainability is amongst the top-most priorities of the conscious nations across the world. Periodic roadmaps to ensure sustainable energy future are designed. Provision of sufficient and secure energy is something governments cannot compromise upon. In a rapidly changing world, they annually review their energy strategies not only to accommodate any uncertainties but also to make the best out of the available opportunities. In order to achieve this, there are rightly qualified, competent and visionary people in place. In their ranks, they have experts who have command not only on a diverse range of energy systems, but also on wider socio-economic and geo-political dimensions of energy. They are thus capable of delivering visionary and successful energy policies to their countries. As a matter of fact often prominent academicians and scientists sit on the policy-making forums. Compared to that, within the policy and decision-making circles of Pakistan, the aforementioned trends are quite alien. Unlike the developed countries, there is no such inclination to get help from academic and research bodies if in-house expertise is not available.

### 5.1.6 THE CURRENT STATE OF AFFAIRS

The examples cited earlier in this chapter indicate how individuals sitting at powerful positions, for their vested interests, don't hesitate in toying with vital national interests and inflicting huge financial and strategic damage to the nation. For the policy and decision-makers, sufferings of the nation are still too little to impress them. Reports emerging through senior energy officials and national media suggest that no lessons have been learnt from past mistakes. The current crisis is reported to have provided another golden opportunity to the rulers to orchestrate mind boggling corruption.[40,41] Hardly any deal/project is being undertaken in a fair and transparent manner. The compact fluorescent lamps (CFLs) project worth Rs6.7 billion, for example, as approved by the Deputy Chairman Planning Commission Sardar Asif Ahmed Ali in November 2009, has been reported to suffer from serious irregularities.[42] Fingers are not only being pointed at the controversial rental power/IPPs programme but also on the projects that the Ministry of Petroleum and Natural Resources is undertaking.[43,44] Not only that, serious irregularities have also been reported with regard to the mega hydropower projects—allegedly the around Rs207 billion Kohala hydropower project has been awarded without bids and without the consent of pertinent authorities. The pertinent Secretary for Water and Power refused to be part of the MoU being of the view that 'since the government's procedure that includes the prime minister and the cabinet's approval and vetting by the law ministry was not followed so he would not be part of any such deal.'[45]

## 5.2. ACADEMIA

Universities are human capacity enhancement centres. By their very nature, universities have the function of providing education through teaching, research and development, and partnerships with other stakeholders of the society. The modern-day world greatly owes to universities for the scientific and technological developments it cherishes. Universities not only serve the physical sciences but also the broad range of social sciences. Across the world, apart from the primary function of capacity building through teaching, universities also provide solutions to industrial and commercial organizations, and develop policies and strategies for public and private sector institutes. Contrary to such trends, universities in Pakistan in general have confined themselves with just the teaching activities, almost completely missing out on research and development, and external partnerships. As a result, the universities, apart from producing graduates, have hardly served the society in any respect. They have traditionally fallen short of developing a conspicuous interaction with industry and other professional and commercial entities in order to deliver optimum solutions to address the issues and challenges facing the society.

Over the last couple of decades, the global energy scenario has been substantially transformed. Energy demand and supply networks have grown manifold at national and international levels, new technologies have emerged, energy-related challenges have increased and so have prospects. Universities across the world have proactively contributed in this progression. The subject of energy has evolved greatly in universities across the world—energy departments have grown both in number and size, the curriculum has evolved, greater numbers of energy engineers and professionals with a wide range of expertise are being produced, research has surged, collaboration with industrial and commercial bodies has boosted, and public awareness has hit new levels. Particularly in the developed countries, universities are leaders in national energy sustainability frameworks in terms of solution provision, human resource development and policymaking processes. Most universities offer undergraduate, postgraduate and research degree programmes in the core areas of energy.

Universities in Pakistan, however, have not given due consideration to energy as it is still being treated as a routine and insignificant subject. Hardly any of the aforementioned trends has found its way into universities. The credentials—a few universities producing power engineers in small numbers and one or two others producing nuclear and petroleum engineers—are far from satisfactory. Recently, a couple of universities have initiated relatively broader energy programmes. It is a commendable effort, however, too little and almost too late.

In the backdrop of the enormous energy-related challenges facing the country along with other stakeholders, universities have a crucial contribution to make. What Pakistan particularly lacks is qualified human resource in the form of energy scientists, engineers and professionals that could analyse energy-related problems facing the country both at the macro and micro levels and synthesise value-engineered solutions. The energy challenges facing Pakistan—a massive gap between demand and supply, depleting gas reserves, rocketing energy prices, energy security and across the board inefficient use of energy—are too mammoth for the energy engineers local universities currently produce.

There is another dimension to the issue of below par performance of universities in the said area that does not allow the entire blame to be placed on them. Universities to some extent have to deliver a product (graduate) that is desirable in the market (industry). Industry in Pakistan has failed to truly comprehend the essence and scope of this area. It has not created a demand for energy engineers and professionals to be met by universities. Thus, in order to bring about a healthy change, industry ought to come forward to help universities not only by accommodating energy graduates but also by supporting research and development activities.

At the same time, universities also have to be appreciative of the need to develop a partnership with industry. The academic-industry partnership would require a profound involvement of government that would help by making conducive policies and by providing financial and other resources as and when required. The triangle of academia, industry and government is thus required to work closely and proactively not only to produce capable and qualified energy professionals but also to provide them a conducive environment and opportunities where they can flourish and serve their purpose.

There are some new universities in the private sector that are in the process of establishing engineering departments. Having performed well in other areas of social sciences, it was expected of them to entertain the subject of energy when taking the physical sciences on board. But surprisingly, none of them have given any deliberation to it and have opted for traditional subjects that are already being widely taught in the country.

Universities both in the public and private sector have to realise that the subject of energy is as much an applied science as any other. They must enlist energy departments in their priorities and make a meaningful contribution to help the country resolve its energy crisis. It is also worth noting that energy is a multi-billion dollar per annum business. Logically and fairly, universities can also win handsome business by providing wide-ranging consultancy services to a diverse clientele including industry, government departments, local and foreign investors and donors. Universities, thus, for their own sakes and for the national interest should rise to the occasion.

## 5.3. INDUSTRY

The industrial revolution, triggered in the West during the late eighteenth and early nineteenth century, has been one of the most important turning points in the history of mankind. It is the time when machines started replacing manpower. The steam engine then propelled the industrial revolution all across the world fundamentally changing dwelling, trading, manufacturing, transportation and agriculture trends. The result was a meaningful effect on socio-economic and cultural conditions setting the cornerstone for the modernization the world cherishes today. In the present age, industry has a very crucial role to play in any country's economic and infrastructural development. For that very reason, a strong industrial base has been the key to the success of the developed countries.

With the invention of the steam engine in the early days of the industrial revolution, a new and dynamic 'energy-era' dawned upon the world. More than two centuries later, the energy-era is at its peak thanks to continuous and rigorous support from industry. Throughout this period, industry in the developed countries has risen to the occasion to improvise solutions—in the form of both quantitative and qualitative growth of energy resources and technologies—as required by the ever-expanding economic and infrastructural basis of the world.

In order to address energy challenges, amongst other sectors, industry in Pakistan also has a very important role to play. The country inherited only a nominal industrial base at its independence. Things had to be built almost from a scratch. Local industry has traditionally put a lot of effort into getting where it stands now especially as government support has not been very healthy. However, having taken into account these drawbacks industry has to face, its overall performance, especially with regard to the energy sector, has not been satisfactory. Since the 1990, local industry has played an important role in the development of the energy sector by setting up new power plants. However, despite this appreciable contribution, its performance, by and large, has not been enviable. The role industry needs to play is much broader as discussed hereunder.

### 5.3.1 INVESTMENT IN THE ENERGY SECTOR

Industry needs to exploit the true potential of investment in the energy sector. Although since the 1990s there has been a significant initiative on the part of some of the large industrial groups to set up IPPs, there is still a great deal of untouched ground. As of 2009, Pakistan experiences a shortfall of over 5,000MW of electricity. With demand on a consistent rise, taking benchmark figures of $1 million per Megawatt, the country would require a multi-billion dollar investment on an annual basis in the coming decades. It is worth noting that energy is one of the most lucrative businesses on the planet—power plants usually have a small payback period and a mountainous reward on the investment. Industry in Pakistan however does not appear to be aware of the true potential of the energy sector. Consequently, a major chunk of the energy business, yielding gigantic sums of profit, is going abroad every year. It is important for industry to also closely follow the modern energy trends across the world. Investment needs to be made in both conventional and non-conventional (renewable) energy systems. The latter has actually been growing at a faster rate than the former—in 2007 investments made in the renewable energy sector grew by 26 per cent against 2 per cent growth (apart from China  and India where the electricity market grew by 6 to 9 per cent) in the area of conventional electricity. In 2008, despite the global economic recession, annual investment in renewable energy jumped by around 5 per cent hitting the $155 billion mark.[46]

Industry, especially the one that has a large energy consumption base, should start producing its own electricity in an attempt to reduce dependency on the unreliable and inadequate national electricity grid and gas network. The national grid is in chaos—on top of planned load-shedding, lengthy and frequent breakdowns without warning have also become a norm. The situation is thus disturbing enough to shake the confidence of industry and hardly leaves it with any margin to stay competitive in local and international markets. Ironically, by the end of 2008, nearly a yearlong persistent pounding by the infuriating crisis forced a substantial number of small and medium enterprises (SMEs) to close down, simply because it was not economically sustainable for them to operate any more. Ironically, there have been numerous cases of companies getting black-listed by business partners in foreign countries for missing deadlines only because of electricity and gas disruptions.

Electricity generation by large-scale industry is not only going to be in its very own interest but will also provide massive relief to the national grid. Some of the large-scale textile mills and a number of other industries are already producing their own electricity and thus are not only self-sufficient but are also in a position to sell their surplus electricity. The trend needs to be widespread. Another aspect of the matter is the ever-increasing energy prices. In recent years energy bills have regularly hit new heights due to jumps in tariff, escalating the production cost of industry. With in-house electricity generation, however, the industry will be in a relatively better position to withstand the shocks of increasing energy prices.

## 5.3.2 TECHNOLOGICAL BASE

One of the most important shortcomings of industry is the lack of a sound technological base. It has traditionally fallen short of making any noteworthy technical/engineering contribution towards tackling the country's energy problems. Although there have been some phenomenal success stories and pockets of absolutely world class expertise, the overall outlook of the industrial base of the country is pretty much unsatisfactory. Amongst the major issues that plague the sector by and large are the built-in passiveness and short sightedness. Concepts like innovative solutions, precision engineering, quality control and standardization appear generally unheard of. In an age of globalization and free economy, local industry, largely for these very reasons, is sharply losing the competitive edge. Often, the SMEs count on technicians and foremen to lead their technical teams—the wider approach is that it would be a lot cheaper to hire a foreman than a qualified engineer. Such a strategy has had numerous ramifications. To mention a few, a large proportion of the industrial base, lacking vision and understanding of contemporary challenges and prospects, has been relying on a copy-cat approach. In many crucial areas such as metals and alloys, coatings and surface treatments, chemicals and synthetic materials, industry relies solely on guesswork. There is also the unhealthy trend of negative competition. Industrial competitors, for example, are not inclined to gain a competitive edge over each other by quality- and functional-enhancement but by reduction in production cost even if they have to compromise on quality, which they often do.

Local industry does not have any expertise in the area of energy technologies whatsoever. It does not know how to produce energy systems'  key components, i.e. turbines, engines, generators and other electronic and control gadgets. The situation with secondary components such as boilers, compressors and heat exchangers is also not enviable. Obviously, in order to tap immediate business opportunities, procurement of power plants from abroad is the only option. Amid numerously emerging new technologies, such as advanced nuclear systems, renewable energy systems and fuel cells, in the medium to long term scenario, the energy sector is going to experience a fast changing and expanding business environment. In order to be well-positioned to tap .upcoming business opportunities, local industry would have to overcome its complacency. Rather than relying on consistent hardware-import, as has traditionally been the practice, emphasis should be placed upon technology transfer so that a few years down the line the country is capable of locally producing the desired level of energy systems.

Industry should also establish an appropriate level of in-house research and development (R&D) base so that pertinent expertise is readily available, also because in many instances foreign technology requires to be indigenized to suit the local environment. Apart from technology transfer, reverse engineering or reproduction is another avenue that can be pursued, which provides solutions with economy as well as ease. It is noteworthy that reverse engineering has played an important role in China's industrial success.

It is worth quoting trends in which, India having realised the importance of renewable energy, took timely initiatives a couple of decades ago and has now become a major exporter of renewable technologies, such as wind turbines and solar photovoltaic. Media reports in 2007–08 suggest that even Pakistan was also considering importing renewable energy systems from India. Interestingly, there is little disparity between the two countries, especially in terms of per capita socio-economic conditions and the calibre of human resources. The noticeable difference one finds is that of vision. For example, Suzlon, the fifth largest wind turbine manufacturing company in the world, was established in 1995 by a textile businessman. By 2007, the company, worth stood at nearly US$2.2 billion.[47] In the field of solar energy, India has managed to attract a number of leading solar photovoltaic (PV) manufacturers of the world and has set up nine production facilities. The state of affairs indicates that Pakistan is going to be a late starter as was the case with the Information Technology (IT) industry. It is time for the industrial sector to rise to the occasion before it is too late. It would have to come out of its inherent laidback stance to contribute, amongst other things, to the technological advancements required to address the country's energy challenges.

### 5.3.3 ENERGY CONSERVATION AND MANAGEMENT

The Industrial sector is the largest consumer of energy in the country. It accounts for nearly 42 per cent of the total national primary energy consumption (excluding the energy being consumed in the power sector). Industry is, however, very low at energy efficiency—the amount of energy required to undertake a certain task is much higher than that required in a developed country for the same purpose.

In terms of wasteful consumption of energy the state of affairs in the small to medium scale factories of Gujranwala and large-scale industries of Karachi and Lahore is alike. Manufacturers of home appliances and surgical instruments are as energy-inefficient as are textile and sugar mills. Cement and heavy metal industries are as unproductive in consumption of energy as are chemical and automobile industries. The industrial sector, thus, needs to substantially improve energy productivity. It can significantly help addressing the issue of energy deficit. Through energy conservation and management measures industry can save over a quarter of the energy it consumes as also discussed in detail in Section 7.1. The practice would not only help lessen the burden on the national grid but would also bring financial gain for the industry and help it remain competitive in an increasingly difficult market.

### 5.4. ENERGY DEPARTMENTS

The energy departments, apart from one or two exceptions, have traditionally fallen short of playing a satisfactory role in meeting national energy requirements. The performance of the major energy departments is looked into in this section.

## 5.4.1 WAPDA and KESC

The two major departments in the power sector, WAPDA and KESC, are well-known for their substandard performance. The story of WAPDA, the backbone of the national power sector is, however, quite interesting and shows that the departments current unhealthy reputation does not justify its brilliant past.

### 5.4.1.1 The Rise and Fall of WAPDA

Before the emergence of IPPs during the 1990s, WAPDA was the main organisation taking care of the national electricity needs. Bearing in mind the threats to Pakistan's water supplies as posed by India immediately after independence, the establishment of WAPDA in 1958 is regarded as a major milestone in the history of Pakistan. It played a key role in promoting the national electricity and water infrastructure. Also, by providing affordable and timely electricity it played an instrumental role in the industrial growth and economic development of the country during the 1960s. Nevertheless, in 51 years of its life the Authority has had a varying degree of performance. Over the years, it has had spells of brilliance as well as dreariness. A former chairman of the organisation, who joined it from the outset, believes that WAPDA did wonders in its early days particularly in terms of the development of some state of the art projects such as Mangla and Tarbela Dams. Dr Pervez Butt, ex-Chairman, Pakistan Atomic Energy Commission (PAEC) reflects on the prosperous era of WAPDA as: 'During 1960s, when I graduated, WAPDA used to be an extremely prestigious body and young engineers used to aspire to join it'. Another former World Bank official, Shahid Javed Burki, states: 'For a number of years, WAPDA was a model public sector institution in the developing world for undertaking developmental work.'[48]

After the 1970s, WAPDA could not maintain its cutting edge thanks to internal as well as external malpractices. Irregularities like financial corruption, operational inefficiencies and lack of sense of responsibility became widespread in the department as has been the case with most of the other public sector departments. Parallel to that, governmental support in the form of conducive policies and provisions of resources started to weaken. Kalabagh Dam, a project that WAPDA dearly wants to pursue considering it as vital for national power as well as a water resource base, has been delayed now for over two decades. This delay has had wide-ranging implications on WAPDA's financial conditions and future outlook. Unfavourable policies and decisions made by political authorities catalyzed the downfall of WAPDA.

Despite its internal shortcomings, many energy officials in Pakistan believe that the responsibility for WAPDA's current turmoil greatly rests with the policy and decision-makers. Making WAPDA generate 40 per cent of its developmental budget from its own resources, barring it from setting up thermal power plants and forcing it to comply with the unhealthy IPPs programme are amongst the major setbacks inflicted on it. The ex-Chairman WAPDA Shamsul Mulk's remarks speak volumes of the pain he feels at the poor state of affairs: 'Relying on the private sector WAPDA was denied the role of setting up thermal power projects without ensuring that the former had the capability to do so in a robust manner. WAPDA was a capable department and the ongoing energy crisis to a great extent could have been avoided had the department not been barred from setting up new power projects.'[35] It is the IPPs compliance that is said to be the main reason for the poor financial condition of WAPDA. More recently, the circular debt created by the Musharraf–Shaukat Aziz regime in 2006–07 further crippled the financial health of WAPDA. It is no less than a tragedy that the once model of a department in the country ended up in a situation where it was labelled a 'white elephant'.

### 5.4.1.2 Issues with WAPDA and KESC

The internal weaknesses of WAPDA are also far too great to be overlooked and are quite similar in nature to those of KESC's. The in-house problems with the two departments are discussed below.

### 5.4.1.2.1 Financial Corruption

Financial corruption is arguably the most important problem these departments face. The problem starts from the bottom in the system— meter readers, linemen and other clerical staff are extensively involved in wrongdoings. Transparency International in its 2002 report suggested that 65 per cent of the users of electricity reported process irregularities in acquiring it. A staggering 96 per cent of clients reported corruption in regular interaction with electricity departments. Here meter readers and billing staff were identified as the key facilitators; extortion was reported by 72 per cent of the victims.[49] Similarly, according to a World Bank report on the power sector of Pakistan, in 2006, 84 per cent of the applicants had to make informal payments in order to obtain new electricity connections.[50]

### 5.4.1.2.2 Losses—Technical Losses, Theft and *Kunda* Culture

After financial corruption, their second major weakness is huge transmission and distribution (T&D) losses. For WAPDA, these losses are reported to be over 35 per cent in many regions and 23 per cent on the country level as indicated in Figure 5.2. The situation with KESC is even worse where losses stand at over 40 per cent.[2,51] Considering both WAPDA and KESC the average countrywide losses turn out to be over 25 per cent. Here it is noteworthy that a combination of different losses such as grid losses, transmission losses and distribution losses are inevitable. Collectively these losses are termed as 'technical losses'. In an ideal scenario, these losses should not be more than 6–7 per cent as is the case in most developed countries. However, with the poor state of infrastructure, these losses are phenomenally high in Pakistan. The World Bank also acknowledges that the technical and collection losses are imposing a severe strain on the financial sustainability of Pakistan's power sector. It declares that the country bears more power losses than all comparators but India.[50]

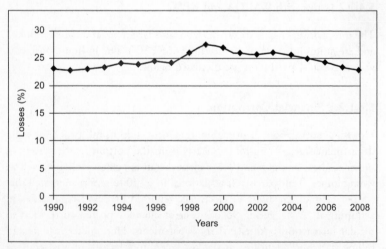

Figure 5.2: Annual T&D losses within WAPDA's domain

The only explanation for the extra hike in T&D losses is theft of electricity which is very much a widespread phenomenon, thanks to the prevalent meter tampering and the 'kunda' (hook) culture as shown in Figure 5.3.[52] On top of theft—a phenomenon mostly facilitated by corrupt elements within departmental ranks—the forceful hijacking of electricity by influential people is also a contributor. In the latter case departmental staff usually turn a blind eye even if they are aware of the crime. Nevertheless, there are many examples of extreme commitment and professionalism within the ranks of these departments. There have been incidents when their staff have been abducted and tortured for not surrendering to the electricity looting mafia. A few years ago a powerful electricity-thief in Gujranwala, for example, for the very reason seriously injured WAPDA's local Sub Divisional Officer (SDO). Gas theft is also a burning issue that annually costs the country billions of rupees. On 10 August 2009, Sui gas workers protested against the murderous attack on a SDO in Lahore. The SDO was attacked as he attempted to curb the theft of gas in his area of jurisdiction. A protest was waged as the culprits were still at large and the local police was reportedly giving the incident a blind eye.[53]

Figure 5.3: An exhibition of the *Kunda* culture

Interestingly and expectedly, there is a long list of influential people who are involved in this brutal exploitation of national assets. In November 2008, a senior federal minister, Syed Khursheed Shah, for example, made headlines in the national print and electronic media for employing '*kunda*' on the occasion of his son's wedding for almost a week.[54,55] Similarly, in March 2010, an election procession, addressed by the former Prime Minister Nawaz Sharif and organized by his political party, was reported in the national as well as international media to have used '*kunda*' for making electricity arrangements for the event. BBC made interesting comments on the incident as: '*Officials of Pakistani opposition leader Nawaz Sharif have been accused of stealing electricity as he addressed a night rally to denounce corruption.*' Nawaz Sharif's party admitted the illegal use of electricity in the said case, however, quite expectedly, refused to take the responsibility. Ultimately a lineman was held responsible for the electricity theft, poor scapegoat. When the Law Minister of Punjab, Rana Sana Ullah, one of the spokesmen of Nawaz Sharif's party was asked to reflect on the issue, he barefacedly said: 'there is nothing suprising, the matter is trivial'. The Federal Minister for Water and Power Raja Pervez Ashraf commented on the incident as: 'Had a common man been found guilty of such illicit activity, the action would be prompt, but no action was taken from Lahore Electric Supply Company (LESCO) this time'. Pervez Ashraf passed such an honest judgement only because Nawaz Sharif belonged to the rival political party. Otherwise, his own character and commitment with the department he is heading and with the rule of law can be gauged from the fact that Pervez Ashraf himself and his brothers, only till a couple months ago, were defaulters of electricity bills for over a year. They cleared the outstanding charges only when the issue was highlighted in the media.

The KESC in July/August 2009 repeatedly blamed influential people/groups as being involved in power thefts. According to the CEO of KESC, the thieves were mainly from the 'upper class' and included multi-national companies, industrialists, and politicians. An initial list of culprits provided to the media included factories, and a hospital, hotel, school and public park.[56,57,58] Similarly, those who should be the symbol of the rule of law have been caught in taking unfair advantage by manipulating policies to facilitate certain sectors. In July 2009, for example, former president of Pakistan, Pervez Musharraf, under whose tenure the current crisis was fostered was found involved in misuse of electricity. The Managing Director of the Pakistan Electric Power Company (PEPCO) announced in a press conference that the company had ordered disconnection of electricity supply to the former president's farmhouse in Chak Shehzad near Islamabad after he failed to clear outstanding dues of Rs500,000. Interestingly but not surprisingly, it was not just him but dozens of other high profile figures—according to an Islamabad Electric Supply Company (IESCO) spokesman, thirty-four consumers in the area were found using illegal electricity tariff without bringing the matter to the notice to IESCO according to the requirement. The luminaries included another former president, an ex-prime minister, retired senior civil and military officials and businessmen. These irregularities, as acknowledged its spokesman, were facilitated by IESCO staff.[59,60]

Of the total losses worth around Rs30 billion, KESC officials suggest that stealing alone costs the department overRs16 billion in 2008–09.[61] Given the level of losses and the tariff structure, the countrywide financial implications in 2008–09 are estimated to be over Rs225 billion. Careful estimates suggests that by controlling stealing alone over Rs100 billion can be saved. It is estimated that by also appropriately renovating the infrastructure, around Rs150 billion can be saved altogether. According to the World Bank the monetary value of these losses is equivalent to 75 per cent of the national education budget and around 200 per cent of the health budget. The losses are further estimated to be equal to electricity sufficient for around three million new connections.[62]

There are growing calls from all corners to curtail losses in response to which once again pledges are being made by pertinent authorities to address the problem. The KESC has come up with an interesting measure as it got a *Fatwa* (religious verdict) from prominent scholars declaring theft of electricity equivalent to *Gunah e Kabeera* (major sin).[61] KESC has also launched a campaign 'Name and Shame' as part of which it plans to publish the names of the culprits in the national press. It is also demanding that the Government of Pakistan make electricity theft a non-bailable offence, as is the case in other countries.

Also, in order to address their liquidity crunch, WAPDA and KESC should resort to curtail their T&D losses rather than shifting the burden onto customers through frequent jumps in tariff. KESC discovered an innovative but naive solution to the issue of lack of liquidity. In December 2008, in order to save money the Corporation skewed its oil-purchase-orders for its power-plants and making a mockery of the affair, KESC publically acknowledged this strategy. KESC thus opted to punish the public for its own inefficiency—rather than increasing its revenues by addressing T&D losses, it decided to make the people suffer up to 18 hours of load-shedding. The poor common man could do nothing at this day-light robbery—KESC got away with this and saw no action from the government.

Concerned authorities should also facilitate recovery of gigantic sums of outstanding charges various departments owe to WAPDA as part of the debt circle.

### 5.4.1.2.3 Other Miscellaneous Mismanagement Issues

On top of financial corruption and power losses, WAPDA and KESC face a number of other management issues that contribute to the poor performance of the two departments. An example of bad management which indeed also shows lack of commitment is that of the recent performance of KESC. As part of the privatization deal, the new management of KESC made three major commitments: firstly, the generation capacity would be increased; secondly, the transmission and distribution system would be upgraded by significant investment; and thirdly, system losses would be curtailed. Interestingly, the new management of KESC has failed to deliver on all three fronts. It is just a matter of sheer mismanagement that KESC which was a profitable institution till 1996 is now in such terrible shape. Its financial status has plunged so greatly that its share that stood at Rs29 in 1996 was merely equivalent to Rs2.58 in August 2009. The losses which were as low as 21 per cent in 1991 have grown to as much as over 40 per cent in 2009.[61]

On top of their fragile transmission and distribution infrastructure, WAPDA and KESC keep on developing unnecessary hiccups for the public. Incidents of destruction of precious home appliances due to issues like low voltage and system-tripping are widespread. In case of rain, lengthy electricity breakdowns and deaths due to electrocution (as shown in Figure 5.4) are also quite common. In the third week of July, for example, the rain triggered system-faults deprived a large proportion of Karachi from electricity for over 48 hours and also resulted in a number of deaths due to electrocution.[63]

Other mismanagement issues such as over billing and untimely load-shedding are like rubbing salt into people's wounds. There have been examples when poor families hardly making Rs5,000–6,000 a month have been issued electricity bills more than their monthly income.[64] Generating correct bills and regulating the load-shedding, that often is orchestrated in an irregular and abruptly fashion, in a systematic way is not something that requires extraordinary financial or technical resources but simply a sense of responsibility and understanding.

Poor management also reflects in mishandling of streetlights—it is quite a common phenomenon that these are unnecessarily operational during bright day-time hours as shown in Figure 5.5. At a time when people are suffering from a severe electricity shortfall, such a waste is extremely unprofessional and indeed condemnable. In Islamabad, for example, on 7 January 2008, on an around 20km-long highway, street lights were functional from as early as 11 a.m. The same day the national media reported similar cases in other cities including Lahore and Karachi.

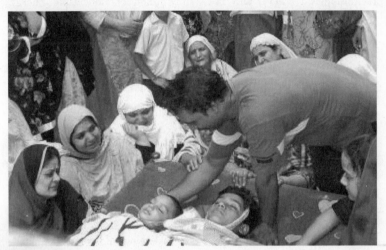

Figure 5.4: Bodies of kids electrocuted by the current in electricity poles, Lahore, 20 July 2010, Courtesy *Urdupoint*

Figure 5.5: On 23 March 2010, as the country faces 5300MW of shortfall resulting in 18 hours of load-shedding, street lights are working in the daytime only a few hundred yards from the WAPDA headquarters. Courtesy *Urdupoint*

## 5.4.2 Renewable Energy Departments

Renewable energy is another area that has faced repeated setbacks at the hands of the concerned departments. A number of initiatives have been undertaken over the last three decades to promote renewable energy. Several departments have also been set up for this purpose including the Appropriate Technology Development Corporation (ATDC), National Institute of Silicon Technology (NIST), Pakistan Council for Appropriate Technologies (PCAT), and Pakistan Council of Renewable Energy Technologies (PCRET). None of these initiatives delivered because of the scarcity of right strategy and due resolve. Of these departments PCRET still exists, though, it has very little, if at all, to show for its existence.[65]

The renewable projects that were launched since the 1970s—mostly pilot projects by their very nature—have had some fundamental shortcomings. No efforts were made to ensure customers' proactive participation and education. There were no operation and maintenance (O&M) training programmes in place to educate customers on long-term utilization of the installed system. There was never a real sense of ownership communicated to customers. Subsequently, hardly any of the installed systems lasted beyond the trial period. The author has seen remnants of a large number of such systems including precious solar photovoltaic (PV) systems, wind turbines and biogas units lying around many parts of the country including remote areas of Sindh and Punjab and even in Rawalpindi. Until a few years ago, even a passerby would observe remnants of a large number of solar PV panels in the junkyard of a university in Rawalpindi. Another renewable energy initiative was taken with the establishment of the Alternate Energy Development Board in 2002. It was hoped that the department would have learnt lessons from the disappointing performance of its predecessors but that has not been the case.

### 5.4.2.1 Alternate Energy Development Board

The Alternate Energy Development Board (AEDB) was established with bold claims and high expectations. Its lacklustre performance, however, is widely seen as an utter disappointment and failure. In the seventh year of its life, the Board has not managed to deliver any tangible output despite having been upbeat about its achievements throughout the period. It was established to promote renewable energy to help address the energy challenges facing the country. A number of ambitious targets were set out, the most outstanding of which was development of a solid wind power base in the country within a matter of a few years. Assurances were also made to advance solar and biomass technologies. Promises were made to develop 100MW and 700MW of wind power by 2005 and 2007 respectively as shown in Figure 5.6.[66] Having not yet been anywhere closer to the wind-power target as of 2010, that was originally to be met in 2005, is either a matter of incompetence and fickleness or over-ambitious and irrational planning.

Anyone closely following the renewable energy developments in Pakistan over the years, can recall media reports from 2005 showing the then president Pervez Musharraf claim that his government was producing electricity from wind. Nearly four years later, by the advent of 2009, one could not find any signs of wind generated electricity. It was only in April 2009 when the first so-called wind farm of a humble 6MW capacity was inaugurated by the Prime Minister Yousaf Raza Gilani.[67] This is still a negligible output compared to the original 100MW and 700MW targets.

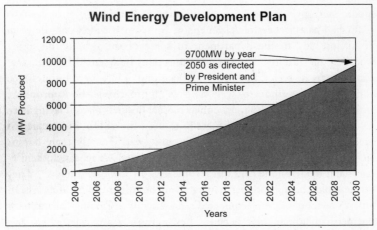

Figure 5.6: Original targets of AEDB towards wind power growth

One of the founding and senior-most officials of AEDB, Irfan Afzal Mirza, when interviewed, admitted that the Board has failed to deliver. He believed it was a combination of lack of necessary homework and unrealistic target setting. He, however, considered a number of other factors to have also played a role in the dismal performance of AEDB such as lack of skilled manpower, lack of financial resources, and reluctant support from other departments, i.e. NDTC, NEPRA, and the Government of Sindh.

The scarcity of professionalism in the Board is evident from the fact that up to 50,000MW of wind power potential claims were furnished in 2004 while by 2008 AEDB was still trying to get the wind data validated from the Rise National Laboratory of Denmark in order to identify the true wind energy potential.[68] To some extent, sympathy can be rendered to AEDB that there was not any concrete wind data available to it in the first place. Without having accurately measured and validated wind data in hand, however, it was not appropriate by any means to make claims and set targets based upon speculative figures.

Sources suggest that corruption and nepotism have also played a major role in the downfall of the Board. Ghost projects are also said to have been part of the catalogue of issues. Various other projects that were proudly projected in the media time and again were said to be in bad shape due to the absence of any maintenance plan, a typical problem that has contributed to the downfall of pervious renewable energy initiatives in the country. Sources claim that the emphasis had been on developing media perception rather on delivering goal oriented projects. An Islamabad-based renewable/clean energy company is widely considered to be a close ally to the department in some of the behind the scenes wheeling and dealing. The strong connections between AEDB and that company are no secret. In August 2009 a group of UK-based businessmen contacted the author to seek help in approaching the appropriate authorities in Pakistan to pursue their biofuel business plans. Having been recommended by the author to get in touch with AEDB, they expressed their despair at its attitude. There response was: 'Frankly there doesn't seem to be much point in contacting AEDB, we have repeatedly sent e-mails and made phone calls but it's like a ghost town—no reply.'[69] They further told the author that having spent months running after AEDB only to be rebuffed, they contacted a few friends in Pakistan to approach the department on their behalf. They were, however, advised to stop wasting time as AEDB was never going to give their business proposals any consideration since most of its business contracts were to, by default, go to the same Islamabad-based company. They were further informed about the unofficial relationship between some of the senior officials of AEDB and the management of that particular renewable energy company.

Quite understandably, from the outset, the AEDB had the disadvantage of shortage of resources, particularly technical expertise and infrastructure. Parallel to these inherent challenges, AEDB, however, also enjoyed significant support from various corners within the government including the former Prime Minister Shaukat Aziz and from some large international development agencies and donors. Figure 5.7 reflects upon the prestigious status AEDB has enjoyed for several years only not to deliver. Given the opportunities and challenges, the Board should have been realistic in setting targets. Yet, whatever the targets were, they could have been reasonably met had there been the right strategy, due resolve, and professionalism. AEDB's approach on the other hand has been utterly directionless and irrational. For example, development of the indigenous technology-base—a vital move that has totally been ignored—could have made things a lot easier. One of the senior-most energy officials in the country is of the view that AEDB has been wasting time and energy with unnecessary issues such as purchasing large land areas for wind farms. Areas covered by wind turbines could have been rented instead of being bought as is the practice in many countries. It would have made the job a lot easier for AEDB bearing in mind the difficulties it has been having with the provincial government of Sindh in purchasing the targeted land for wind farms. Sharing his experience of seeing wind turbines in JhimPir in 1951—built before 1947 for water pumping—he was of the view that the development of wind power in Pakistan, as was the manifesto of AEDB, should have not been such a challenging task as the department has made it appear.[70]

Figure 5.7: Bio-diesel run car on display outside AEDB's initial office in the Prime Minister's Secretariat reminds one of yet another cosmetic project by AEDB which could not deliver

The degree of AEDB's realism can be gauged from a characteristic upbeat statement that the Secretary of AEDB gave in an interview in 2005 that: 'With only six people AEDB did a number of things during the last year or so' and that 'it intends to double this effort with 12 engineers on its payroll. The results will certainly speak for themselves.'[65] One can't help being shocked that an energy department at the national level was  relying on 'six' people to develop wind power projects of around 1,000MW especially when none of them had any notable experience of dealing with the technology. As a matter of fact, energy departments in other countries would have several hundred engineers and experts working for them for projects of a similar magnitude. Coming to the second part of his statement, yes, the results definitely speak of an utter letdown and mismanagement but the concerned gentleman, like the chairman of the AEDB, is not on the Board any more to own the failure.

One of the greatest reasons behind the downfall of AEDB is a lack of a competent and robust strategy. Emphasis has been on expensive and fashionable technologies without taking into account their technical and economical viability while ignoring either by design or by incompetence much needed and technically and economically mature technologies. The list of over-ambitious and uncalculated plans of AEDB also included pursuance of projects which are technically and financially far from being viable even for the richest and the developed countries of the world. Tidal  power and fuel cells, for example, were on the list of priorities of AEDB as its founding Chairman Air Marshal (retd.) Shahid Hamid and Secretary Brigadier (retd.) Naseem Khan informed the author in 2005. The author was even invited by them to join AEDB to take on the fuel cell and wave the tidal projects. Owing to his reservations on the professinalism of AEDB in general, and viability of these projects in particular, the author, however, declined the offer. Overlooking much needed and viable technologies—like solar water heating, solar photovoltaic (PV) and biogas—and running after technologies that are only at the research and development phase and are decades away from their commercial viability is a strategy that makes little sense to the author. The demise of AEDB indeed should not be of any surprise when such an unrealistic and fantasized was the approach of its top management. All it has been having—as can also be observed from its current list of projects in the pipeline and future plans—is a long wish-list with negligible homework, minimal, if any, expertise and no real intent.

It is also noteworthy that contemporarily a large number of countries have made significant progress in renewable energy including South Asian countries of Bangladesh, India, Nepal, and Sri Lanka. The accomplishments of AEDB as highlighted in Section 3.1.4 compared to what has been achieved in these countries as discussed in the following section are nominal. Over the years, with growing competition in the international market, technology transfer has become a lot more expensive and complicated. Therefore, many experts believe that AEDB has wasted precious time.[71] They also believe that a great degree of damage has already been done to the renewable energy aspirations of the country. Opinion also exists that the credibility of the country has also been considerably damaged within the international wind power market thanks to lack of professionalism on the part of AEDB. It is thus all but obvious that, just like its predecessor departments, AEDB's story has been a tale of failure, which in numerous ways has damaged the long-term prospects of renewable energy in the country.

### 5.4.2.2 Renewable Energy Developments in South Asia

With the advent of 2010 as Pakistan continues to struggle to get inroads into renewable energy, countries across the world have made remarkable progress in the area. It is not just the developed countries that have managed to streamline renewable energy as an important part of their energy base but a large number of developing countries have also made significant accomplishments. There are some very successful renewable energy programmes in place in the developing countries of Africa, Latin America, and Asia. A number of South Asian countries are also benefiting from various types of renewable technologies. India, for example, has made remarkable progress in the area of renewable energy, thanks to the initiatives taken by its dedicated and visionary Ministry of New and Renewable Energy (MNRE). Over 9 per cent of India's total power generation capacity comes from renewable energy, around 70 per cent of which is contributed by wind power. Presently, India is the fifth largest country in the world in terms of wind power with an installed capacity of over 9.6GW. It has also excelled in the area of solar and biomass energy. The installed PV capacity in India is estimated to be around 100MWp of which 2.39MWp is grid connected. A highlight of its future ambitions is its plan to grow its grid connected PV capacity to 50MWp by 2012. An overview of India's decentralised renewable energy systems is given in Table 5.4. On top of these, it has also installed around 3.12 million square meter of solar water heating collector area.[72] It has nine solar cell manufacturing and eighteen solar module production facilities. From the indigenous manufacturing of wind turbines and solar PV India is not only meeting its own needs but is also getting huge revenue by exporting these technologies. Currently, for example, over 70 per cent of its solar PV production is exported.[73]

**Table 5.4: Overview of decentralised renewable energy systems in India**

| Technology/system | Installation in numbers |
| --- | --- |
| Family biogas plant | 4,142,000 |
| Solar Home Lighting System | 510,887 |
| Solar Lantern | 767,350 |
| Solar Street Lighting System | 82,384 |
| Solar Pump | 7,247 |
| Solar Water Heating—collector area | 3.12 million square meter |
| Solar Cookers | 657,000 |
| Wind Pumps | 1,347 |

Commercial projects of micro-level decentralised renewable energy systems of various types such as solar home systems, biogas plants, village hydropower plants and efficient biomass cookers supported by governmental and nongovernmental organisations (NGOs) are being successfully run in Bangladesh, India, Nepal, and Sri Lanka. Biogas Sector Partnership (BSP) of Nepal and Energy Services Delivery (ESD) of Sri Lanka, for example, have respectively installed over 180,000 biogas plants and 106,000 solar home systems.[74,75] In doing so, these countries have managed not only to mobilise handsome foreign funding but also to develop a huge infrastructure and human resource base in the area of renewable energy in terms of manufacturing facilities, trained human resource, entrepreneurs and micro-finance institutions (MFI).

### 5.4.2.2.1 Grameen Shakti

Grameen Shakti (GS), the energy arm of Grameen Bank, is undertaking a micro-generation renewable energy programme in Bangladesh. Grameen Shakti, started in 1996–97, is now the largest programme of its type in the world and deals with three technologies: solar home systems (SHS), biogas and improved cooking stoves (ICS). Through its flexible business model, GS offers a number of financial packages under which customers can have the system of their choice by paying upfront as little as 15 per cent of the total system cost. The remaining payment can be made in monthly instalments within three years. Through its novel business model, GS has made solar PV—often considered to be an expensive technology—affordable for the lower middle and lower class of Bangladesh. As of January 2010, in terms of installed systems, GS's accomplishments are as follows:

- Over 300,000 solar home systems (see Figure 5.8)
- Over 10,000 biogas units
- Over 45,000 improved cooking stoves

Apart from its contribution towards energy security and the fight against climate change, GS has excellent social service dimensions in terms of community development, poverty alleviation, and contribution towards

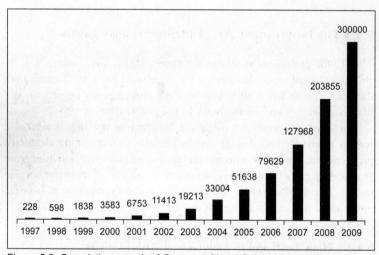

Figure 5.8: Cumulative growth of Grameen Shakti Solar Home systems

improvement of education and health conditions. GS has also created a large micro-utility network with over 10,000 of the installed solar home systems and biogas units operating as micro-utility. They have created over 5,000 'Green Employees' including 3,900 trained technical staff. The total number of people benefiting from GS is around three million. GS further aims to empower over 1.5 million homes from renewable energy by 2012 and to create over 100,000 green jobs by 2015.[76]

### 5.4.3 ENERCON

A number of small but important departments have been in place for a reasonably long period of time in Pakistan. ENERCON, for example, was established in 1986 with a clear mandate of promoting energy conservation and management. Over this period, ENERCON claims to have undertaken a large number of project ranging from newsletter circulation and organization of workshops to energy audits and boiler tune-ups.[77] In recent years, daylight saving time measures have also been adopted. The effectiveness of these activities is yet to be established—the fact that no data is available on the tangible benefits from ENERCON's activities in terms of saved energy, places serious question marks against the performance of the department. Considering its wider scope and extremely crucial status in the national energy scene, the performance of ENERCON is far from being impressive.

### 5.4.3 THE INDEPENDENT POWER PRODUCERS PROGRAMME

The 1990s Independent Power Producers (IPPs) programme, for its enormous significance, has been a much debated topic in Pakistan over the years. There has been strong criticism from various corners on the financial viability and transparency of the programme.

The most important benefit of the programme was that it averted a serious electricity shortfall. It also helped the country enjoy electricity prosperity for more than a decade and facilitated economic activities grow at a healthy rate. Bringing in investment is also one of its major success factors. The disadvantages of the programme, however, appear to have far outweighed its said advantages as discussed hereinafter.

#### 5.4.3.1 High Tariff and its Commercial Ramifications

The first and most important repercussion of the IPPs was the higher tariff structure. Irrespective of the technology of the power plant and the type of fuel used, a tariff of 6.5 cents/kWh (Rs1.952/kWh) was offered to the IPPs. This price had two components: capacity purchase price and energy purchase price. The capacity price was to be paid on a monthly basis to cover fixed costs, debt servicing, insurance expenses and return on equity irrespective of the quantum of energy purchased by the Government of Pakistan (WAPDA and KESC). The energy price was to be paid in Rs/kWh based on actual energy sold to WAPDA/KESC.[78] The most disturbing aspect of the tariff, experts believe, was the capacity payment equivalent to nearly 60 per cent of the total tariff—WAPDA was to pay the capacity price to IPPs even if it did not purchase any electricity from them. Moreover, the mechanism of indexation—of certain components of tariff based upon the Rupee/Dollar exchange rate, fuel price variations, interest rates and inflation—meant the overall tariff would remain prone to increments. Consequently, the tariff of 6.5 cents/kWh in 1994 has risen to around 14 cents/kWh by 2009.

The tariff offered to the IPPs appears to be unhealthy on two fronts. Firstly, to purchase electricity from the IPPs initially at 6.5 cents/kWh was quite an expensive choice for WAPDA that was producing its own thermal power at a much lower cost. WAPDA at the time was producing its own electricity at a price of Rs0.59/kWh (1.96 cents/kWh) and Rs0.73/kWh (2.4 cents/kWh) using gas and furnace oil respectively.[2] Furthermore, the electricity being offered to WAPDA from foreign energy companies through the earlier mentioned indigenization plan was at a price under 4 cents/kWh. Considering the monetary value of the additional benefits being offered—technology transfer, local manufacturing, and human resource development—it was an extremely economical and sustainable option compared to the IPPs. Senior WAPDA officials suggest that WAPDA had originally objected to the tariff structure being offered to the IPPs but at the end of the day had to oblige at the orders of the political superiors. Infact, during the course of the agreements some of WAPDAs officials were penalized by being removed from their positions for opposing the controversial tariff.

The most prominent direct impact of the higher tariff was a colossal financial loss to WAPDA that inevitably resulted in a considerable and gradual increment in electricity prices at the consumer end. Since, WAPDA was made to purchase too much and very costly electricity, it pushed the average selling price of electricity from Rs1.4/kWh in 1994 to Rs2.8/kWh and Rs4.02/kWh respectively by 1999 and 2004.[2] Shahid Javed Burki who also served as Pakistan's Finance Minister says: 'The government allowed IPPs to charge tariffs that were well above WAPDA's usual cost for power generated by its own sources. This created huge financial burden for WAPDA and a fiscal liability for the government since WAPDA's losses were met from budget. Even the World Bank, which helped Pakistan formulate the policy that led to the IPPs, failed to anticipate the long-term burden this policy was likely to impose.'[79] Tahir Basharat Cheema, the current Managing Director of PEPCO, wrote in an article:

The power policy of 1994 also did not specify or fix the locations in conjunction/consultation with the utilities and nor any specific technology was considered as appropriate to be inducted by the IPPs. This led to the most inappropriate of the tariffs, which was surely beyond the means of the public. In other words, the exorbitant tariff concluded between HUBCO, these IPPs and the utilities viz. WAPDA and KESC resulted in such an increase in power rates that the same became unaffordable not just for the general public but also for the industry and agriculture. Incidentally, that WAPDA alone had to pay a colossal sum of Rs 810 billion as HUBCO/IPPs payments during the last 10 years for only 202 billion electricity units is the reason which made the utility non-profitable.[80]

### 5.4.3.2 Excess Generation Capacity

Secondly, taking into account the then electricity shortfall (1,000-1,400MW) and the power generation projects that were in the pipeline by the public sector, a 2,000–2,500MW from IPPs would have been sufficient. Contrary to that over 4,300MW of projects were developed through the private sector. While including the 1,638MW KAPCO project that became operational in 1996, the total capacity in the private sector neared 6,000MW.

There was no need for most of this electricity for several years but WAPDA was made to pay for it, at least the capacity payment. This was probably the most preposterous compliance that WAPDA could have been forced into. Consequently, WAPDA's financial health deteriorated substantially because of having to pay gigantic sums of money to IPPs for years and without needing a unit of electricity from them. It created a huge cash flow problem for WAPDA which was obliged to pay the IPPs on a monthly basis. Julia M. Fraser, a senior financial analyst of the World Bank (WB), states: 'The financial difficulties of WAPDA were exacerbated by too many IPPs coming on stream simultaneously at a time when demand did not grow as anticipated. This resulted in excess generating capacity that, in the minds of most Pakistan officials, they neither needed  nor could afford.' The analyst also acknowledges that: 'One could argue that had the implementation of the 1994 Policy been limited to about 2,000MW—as advised by the Bank Group—WAPDA may have been better able to absorb the capacity charges under the long-term power purchase agreements.'[81] Tahir Basharat Cheema, Managing Director PEPCO, is also of the view that: 'Tens of billions of Rupees were doled out to these IPPs for purchasing electricity not needed by WAPDA'.[82]

### 5.4.3.3 Technological Ramifications

There have been a number of other subsequent ramifications of the IPPs programme. It, for example, increased the share of thermal power in the total generation mix of the country. With the installed thermal power largely being dependant either upon imported oil or inadequate and fragile local gas supplies, such a move was in principle against the concept of energy security. It also added to the amount of oil imports thus adding to the national trade deficit.

If thermal power was to be pursued, emphasis should have been upon exploitation of indigenous coal. Though it would have taken a few years, given the fact that some of the IPPs signed under the 1994 policy became operational as late as 2001, going for coal would still have been a viable and more constructive option. The IPPs programme also adversely affected the development of hydropower. As a result of that, between 1996 and 2001, the share of hydropower, an indigenous and most economical source of electricity, decreased from 47 to 29 per cent. With emphasis on thermal power and creation of excessive generation capacity, the prospects of any meaningful exploitation of hydropower were placed on the backburner for a good number of years.

### 5.4.3.4 Allegations of Corruption

Owing to the aforementioned baggage, the IPPs programme attracted a huge amount of criticism from various corners in the country including political parties, energy and economic circles, media and civil society. Factors like political influence and behind the scenes wheeling and dealing are also said to have played a major role in it. The later government that was sworn into office in 1997 put forward allegations of serious misconduct in the IPPs deals. Julia Fraser acknowledges that, 'The basis on which projects were selected and accorded attention was not transparent and subject to political influence which led to perceptions of corruption by successive governments.'[81]

How desperate certain circles were to get the IPPs programme underway irrespective of its far-reaching and wide-ranging implications can be seen from the pressure exerted on the KESC. The KESC, a public body at the time, was asked to sign 5,000–10,000MW of IPPs as disclosed by a former top official of the Corporation. The KESC, having an immediate shortfall of less than 200MW, estimated that over the next 10 years its need may rise by as much as 500–600MW, or at most by as much as 1,000MW. Also, the Corporation simulated its transmission and distribution system and found that the infrastructure could not induce more than 780MW of new power. The KESC, thus, found no reason to purchase such a large amount of extremely expensive electricity from the IPPs when neither there was a demand for it nor the system could absorb it. The KESC Board of Directors thus refused to endorse the IPPs MOUs that were already signed by the Government of Pakistan. Various kinds of temptations and arm twisting on the part of the concerned group of influential political and bureaucratic figures, some of whom are enjoying powerful positions in the present system, failed to persuade the KESC to go for such an unhealthy move. The KESC officials were even given death threats during the course of the campaign.[83] Later, however, KESC agreed to the proposal, as the Government of Pakistan promised that WAPDA would purchase the excess electricity and that KESC would not be responsible for it.

Another issue that substantiates the allegations of corruption is the fact that the IPPs were not invited through competitive bidding. Offering a generous ceiling tariff without concern for vital project details, i.e. plant size, technology and the fuel employed was an unprecedented move even by the standards of the contemporary IPPs being installed in other countries such as Bangladesh, Egypt, Turkey, Indonesia, and Philippines. These countries had invited IPPs through transparent tenders and competitive bidding.

Another factor that has been underpinned by the critics is the high capital cost of IPP projects. The capital cost assumed for IPPs under the 1994 power policy was US$1Million/MW. Just before the IPP deals were signed, WAPDA had installed several thermal power plants at various locations. According to WAPDA officials and various others sources, for like with like technologies, the capital cost WAPDA paid, was 25 to 50 per cent lower than that agreed in case of IPPs.[77] Julia Fraser argues that: 'The assumed project cost under the 1994 Policy was US$1,000 per kW  (US$1Million/MW), but starting about 1997, capital equipment costs for combined cycle plants dropped to about US$450 to US$600 per kW (US$0.45–0.6Million/MW).'[81] Few would believe the credibility of the IPPs price tag of US$1 Million/MW when the projects accomplished by WAPDA and other international bodies, respectively before and after Pakistani IPP deals, incurred a substantially lesser capital cost. Over-invoicing of project costs is, thus, said to have taken place. Reflecting upon this issue, Syed Tanzeem Naqvi, ex-Member WAPDA, states that the Auditor General of WAPDA reported HUBCO to have over-invoiced by 237 per cent.[21] Tahir Basharat Cheema reflects upon the dodgy HUBCO affair as: 'This was a disaster, because the power purchase agreements (PPAs) with HUBCO and the IPPs had been arranged for one under wrongful assessment; the costs were over-invoiced and accepted to be around US$1.2 million per MW, when in reality the world prices of such plants were in the vicinity of US$0.6 million per MW or so.'[80] Such over-capitalized prices were bound to have a long-term bearing upon the tariff and thus upon the financial conditions of WAPDA and the country.

As evidence of misconduct in respect of the IPPs programme, WAPDA officials also highlight the issue of HUBCO amendments 1 and 2 that came into existence in 1994. These amendments were mysteriously introduced a few months after the tariff had been finalized and as a result of which the tariff was raised by around 45 per cent. What truly frustrates senior WAPDA officials is the fact that these amendments were put into practice without the consent of the department. The fact that WAPDA was not even notified about the amendments by the Ministry of Finance makes many believe that the decision-making was undertaken somewhere else rather than at the concerned forums. The financial implications of these amendments on WAPDA are reflected in a statement by a former Managing Director of PPIB: 'When WAPDA refused to accept the amendments and challenged them in court the monthly instalment it would pay to HUBCO dropped from Rs1.6 billion to just Rs0.74 billion.'[21] Interestingly, the HUBCOs affair has been internationally presented in the literature of economic law as a classic example of an arbitration case to illustrate the legal problems arising from corruption. The book *Arbitrating Foreign Investment Disputes* states in one of its chapters: 'Corrupt Practices in the Foreign Investment', 'Amendments to the tariffs were made in order to grant HUBCO higher prices under the Bhutto government in 1993 and 1994. Allegedly part of the tariffs paid by the state-owned power distributor were used as kick-backs to the Bhutto family.'[85] Again, the case of HUBCO has been cited in *Financial Times* as an example in following terms:

Export Credit Agencies (ECAs) have even pressured Southern governments to drop corruption investigations into companies that ECAs have backed. In Pakistan in 1998, for instance, aid donors such as the World Bank and various Western countries including Britain put pressure on the government to abandon investigations into the HUBCO power plant, built in Pakistan in 1997, owned by a consortium that included British energy company National Power, and backed by the ECAs of France, Italy and Japan. Pakistan's

Accountability Bureau had claimed that HUBCO's project costs were marked up by $400 million, and there were suggestions that the companies involved had paid kickbacks to Benazir Bhutto's government of the time.[86]

The World Bank also appears to be convinced over allegations of corruption as it notes:

> Rather than proceed through competitive bidding for private power, Pakistan instead set a bulk tariff ceiling for investors in an effort to accelerate the private power programme and reduce transaction costs in order to quickly address the blackout situation facing the country. This was a very successful tactic in attracting foreign investors, but too many projects were approved and the selection process was not transparent. It is likely that some projects for which Letters of Support were issued, and indeed some of those which ultimately reached financial close, benefited from political support since no clear criteria existed to determine which projects to prioritize when the Government was faced with negotiating project agreements with almost 80 potential IPP developers. In addition, setting prices rather than bidding allowed for inefficiencies (e.g. projects which were too small and not least cost) and corruption opportunities on non-price issues (e.g. securing the necessary fuel supplies and WAPDA's transmission investments).[81]

### 5.4.3.5 Tariff Renegotiation

With the change of government, the new government, in conjunction with WAPDA, in 1997–98, decided to look into the controversial tariff structure in place. The new government brought in criminal allegations of corruption, bribery and kickbacks against IPPs including HUBCO and the majority of them were issued notices of intent to terminate their contracts.[80] Court battles in case of HUBCO—won by WAPDA/Government of Pakistan—also made headlines bringing in rather negative publicity for all stakeholders. In the end, as a result of tedious negotiations between WAPDA/Government of Pakistan and pertinent IPPs the disputes were resolved in a relatively amicable fashion. The World Bank played a vital mediatory role in some of these negotiations especially in the case of HUBCO. All the concerned IPPs agreed to reduce the tariff, the major players reduced the tariff by 6 to 10 per cent as indicated in Table 5.5. WAPDA managed to secure a wee bit of relief in the form of the renegotiated tariff. The tariff negotiations have resulted in a reduction of future fixed liability of WAPDA to the extent of over US$6.0 billion over the life of these projects.[88]

**Table 5.5: Original and renegotiated tariff for IPPs**

| IPP Project | Original Tariff (US cents/kWh) | Revised Tariff (US cents/kWh) |
|---|---|---|
| HUBCO | 6.500 | 5.900 |
| KAPCO | 5.600 | 5.040 |
| Southern Electric Power | 5.577 | 5.199 |
| Habibullah Coastal | 5.577 | 5.171 |
| Saba Power | 5.578 | 5.080 |
| Japan Power | 5.560 | 4.300 |
| Power Generation | 5.570 | 4.000 |
| Altern Energy | 5.577 | 2.894 |
| Liberty Power | 5.578 | 4.702 |
| Davis Energen | 5.578 | 3.298 |
| Northern Electric | 5.912 | 3.946 |
| Rousch Power Limited | 5.578 | 5.188 |
| Fauji Kabirwala | 5.578 | 5.137 |
| Uch Power | 5.578 | 5.127 |
| Kohinoor Energy | 5.551 | 5.199 |

However, the IPPs controversy brought bad publicity for the IPPs, WAPDA, and the Government of Pakistan. The lack of transparency on the part of the pertinent ruling regime and the IPPs was well exposed. It also tarnished the image of the country as there were sovereign guarantees to purchase electricity at rates originally decided in the agreements. It shook the confidence of local investors in general and foreign investors in particular. Consequently, for over a decade Pakistan could not attract any foreign investments in the energy sector[89]—there was no new foreign direct investment in the energy sector from 1997 to 2007.

A number of senior energy officials, on the basis of their personal experiences, are convinced that a certain group of politicians and bureaucrats determined the trajectory of the IPPs programme making what actually could possibly have been a productive affair if handled professionally and dedicatedly ultimately counterproductive.

### REFERENCES

1. Data provided by PEPCO Officials, WAPDA House, Lahore, May 2009.
2. Electricity Marketing Data, 33rd issue, NTDC, 2008.
3. Aftab Sherpao, Presentation by the Minister for Water and Power, Pakistan Development Forum, 18 March 2004.
4. Former Member (Planning) WAPDA, interview, Lahore, May 2009.

5. Former Acting Chairman WAPDA, Email Correspondence, 21 September 2007.
6. Former Member (Finance) WAPDA, Email Correspondence, April 2009.
7. Proceedings of a Power Sector Forum, Lahore, May 2009.
8. 'Power prices in Pak to go up by 31 pc', *The Indian News*, 31 August 2008.
9. 'Protests across Punjab as outage hours multiply', *The Nation*, 5 September 2009.
10. *The News*, 24 October 2008.
11. 'A blue-eyed baboo with three heavy hats', *The News*, 17 February 2008.
12. Mushtaq Ghumman, Khalid Saeed retained as NEPRA Chairman, AAJ TV, 7 January 2009.
13. 'Senate demands removal of illegal NEPRA chief', *The News*, 3 March 2008.
14. *The Wall Street Journal*, 26 February 2009, http://online.wsj.com/article/ SB123561113179577559.html (accessed on 5 December 2009).
15. *Asia Times*, 22 September 2009, http://www.atimes.com/atimes/South_Asia/KI22Df01. html (accessed on 5 December 2009).
16. Former Member (Finance) WAPDA, Email Correspondence, 27 July 2009.
17. Senior Planning Commission Official (who preferred to remain anonymous), Interview, Islamabad, May 2009.
18. *The News*, 24 September 2009.
19. Global Corruption Report 2009, Transparency International.
20. A UK-Based Energy Consultant, Telephonic Interview, March 2009.
21. Syed Tanzeem Hussain Naqvi, ex-Chairman KESC, Interview, Lahore, May 2009.
22. Javed Nizam, ex-Member WAPDA, Telephonic Interview, July 2009.
23. 'Ex-KESC Chief Discusses Crisis', *Dawn*, 25 July 2006.
24. Capital Talk, Geo TV, 30 July 2009.
25. Former Member WAPDA, Interview, Lahore, 8 May 2009.
26. Report on the Indigenization Plan for Achieving Lower Cost of Power Generation, State Engineering Corporation, Ministry of Industries and Investment, February 1997.
27. Letter from the Chairman State Engineering Corporation to the Chairman WAPDA, REF: COM—018 (11), 31 March 1994.
28. Letter from Member Power (WAPDA) to the Chairman State Engineering Corporation, REF: MP/PS/GMD&D.TH, 13 November 1993.
29. Letter from the Chairman WAPDA to the Chairman State Engineering Corporation, REF: C/94/12256, 12 June 1994.
30. Summary for the ECC of the Cabinet, Ministry of Industries and Production, REF: 3-17/92-SEC, 23 April 1995.
31. Letter from the Secretary to the Ministry of Water & Power to the Secretary to the Ministry of Industries & Production, REF: Z(Z04)PPIB/95, 14 May 1995.
32. 'Finally, dreaded NRO list is out and official', *The News*, 20 November 2009.
33. Former Chairman State Engineering Corporation, Interview, Islamabad, May 2009.
34. 'Kalabagh Dam Scrapped: Minister', *Dawn*, 24 May 2009.
35. Former Chairman WAPDA, Interview, Islamabad, May 2009.
36. Former Member (Finance) WAPDA, Email correspondence, 15 May 2009.
37. Former Member (Planning) WAPDA, Interview, Pakistan, May 2009.
38. One of the senior-most serving energy officials (preferred to remain anonymous), Interview, May 2009.
39. Former Chairman Planning Commission, Interview, Islamabad, May 2009.
40. Bolta Pakistan, AAJ TV, 21 July 2009.
41. 'Government, PML-Q engage in blame game over power crisis', Irfan Ghauri, *Daily Times*, 8 August 2009.

42. *Dawn*, 2 December 2009, http://www.transparency.org.pk/news/newsdec09.htm#189 (accessed on 5 December 2009).
43. Daily *Jang*, 29 July 2009.
44. *The News*, 1 and 5 August 2009.
45. *The News*, 16 September 2009.
46. 'Global Trends in Sustainable Energy Investment 2009, Analysis of Trends and Issues in the Financing of Renewable Energy and Energy Efficiency', United Nations Environment Program, 2009.
47. Company Profile, Suzlon.
48. Robert Hathaway and Michael Kugelman (ed.), *Powering Pakistan*, Oxford University Press, 2009, p. 32.
49. 'Corruption in South Asia: Insights and Benchmarks from Citizen Feedback Surveys in Five Countries', Transparency International, December 2002.
50. *The News*, 8 July 2009.
51. 'KESC to use hi-tech system against power theft', *Dawn*, 5 August 2009.
52. Presentation on Power Sector Development in Pakistan, Minister for Water and Power, Pakistan Development Forum, Islamabad, 18 March 2004.
53. Daily *Jang*, 10 August 2009.
54. Cowasjee, *Dawn*, 16 November 2008.
55. *The News*, 13 November 2008.
56. *The News*, 8 July 2009.
57. *The News*, 30 August 2009.
58. *Dawn*, 30 August 2009.
59. Ansar Abbasi, *The News*, 19 July 2009.
60. *Daily Times*, 19 July 2009.
61. BBC, Urdu News, 9 July 2009.
62. Penelope J. Brook, 'Power Sector Challenges', Presentation to the Pakistan Development Forum, World Bank, 18 March 2004.
63. 'Demand for judicial probe into KESC affairs', *Dawn*, 21 July 2009.
64. *Express*, 23 October 2008.
65. Muhammad Badar Alam, 'On Board Off Board, On The Brink', Panos South Asia.
66. Power Sector Situation in Pakistan, AEDB and GTZ, Islamabad, 2005.
67. AEDB website, http://www.aedb.org/(accessed on 7 December 2009).
68. AEDB contacts Denmark lab for data validation, *Daily Times*, 7 January 2008.
69. A Glasgow-based entrepreneur, notes from meeting and e-mail correspondence, August 2009.
70. One of the top energy officials in Pakistan, Interview, Islamabad, May 2009.
71. John Furze, Wind Energy Expert, Interview, Denmark, August 2008.
72. Ministry of New and Renewable Energy Website, India, http://mnes.nic.in/ (accessed on 7 December 2009).
73. The Solar PV Landscape in India, PV Group, April 2009, India.
74. Biogas Sector partnership, Nepal, http://www.bspnepal.org.np/ (accessed on 7 December 2009).
75. Energy Services Delivery, Sri Lanka, http://www.energyservices.1k/gridconnect/esd.htm (accessed on 7 December 2009).
76. Grameen Shakti, Bangladesh, http://www.gshakti.org/ (accessed on 11 December 2009).
77. ENERCON website, http://www.enercon.gov.pk/intro.html, (accessed on 11 December 2009).

78. Policy Framework and Package of Incentives for Private Sector Power Generation Projects in Pakistan, GOP, 1994.
79. Robert Hathaway and Michael Kugelman (eds.), *Powering Pakistan*, Oxford University Press, 2009, p. 25.
80. Tahir Basharat Cheema, 'Pakistan's Quest for Affordable Power', Institution of Electrical & Electronics Engineers Pakistan.
81. Julia M. Fraser, 'Lessons from the Independent Private Power Experience in Pakistan', World Bank, Energy and Mining Sector Board Discussion Paper, Paper No. 14, May 2005.
82. Tahir Basharat Cheema, *Dawn*, 12 February 2007, http://www.dawn.com/2007/02/12/ebr13.htm (accessed on 11 December 2009).
83. Ex-Chairman KESC, Interview, May 2009.
84. Sartaj Aziz, 'The Perils of High Cost Imported Energy', *The Nation*, 28–29 November 1994.
85. H. Raeschke-Kessler, 'Corrupt Practices in Foreign Investment, Arbitrating Foreign Investment Disputes', Edited by Norbert Horn, ISBN 90-411-2293-1, Kluwer Law International, Netherlands, 2004, p. 474.
86. Andrew Taylor and Mark Nicholson, 'HUBCO seeks World Bank Intervention', *Financial Times* special report, 14 October 1998.
87. David Newbery, 'Power sector reform, private investment and regional cooperation', SAARC Business Leaders Conclave, South Asia Regional Integration and Growth, 17–18 November, Delhi, India, 2005.
88. WAPDA website, www.wapda.gov.pk (accessed on 7 December 2009).
89. Robert Hathaway and Michael Kugelman (eds.), *Powering Pakistan*, Oxford University Press, 2009, p. 28.

# 6

# Road to Energy Sustainability

Given the magnitude and dimensions of the challenges faced by Pakistan, the road to a sustainable energy future is not an easy one. The scale of the damage that has already been inflicted is enormous and it is going to take quite a few years before it can be repaired. In this chapter the author proposes a rigorous and coordinated line of action to overcome the self-inflicted energy problems of the country. It illustrates that to reverse the adverse trends continuously marring the energy sector, tough decisions based on vision, pragmatism, and conviction, are required to be made and steadfastly pursued. A set of rational solutions to achieve energy sustainability has been presented in this and the following chapter.

## 6.1. HOUSEKEEPING

The most peculiar dimension of the energy crisis in Pakistan is the reality that the country faces a near bankrupt power sector despite having a significantly healthy resource-base and a considerable number of very competent and dedicated people in the relative departments. Compelling evidence suggests that the root cause of the downfall of the energy sector is the wrong attitude—it is a combination of lack of commitment, poor policies, bad management and pursuance of vested interests on the part of a section of pertinent authorities that has created this quagmire. Although there are some extremely proficient and dedicated people within the ranks of all concerned stakeholders, they are marginalised when it comes to vital policy and decision-making. Sometimes these sincere officials have to pay a huge price for taking a stand in the best interest of the country in different ways such as transfers and forced resignations. In extreme cases they, as personally reported by them, have had to face death threats.[1,2]

To head to a sustainable energy future it is imperative to do the housekeeping first. As Albert Einstein once said, 'we cannot solve our

problems with the same thinking we used when we created them.'
Thus, the attitude needs to be corrected in the first place in order to make
the effort to address the energy problems of the country effective. The
starting point of any remedial programme should be an acknowledgement
of the fact that the energy crisis of the country is a self-inflicted one.
Although such an acknowledgement may not be appreciated by concerned
quarters, what they cannot deny is the fact that something has been wrong
down the line that led to this devastating situation. Since the heavens
don't fall by committing mistakes but by repeating them, it is important
that lessons be learnt from past mistakes on the part of relevant circles.

In a roadmap to ensure a sustainable energy future, before
recommending a set of solutions for overcoming the energy problems, this
chapter talks about the measures that need to be adopted to address the
matrix of chronic attitude problems on the part of pertinent stakeholders
as indicated in Figure 6.1. Burying the real issues under the carpet and
 presenting artificial and detrimental measures as solutions—like on top
of Friday's half working day, having two holidays a week,[3] and reckless
addition of generation capacity at an absurd cost and continuously
increasing energy tariffs rather than addressing losses and inefficiencies—
is not the way ahead. Already, attitude-related malpractices have driven
the energy sector in general and the power sector in particular into deep
trouble. A complete disaster is inevitable unless the mindset is corrected.
As a matter of fact, if the concerned circles stop prioritising their personal
gains against their professional commitments and vital national interests,
most of the country's energy problems can be automatically resolved.

### 6.1.1 AUTHORITY WITH ACCOUNTABILITY

Every citizen in Pakistan is wary of a certain class of influential people
who come from diverse backgrounds and are powerful enough to have
made the whole country hostage to their endless treachery and greed.
They, with a substantial representation from the ruling elite, are amazingly
clever at securing undeserved benefits and in doing so they do not mind
bulldozing anything that comes their way be it an individual's fundamental
rights or vital national interests. Hardly any day goes by when the national
media does not report the immoral and unjust activities of this network.
Almost all sectors and government departments have been severely dented
by their corruption, much of which remains unearthed due to their
influence. The recent sugar and flour scandals, for example, provide a wee
reflection of the degree of their real moral bankruptcy. Riding on their

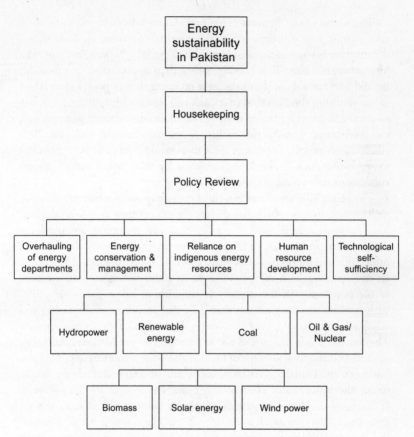

Figure 6.1: Route to energy sustainability in Pakistan

credentials such as position/influence in the system; partnership with mafias of both illegal and legal outfits; and unjustly earned wealth, they can easily get away with anything. The authorities who are supposed to bring such elements to justice are either too weak to tackle them or are in their pay.

Having invented an extravagant VIP culture to suit their desires, they have made tax-paying and honest Pakistanis feel like second-rate citizens. Pakistan—that the founder of Pakistan Quaid-i-Azam Mohammad Ali Jinnah wanted to be one of the most respectable and successful countries in the world—has been continuously and mercilessly undermined by the ruling elite so much so that it is now regarded amongst the most undisciplined, illiterate and poor countries of the world.

The writer Owen Bennett-Jones provides an interesting account of an educationist who was deputed by the government to set up schools in a deprived area. The educationist approached the local Nawab (lord) to brief him about his task. The Nawab, rather than appreciating his mission, invited him for a duck shoot the next morning. It was peak winter when in the morning the Nawab shot a duck and signalled his flock of servants to collect it, at which more than ten of them immediately jumped into the cold water. The Nawab turned to the educationist and said: 'If I educated my people, not one of these men would have gone into the water to fetch the duck.'[4] The logic furnished by the Nawab indeed speaks volumes of the typical mindset of the ruling elite.

The ruling elite are the architects of the raging socio-economic injustice in Pakistani society which has driven the masses into a state of despair. The national wealth and resources that are meant to be used for development and welfare of the people are snatched away by the elite and other influential groups leaving the capable and hardworking masses in an endless struggle to meet both ends. At a time when over 40 per cent of the population in the country is languishing below the poverty line with families surviving on less than $2 a day, members of the ruling and economic elite have got away with gigantic sums of the public money. The details of this disgraceful act as presented in the National Assembly disclose that the total amount of loans written-off to influential politicians, businessmen, feudals, civil bureaucrats and military officials by banks under the influence of successive regimes stands over Rs120 billion.[5,6] While some estimates suggest that the total amount of the loans waived since the 1980s is as much as Rs250 billion.[7] Considering the devaluation the Pakistani Rupee has experienced over this period, the public money robbed in the form of written-off loans could be well over $5 billion. Similarly, Transparency International refers to a World Bank report that tax-theft in Pakistan during the financial years 2007 and 2008, amounted to around Rs760 billion.[8]

Often the same pages of national newspapers disclosing details of corruption worth billions of rupees repeat stories of parents who committed suicide because they could not feed their young children for several days and of well-educated professionals who had to support their families but were jobless for years. On 12 August 2009, for example, two days before the 62nd Independence-Day of the country, when the concerned authorities were deliberating how to arrange an amnesty for a section of the ruling elite over charges of wide-ranging crimes and gigantic financial corruption, Shahid, a 30-year-old jobless Pakistani, committed suicide at the most important national monument, '*Minar-e-Pakistan*'—he took his life while holding the flag of Pakistan high in his hands and shouting 'Long live Pakistan...death to unemployment...I am killing myself because I have not been able to find any job for years.'[9]

With their strong representation in political parties and bureaucratic and feudal circles, the rich and influential can even get legal indemnity for all their transgressions. Sources suggest that the members of this powerful network from within the ranks of the policy and decision-making circles have also badly betrayed the energy sector, thanks to the prevailing trend of authority without accountability. Apart from one or two exceptions, in every energy department there are examples of people abusing their authority in numerous ways, i.e. misconduct, corruption and inefficiency. They inflicted huge damage, in some cases irreparable, to the energy sector and yet got away with a clean sheet.

Some of the scandals in terms of their magnitude and implications are literally mind-blowing. While the wrongdoings happen at all levels in the chain of command, the higher the status one holds in the hierarchy the greater the level of immunity he/she enjoys. However, interestingly, it is not only the officials within the energy departments who are involved in misconduct but fingers are also pointed at some of the highest offices in the country. The allegations of corruption, bribery and kickbacks in the IPPs affair of the 1990s have made headlines for years. Here, the allegations of misconducts as later brought forward by the Nawaz Sharif regime as well as independent sources rested with Asif Ali Zardari—the current president of the country who also was a federal minister in his late wife Benazir Bhutto's cabinet at the time the IPPs programme was finalised—and a group of bureaucrats led by Salman Farooqi who is currently principal secretary to the president. A large number of senior energy officials believe that the financial crisis WAPDA and other departments are facing, a vital aspect of the current crisis, is a consequence of those detrimental deals.[1,10,11]

More recently, the most painful dimension of the current crisis, the gap between electricity demand and supply, could have been easily avoided had the growth in demand over the last few years been reacted to in a timely fashion, as discussed in detail in Chapter 4. The way relevant authorities gave a blind eye to the gathering storm especially over the last few years is appalling. What a downfall it has been that Pakistan, having enough of an electricity surplus in the year 2001 to negotiate its export to India, was facing a deficit of over 5,000MW by 2007. Not reacting to the rapidly growing demand and thus pushing the country into energy bankruptcy with an overall deficit of over 40 per cent is either a matter of sheer incompetence or vested interests on the part of pertinent policy and decision-makers. Bearing in mind the consequences of the situation for the country, many believe that the possibility of it being a deliberate attempt to destabilize the country cannot be ruled out.[10]

There is almost a unanimous understanding in the country that it is the former regime that has cultivated the current crisis. The ultimate responsibility is being put on the ex-President Pervez Musharraf and the ex-Prime Minister Shaukat Aziz who throughout their tenures kept preaching to the nation of their respective credentials of 'having a control over everything' and 'taking the trickle-down impacts of the brilliant economic policies to the grass roots level'. The devastating energy crisis they eventually created, however, tells of their incompetence and bad management more than anything. WAPDA officials closely related to the policy and decision-making processes over the last few years reveal some shocking experiences they have had with the top office bearers in the country. Some are even not shy of saying that Shaukat Aziz deliberately jeopardized a number of crucial energy projects pushing the country into deep crisis.[10,11] He, after having 'served' the country with his self-declared wonderful economic policies, has abandoned Pakistan and enjoys a lavish lifestyle abroad. For their very services of fostering the energy crisis, during the parliamentary debates on the issue, Pervez Musharraf and Shaukat Aziz have been declared to have committed 'criminal negligence' by having overlooked the gathering storm.[12]

However, WAPDA finds itself the target of public anger as those responsible have got away. In July 2009, concerned Pakistanis were dismayed to see Shaukat Aziz on a TV channel watching the Ashes Cricket Match while over 18 hours of daily load-shedding was leading to countrywide violence in Pakistan of various forms such as agitated protests, attacks on utility offices and infrastructure and beating of their staff, blockade of roads and train tracks, and attacks on public transport. In the preceding months, hundreds of thousands of people had lost jobs, majority of the industry had closed, and all sectors including agriculture, education and health were in a state of turmoil.[13] Reflecting upon the irresponsible attitude of the ruling elite the ex-Chairman WAPDA Shamsul Mulk, who has also served as caretaker Chief Minister of NWFP, says: 'By and large politicians don't have a sense of responsibility and don't feel accountable for anything. They are not afraid of being the victim of failure'. Also reflecting upon energy departments he says: 'there is a lack of institutional responsibility.'[14]

There is also a growing degree of understanding within Pakistan that the tenure of every regime has been marked by scandals and allegations of corruption. Once again the energy sector is under the spotlight due to allegations of serious corruption. Sincere energy officials are dismayed as they believe that the elements that previously organized gigantic corruption in the IPPs programme and managed to get away despite having inflicted huge damage to the power sector and the country are back in business. Hands have been joined again to give it another go, this time with a lot more freedom.[10,15,16,17,18,19] In November 2009, a Transparency International (TI) report suggested corruption scams of billions of rupees in various projects including the rental power programme. In response to that, the federal finance minister Shaukat Tareen acknowledged that the money being made by corruption is largely going into the pockets of a few 'influential' people.[20,21,22,23]

The energy crisis is the consequence of vested interests and professional and administrative negligence, at the hands of certain individuals. The public, the energy departments and the country have all been made to pay huge price for the unwarranted acts of policy and decision-makers. To head to a sustainable energy future it is imperative to have a stringent check and balance system in place. It is essential to establish the deterrent of meaningful accountability—irrespective of how influential one is, everyone must be answerable for their actions in order to minimize possibilities of misconduct. The higher the office the greater must be the degree of accountability. A culture of honesty, loyalty, and discipline needs to be firmly established. As a starting point, the culprits behind the ongoing electricity crisis should be brought to immediate justice. All those who have contributed to the raging load-shedding, either due to their vested interests or incompetence and negligence, should be made an example of, be it senior bureaucrats and politicians or ex-Prime Minister Shaukat Aziz and ex-President Pervez Musharraf, naturally and logically, the bucket has to stop at the very top! Also, irrespective of their status and influence, all the culprits behind the blatant as well as white-collar corruption in energy projects should be dealt with heavy handedly. A similar treatment is necessary for all those who have havocked the energy sector in the previous decades. If the allegations of corruption and wrongdoings over the currently pursued projects, in particular rental power programme, hold water, the perpetrators must also be brought to justice be it ministers and secretaries or higher bosses. The corrupt elements that have cost the country tens of billions of dollars and have made life extremely difficult for the masses deserve no mercy.

A stringnet accountability of the perpetrators behind the energy crisis may help lessen the sufferings of hundreds of thousands of people who have lost their source of income due to the crisis and of many more who are also in pain due to their disfigured daily routines. Also, not only would it help seek pragmatic solutions to the energy challenges but also help restore the trust of important stakeholders including public, investors and industrialists in this sector.

## 6.1.2 Rule of Merit

The trend of offering important positions to favourites and ignoring merit, moral values and institutional regulations is quite common within the energy sector. The practice of nepotism, which is also often maintained while making promotions, has disastrous implications in many respects. Anyone who is a product of favouritism rather than merit can never be fair and robust in professional practices. Here a quote of an ex-Chairman Pakistan Atomic Energy Commission (PAEC), which, though passed in a different perspective, is quite relevant. While he was the head of the PAEC, in his welcome speech to the new batches of engineers and scientists, he always said: 'Your aim should be to ultimately reach where I stand.'[24] Reflecting upon this statement, what is apparent is that depriving committed and capable career officers—who give decades of their lives to the departments—from reaching the top positions they deserve is utterly destructive for departmental growth.

A number of irrational appointments in immensely important offices, at a time when the country faces the toughest energy crisis of its history, have been discussed in Section 5.1.3. There are also examples of people with a dubious track record having been appointed to head energy departments. Here it is vital to remember that the energy sector has always had a large number of dedicated and capable people who worked for the progress of their respective departments tirelessly for decades. The author has personally come across quite a few brilliant people who exhibit an extremely impressive track record yet are victims of nepotism. Considering the crisis the country is facing, capable and deserving officials must be appointed to run the energy offices.

Merit also needs to be implemented during policy and decision-making. Violation of merit at these critical stages in terms of procedural irregularities is very common. Often the fate of vital projects is decided without having the consent of pertinent departments/authorities and a meaningful discussion in parliament. In almost all of the major energy projects recently dealt with such as the shelving of the Kalabagh Dam, approval of rental power projects and allocation of the Kohala hydropower project the spirit of merit has not been maintained.[25,26]

### 6.1.3 ERADICATION OF FINANCIAL AND ADMINISTRATIVE IRREGULARITIES

The performance of the energy sector is dented by in-house irregularities as much as by anything. The irregularities are widespread and are of various types such as financial corruption and operational inefficiencies. The financial corruption in WAPDA and KESC, for instance, is deeply embedded in the system from the highest to the lowest levels. Corruption often plays a decisive role in the development of projects at the highest possible policy and decision-making levels in the form of kickbacks. Bearing in mind the business potential of energy projects, kickbacks in the multi-million dollar range over a single project, as reported by various sources, do not appear implausible.[10,27] What however is truly agonizing is that some corrupt elements don't even bother to make deals as a result of which the department and country is going to face tens of times more loss compared to what is unofficially going into their personal pockets. Sadly such cases are not rare, and more so, have even been patronized by the highest possible office bearers in the country.

Another major weakness of the electricity departments is their huge Transmission and Distribution (T&D) losses, as discussed in detail in Chapter 5. Majority of these losses—in the form of electricity thefts—are controllable and are either facilitated by their own staff or are allowed to take place for various reasons. A two-pronged approach needs to be adapted to address the issue. Firstly, there has to be a tighter control on electricity thefts and leaks. In order to truly address the T&D losses, system loopholes, such as corruption, blind-eye-attitude towards 'influential' customers and the '*kunda*' (hook) culture need to be cracked down on. Ironically when corrupt elements get electricity through theft, they use it mercilessly. For instance, if they were to run an air-conditioner for 4-5 hours through legal connection, now they run it for much longer.

The power sector cannot recover from the crisis it faces unless these loopholes are sorted out. It is simply a matter of implementation of the writ of the government. For this purpose the first and far most important point is to ensure solid commitment on the part of the concerned departments. The *kunda* culture can also be rationalized by allowing legal connections to tens of thousands of consumers living in slums free of cost. Procedures like intelligent metering, task forces, vigilance teams and random checks can be incorporated in an effective T&D losses-control programme. Secondly, the ageing transmission and distribution infrastructure needs to be refurbished in order to curtail technical losses. The existing infrastructure is insufficient and often leads to problems due to overloading. Syed Tanzeem Naqvi, for example, presents a very dismal picture of KESC. According to him, during 2006–07, of 54 132kV grid stations, 44 were overloaded. In terms of 11kV lines, of the total 2,000 km, 1,800 km were overloaded. Similarly, of 15,000 distribution transformers, 12,000 were overloaded. The situation is alike in many of the WAPDA controlled areas.[1] The solution to these issues lies in overhauling and capacity building of the infrastructure. There is a desperate need for new grid stations and extension in transmission and distribution lines.

The laidback attitude is also a chronic problem. Officials are not held responsible when they fail to meet the objectives of their positions/departments resulting in wastage of public resources, time and money. Rather overcoming these irregularities the officials prefer to bury the things under carpets and remain upbeat about promises that they would never deliver. The author had an interesting experience in the second quarter of 2009 at a meeting with a key official in the Alternate Energy Development Board. The official expressed great distress over the dormant state of affairs in the Board particularly reflecting upon lack of financial and technical resources, lack of support from higher authorities and poor coordination with other stakeholders in the energy sector. Towards the end of the meeting, he said: 'It is enough; I want to leave the job as things are incorrigible.'[28] Less than a week later, the author was attending an energy forum where the Federal Minister for Industries and Production Mian Manzoor Ahmed Watto was also present. In response to the author's wake-up call for energy departments including AEDB to overcome their chronic irregularities, quite amazingly, the federal minister in his speech expressed great pride in AEDB's achievements and made huge promises saying 'our experts and scientists are working hard days and nights to meet the expectations of the nation.'[29] It was all but political rhetoric—an exhibition of the typical mindset of the ruling elite. The frustration of some devoted people can be gauged from a statement that a couple of years ago one of the senior-most officials of ENERCON, while discussing the below par performance of his department over the years, gave to the author 'To be honest our department does not deserve to exist.'[30]

## 6.1.4 END TO POLITICAL INTERFERENCE

Political interference has also significantly contributed to the downfall of the energy sector. Undue pressures are exerted on energy departments by political and other powerful quarters to reap wide-ranging unreasonable favours that ultimately cause a detrimental impact on the performance of the department. Another harmful practice is that of political appointments—over the years, thousands of jobs have been given by different regimes to the political workers of their parties in various energy departments. The criteria in doing so has not been qualifications or skills but political contacts and affiliations. Quite often corruption plays the decisive role in these appointments—people have to offer bribery to get these jobs. The responsible authorities don't care about the implications of these employments on the concerned departments in terms of an incapable and potentially corrupt workforce and the associated financial burdens. An interesting demonstration of political appointments was seen in Pakistan Railways, an organisation on the verge of financial bankruptcy, in media headlines in September 2009. In this case the appointments were made at the personal orders of the pertinent minister who had forwarded a list of people that he wanted to be appointed irrespective of merit. A senior official who refused to accept these illegal orders and insisted upon appointments on merit was removed from her position. When asked about the issue in a live TV programme, the Federal Minister for Railways Ghulam Ahmed Bilor, without any remorse, replied: 'After all we have to accommodate the people from our constituencies.'[31] Even at the height of the energy crisis, the malpractice of political appointments in pertinent departments continues. Reports emerged in the national media in January/February 2010 that the Minister for Water and Power Raja Pervez Ashraf has pressurized WAPDA to appoint several hundred people in clear violation of merit and procedures. The appointees in Gujranwala Electric Power Company (GEPCO) and Lahore Electric Supply Company (LESCO), for example, also include people from his election constituency.

With the change of regimes—a frequent phenomenon over the last two decades—shuffling of bureaucracy and appointment of favourite officials at key positions is also a norm. It almost inevitably results in the introduction of new sets of policies and trends. The disruption of policies tend to sabotage vital energy projects. Sources also mention cases where political forces have interfered with the mandate and policies of energy departments for their vested interests thus inflicting substantial damage to the energy sector. A number of senior energy officials tell of their personal experiences of being put to immense political pressure to either go for unhealthy projects or to drop profitable ones. An ex-Deputy Chairman Planning Commission reflects on the issue in the following terms: 'The system is being inflicted with ever more political interference in the form of appointments on personal likes and dislikes and reshuffling of bureaucracy with every change in government.'[32]

### 6.1.5 Enhanced Coordination

The progress of the energy sector in Pakistan has also been undermined by the lack of coordination both at the policy and decision-making, and implementation levels. The power sector is mainly the responsibility of the Ministry of Water and Power while that of oil and gas is looked after by the Ministry of Petroleum and Natural Resources. Each of the two ministries takes care of its respective tasks through several departments it houses. The lack of coordination is considerably more visible in the case of the power sector. The situation with the Ministry of Water and Power has become a little more complicated as in recent years it has restructured WAPDA creating a number of new departments out of it. Any tangible benefits the development has brought to the power sector in general and WAPDA and its offshoots in particular are yet to be established. What is, however, quite obvious is that it has inevitably resulted in more hiccups and lower levels of overall productivity.

In recent decades on numerous occasions there have been disagreements over priorities between WAPDA and its superior ministerial offices. Sources from within the power sector tell of several projects and policies that WAPDA had to agree to despite considering them counterproductive. Whilst in other instances the Authority wanted to pursue certain projects but was not permitted to do so. Similarly, a lack of support from WAPDA and KESC to their nominal superior offices over various issues has also been reported.[33] KESC has recently been privatised; however, the situation was not different when it was in the public sector domain. Occurrences of a corresponding nature happen with other energy departments as well. An example of ineffective coordination can be seen in the form of conflicting signals that ministers and energy departments have been giving over the issue of load-shedding. Throughout the latter half of 2008 and the first half of 2009, the Minister for Water and Power Raja Pervez Ashraf kept claiming to sort out the problem of load-shedding by December 2009. His claim was, however, time and again rejected by his fellow ministers and PEPCO officials.[34,35,36,37,38] Such poor coordination between these stakeholders only adds to the confusion and suffering of the masses. It also causes implications for industrial and economic activities.

Although the administrative and operational responsibilities of the larger energy sector mainly lie with two ministries—Water and Power, and Petroleum and Natural Resources—other stakeholders also play a role in running the energy business in the country. The enactment of the national energy policy is primarily undertaken by the following bodies.

- Planning Commission
- Ministry of Finance
- Ministry of Water and Power
- Ministry of Petroleum and Natural Resources
- Ministry of Science and Technology
- Ministry of Environment
- Pakistan Atomic Energy Commission

The involvement of so many players leads to inefficiency and confusion. Furthermore, the existence of so many ministries is unnecessary. After independence, during the first three decades the number of ministries in every government apart from one exception always remained under 20. It was during 1957–58 when the federal cabinet housed over 20 ministers and only for a few months. Some of them actually held offices for even less than a month. Even during the 1960s—which is said to be the best part of country's history in terms of economic and industrial development—the number of ministers remained between 11 and 17. The 1990s saw cabinets larger than ever before as governments attempted to accommodate more allies—the trend of offering ministerial offices as incentives in political deals saw the cabinet size growing to as much as 49 during the decade. Cabinets grew either due to the creation of more ministries (in some cases two to three ministries were created out of one) or by the appointment of two ministers for the same portfolio. The trend became so widespread that the Shaukat Aziz government benefited from the services of 58 ministers and 20 special advisers thus taking the tally to 78.[39] Interestingly, the regime equipped with such a massive cabinet greatly contributed towards the development of the current energy crisis.

The author has discussed the issue with a number of officials from diverse backgrounds including the energy sector, politics, academia, industry and media. There was a unanimous understanding that over the years the policy and decision-making process in the energy sector has suffered at the hands of the increased bureaucratic layers. In theory each of the departments and ministries dealing with the energy sector carves its plans in response to the objectives and strategies established by the Planning Commission. In practice, however, little coordination exists. In many cases the lack of coordinated and consistent efforts on the part of pertinent stakeholders has created problems that inflicted colossal damage not only to the whole energy sector but also to vital national interests. The solution to the below par performance and inefficiencies within the energy sector does not lie in the creation of more offices but in inculcating a culture of dedication and professionalism. It can be noted that the energy sector in Pakistan did better when dealt with by a lesser number of ministries and departments. In a business as usual scenario—if ministries and/or subsequent departments of similar functions can't be merged—it would be advisable to at least have a fully integrated and powerful inter-ministerial body with the mandate to decide on energy development strategies, ideally manned by professionals.

## 6.2. POLICY REVIEW AND POLICY ENDURANCE

A chronic problems in Pakistan's official circles is the dearth of vision and sense of responsibility. The energy history of the country reveals that apart from a couple of exceptions, no regime has done justice to this important sector. The traditional practice has been to rely upon makeshift arrangements rather than making long-term and goal-oriented policies. Where far-sighted policies have been made due sincerity and resolve to ensure their implementation has not been demonstrated. The gigantic energy challenges the country is facing cannot be addressed by the traditional quick-fix approach. A durable and sustainable solution requires a vibrant and coherent energy policy followed by stringent implementation. Some of the key dimensions of the policy should be as follows.

• Apart from comprehending the true nature and intensity of the challenges, the policy should also meticulously explore the range of opportunities available to address them.

- In an era of globalization and free market economies, the national energy policy should also take regional and global trends into consideration.
- Energy security must be at the heart of the policy. To bring that about, it should focus on increasing the share of indigenous resources in the supply mix as far as possible. Efforts should also be made to in developing a culture of energy conservation and management. To operate robustly, relevant departments and bodies need to be overhauled. Emphasis should be placed on the development of a strong pool of human resource and local technological base.
- Energy is vital for the strategic and economic interests of a country, as discussed in detail in Chapter 2. Nations across the world are keen to safeguard their energy interests and to ensure the supply of required amount of energy from the resources existing within and outside their geographic borders. Energy is, therefore, at the heart of the foreign policy of a great number of countries in the world. Pakistan, on the other hand, has yet to realise the importance of the partnership between the foreign office and energy departments. In the backdrop of current challenges such as regional geo-political volatility, pressures on Pakistan to withdraw from the gas pipeline project with Iran, and the increasingly intimidating behaviour of India towards Pakistan's water resources, unreserved support from the foreign office becomes extremely vital in safeguarding national energy interests. The recent US–India nuclear deal also demands a united stance on the part of Pakistani foreign- and energy-policy-makers. To ensure a proactive partnership between them, it would be advisable to have a permanent energy desk in the foreign office. It could also be helpful to have special energy attachés deputed in countries Pakistan has strategic energy interests with.
- Also encompassing short- and medium-term goals, an important niche of the policy should lie in its long-term (at least for twenty-five years) approach. It can only be accomplished by having a certain degree of rigidity as well as flexibility in the policy. The aforementioned underlying aspects to ensure energy security should not be compromised on. Targets, for example, could be set to maintain a certain proportion of energy to come from indigenous resources in the overall supply mix. Similarly, in terms of project development, targets could be set to ensure a certain proportion of technical expertise and equipment to come from local sources. Targets could also be set to save energy

through energy conservation practices. Prioritization of strategies and projects towards meeting the set targets can be flexible.

- There have been numerous energy policies in the country, especially over the last two decades. None, however could be sustained. Rapid changes in government owing to political instability saw the power policies of previous regimes binned frequently. There must be across the board agreement on issues of vital national interest. Policies should be framed with all concerned stakeholders on board, most importantly the mainstream political forces.

- Once agreed upon, such policies should be rendered constitutional indemnity so that future governments do not jeopardize them due to naïve political interests as has been the case in past when many projects of national importance have been abandoned for that very reason. Such an unprecedented move appears logical when one sees the nature of investment required to secure the energy future of the country. According to the Medium Term Development Framework (2005–10) of the Government of Pakistan the electricity generation capacity demand will increase by a factor of 8, from 19,540MW in 2005 to 163,000MW by 2030. The projection, assuming an average economic growth of 7 to 8 per cent per year, thus indicates an additional requirement of 143,460MW over this period.[40] Bearing in mind the expected impediment in global economical growth especially due to the 2008 credit crunch, such a high target for economic growth may not be easily achievable. In a conservative scenario, assuming economic growth at half that of the above assumed rate, an additional 72,000MW of installed capacity would be required. Obviously, this electricity would have to come from a diverse range of resources including hydropower, thermal power, nuclear power, and renewable energy. These technologies considerably vary in their economics. However, assuming a benchmark price bracket of $1–1.5 Million/MW, the country would need an investment of $72–108 billion within the next 21 years.

## 6.3. Reliance on Indigenous Energy Resources

Reliance on indigenous energy resources must be at the heart of the designed energy policy. The steadily rising demand for fossil fuels in combination with their low reserves is bound to usher in a new energy era in the world. Given the volatility in oil prices and fierce competition for access to its deposits, global geo-politics is set to be ever more driven by the energy factor. The likelihood of all-out wars over energy resources cannot be ruled out. In such a scenario, it is critical for a country like Pakistan to rely on indigenous resources as far as possible. Pakistan is a country richly blessed with coal, hydropower, and renewable energy resources. These resources in conjunction with relatively mediocre oil and gas reserves have a very healthy potential to meet the country's present as well as future demands satisfactorily as discussed in detail in Chapter 7.

Timely attention needs to be paid to the exploitation of the aforementioned internal resources. The steep rise in energy prices—one of the major challenges the country is facing at the moment—has largely to do with the ever mounting share of imports in the supply mix. A strategy of getting most of the national energy needs supported by indigenous resources would not only ensure cheap energy, but also benefit socio-economic conditions both at the macro- and micro-level. Through provision of energy security, it would also substantiate national sovereignty.

## 6.4. Human Resource Development

Unrefined human resource is one of the weakest links in the energy equation of the country. Pakistanis in general are extremely capable when it comes to delivering a task. Despite the lack of resources, facilities and opportunities, they have made world class achievements in numerous areas including education, science and technology, literature, and sports. Examples of such achievement, however, are often rare exceptions, as owing to lack of education, direction and encouragement, most of the national manpower base remains weak thus unable to make any noteworthy contribution towards national development. The example of Japan is worth quoting here. The country does not have any noteworthy natural resources but with its refined human resource has been one of the leading economic and industrial superpowers of the world for several decades. Pakistan is in a much better position compared to Japan in terms of available natural resources but does not have refined human resource. Appropriate opportunities, resources and appreciation to the Pakistani people can do wonders for the country.

In recent decades the global energy sphere has immensely expanded both in terms of size and dimensions. Contrary to that the national human resource has not been duly transformed on either of the two fronts. There is a great dearth of expertise in many fields within the wider area of energy. For example, apart from nuclear power, there is no research and development base whatsoever. Likewise, there is a huge vacuum of expertise pertinent to the emerging technologies and modern trends i.e. renewable energy systems, energy conservation and management, energy marketing and trading, and energy policy. Thus, the energy sector largely remains dependent upon foreign expertise on almost all fronts such as the development of project proposals and feasibility studies, design and engineering, manufacturing and commissioning.

There are, however, some pockets of extremely brilliant academic and industrial working groups, furnished with diligent and visionary professionals, operating both in the public and private sector, though hardly any of them deal with energy. These few need to be cloned in big numbers. Government must commit the necessary technical and financial resources to help the existing platforms grow besides setting up new ones to deal with the demands of the energy sector. Within the defined mandate, a certain degree of freedom and autonomy of policy and decision-making would also have to be ensured to make them work.

To ensure a sustainable energy future, a strong human resource base is imperative. Universities have a great role to play producing competent and qualified engineers and professionals with expertise in a diverse range of energy areas. They should produce experts in the areas of both conventional (hydropower, oil, gas, coal, and nuclear) and non-conventional (solar, wind, biomass and wave) energy systems, energy trading, energy conservation and management, energy security and risk assessment. These experts should be aware of the crucial role of energy in economic, social, and environmental development. They should be aware of the global geo-politics of energy and of the challenges facing national as well as global energy scenarios and the opportunities so as to be able to deliver visionary policies and solutions to bail the country out of the energy crisis. A multilateral effort on the part of government, academia and industry would be essential to produce a pool of competent and visionary experts who could provide optimum solutions to the energy challenges facing the country.

The problem of brain drain in Pakistan has intensified over the last couple of decades, as a result of which extremely precious and capable human resource is being lost. The government needs to reverse this trend or at least put a stop to it. Arrangements must be made to protect a critical mass in the country sufficient enough to undertake the whole range of energy developmental projects. As a matter of fact there are many

Pakistanis working abroad who want to come back and serve their country. They are even happy to work at a much lower financial package compared to what they are getting abroad. All they want, however, is an assurance that they would be allowed to deliver—they are wary of the typical bureaucratic hurdles and departmental politics that do not allow proactive and dedicated professionals to make a contribution. These are committed people who want to return to their country and want a reasonable level of commitment on the part of institutions in Pakistan.

## 6.5. TECHNOLOGICAL SELF-SUFFICIENCY

Reliance on imports of energy systems is another costly affair that requires immediate attention. Presently, in the absence of a local relevant technological base, all types of energy systems i.e. thermal power plants, nuclear power plants or hydropower facilities, have to be largely imported. In the case of renewable energy technologies the state of affairs is further unsatisfactory. This implies wide-ranging financial implications such as huge capital and life cycle cost of projects and increased trade deficit. The price of missing out at the local technological base can be seen again in the wake of the prevalent electricity crisis. Statistics reveal that during July 2008–April 2009, Pakistan spent $1.43 billion on the import of electricity related machinery. The bill, mostly counting for generators and  Uninterrupted Power Supply (UPS) systems, recorded a staggering 67 per cent increment compared to the same period over 2007–08.[41]

Amid fast changing and expanding international business environment, in order to achieve energy sustainability, it is crucial to become technologically self sufficient. Emphasis should be placed upon options like technology transfer and reverse engineering. Concerned energy circles believe that policy and decision-makers have not been eager to promote technological developments within the country or to pursue technology transfer because that would diminish prospects of future kickbacks that  continuous reliance on imports generate. Evidence of this unpatriotic approach is the sabotage of the power plants indigenization plan developed by the State Engineering Corporation in the 1990s as discussed in detail in Section 5.1.4.1.

 As with the phenomenal developments that Pakistani engineers, scientists and professionals have accomplished in the areas of nuclear power and military defence, it would have been easily possible to attain a high lavel of technological self sufficiency in the area of energy had the policy and decision-makers given them the mandate, autonomy, and resources. This unhealthy attitude needs to be addressed. Without attempting to reinvent the wheel, however, where essential, a research and development base also needs to be established in order to strike value engineered solutions.

In the wake of continuous devaluation of the Pakistani Rupee, and volatility in material prices and international freight charges, imports are becoming ever more unrealstic. The sooner the country pursues technological self-sufficiency the quicker it would head for a sustainable energy future.

## 6.6. REVAMPING OF ENERGY DEPARTMENTS

The by and large mediocre role of relevant and constituent departments has been part of the greater energy problem of the country. They have regularly struggled to respond to the challenges facing the country as is also evident from the current state of affairs. Parallel to the governmental/ political interventions, their own institutional weaknesses are to be blamed for the dismal condition of the energy departments. Their refurbishment is of the utmost importance in any attempt to improve the national energy scenario.

As a starting point, the departments have to be freed from political pressures—they have to be given a reasonable level of policy and decision-making autonomy which is not the case at present. The limitations of financial and technical resources which have traditionally constrained their progress also need to be addressed. Lack of funds has often delayed not only orchestration of crucial new projects but also timely overhauling and up-gradation of the existing ones. Similarly, the ageing infrastructure, particularly in terms of an inefficient transmission and distribution system mainly roots from lack of funds.

The performance of the energy departments have been greatly undermined by customary lack of commitment and poor management. The consequent wide-ranging administrative inefficiencies and financial irregularities must be eradicated to bring about a positive change in the national energy equation. Another major shortcoming is the scarcity of technical expertise—neither do they have a satisfactory technological base nor a rich enough pool of skilled human resource to tackle the current as well as future challenges.

The situation thus demands a holistic overhauling of the energy departments. Some of the key steps that could be taken in this regard are as follows.

- Energy departments must be purified from corrupt elements irrespective of their positions and status. In a top down approach, scrutiny should begin with departmental heads and end at the clerical and field staff. Housekeeping measures, authority with accountability, rule of merit, eradication of financial and administrative irregularities, and an end to political interference must be strictly followed.
- Arrangements have to be made to ensure across the board transparency. Particular attention needs to be paid to areas like project bidding and development, and tariff determination.
- An appropriate level of automation should be introduced in order to minimize the involvement of the human factor in issues prone to corruption.
- Carefully calculated structural changes in departments, to seek improved productivity, can be pursued. Priority in doing so should be to lessen bureaucratic layers rather than the other way round.
- In view of their technical nature, energy departments must be run by engineers and professionals rather than bureaucrats and non-technical people. Dealing with areas like project planning and development, energy management and tariff determination should be the job of hard core professionals.
- Robust staff development programmes should be in place.
- Partnerships with external actors such as academia and industry should be established to promote the technological and human-resource base.
- Inter-departmental coordination should be improved.
- Fresh blood, as and where required, should also be injected in order to assist seasoned staff with new ideas and enthusiasm.
- Bearing in mind the huge cost-cutting and losses-control opportunities, performance based incentives should be introduced.

## 6.7. PUBLIC EDUCATION

Another area that needs attention is public education on the subject of energy. In Pakistan, the common man's understanding of energy is very weak. As an important stakeholder—the consumer—he has a very important role to play in the success of the national energy strategies. Some of the major contributing factors in his below par awareness on crucial issues are as followings.

- Poor literacy rate
- Lack of energy related courses at university and college levels
- Lack of government/departmental initiatives for public awareness

The energy consumption patterns in Pakistan are very inefficient. There is simply not enough respect offered to this vital and precious commodity. Energy saving through improving its consumption style and habits is the need of the hour. It would benefit not only the national grid but also individuals.

The poor literacy rate is a factor that amongst other areas also affects the national energy consumption culture. On this front, there is hardly anything that can be done in the short-to-medium term. Still, a considerable change can be brought with the help of the educated segments of society. There is a clear scarcity of energy related courses in education at all level. Universities don't offer many energy focused programmes. The situation at technical colleges is more disappointing. Things can be improved by starting new programmes or even by introducing energy modules within the existing programmes. Graduates with a better understanding of energy can significantly contribute in bringing a positive change in the energy consumption culture of the country. Children can also play a very important role in improving energy consumption attitudes in the household. It is noteworthy that in the energy conscious countries, methods to save energy are taught in a very easy and friendly manner as part of the school curriculum. Government/ departmental initiatives in the form of public awareness campaigns and incentives can also be very helpful. Over the last few years, there have been examples of energy saving campaigns in the media which is a commendable effort on the part of pertinent departments. These campaigns need to be made more appealing and should be launched on a more frequent basis. Distribution of effectively designed leaflets in conjunction with the monthly utility bills can also be a beneficial approach.

It is crucial to raise public awareness not only from the energy conservation perspective but also in terms of a wider understanding of the challenges facing the country. Since 2006, there have been violent protests against the disturbing energy crisis across the country on a regular basis.

These demonstrations clearly indicate the widening communication gap between the policy and decision-makers and the common man. It is crucial to win the confidence of all stakeholders of society in the fight against the energy crisis. Pertinent authorities need to initiate a constructive dialogue with various segments of society.

The people need to be educated so they understand that violence and attacks on energy infrastructure and national assets are not going to help things get any better. They must learn to record their protest in a peaceful and effective manner.

It is vital to educate people not only on their social responsibilities but also rights. They can exercise their right of accountability through the ballot or other legitimate means against those politicians and policy-makers who deliberately or incompetently create crises.

## 6.8. THE NEW RENTAL POWER PROGRAMME

In order to address the severe electricity shortfall, the present government has decided to have a second wave of IPPs. Rental power plants are also being actively pursued as a quick-fix solution. Collectively, the IPPs and the rental power programme are to contribute 6,233MW of new power plants by 2011 of which 2,700MW are to come through the latter.[42] Rental power projects for 2,250MW have already been approved.[43,44] The government appears to believe that rental power is the only solution to the crisis, as the Minister for Water and Power told the National Assembly in August 2009. According to the government all other options including thermal, hydro or coal would take at least three to five years to generate electricity.[45,46]

In the backdrop of the immense socio-economic implications of the deepening crisis there is no one to deny the need for an urgent solution. What is important, however, is that the urgency must carry an element of robustness and pragmatism. This is where the government's IPP/rental power approach is far from convincing and has duly drawn overwhelming criticism. Concerns are being raised on the financial viability of rental power in particular for two reasons: their below par efficiency and high tariff structure. Energy circles are wary of the operational performance of these plants. Some even say that most of the plants being rented are almost worn out. They also believe that the sort of tariff structure being proposed is set to have huge financial implications for WAPDA, the power sector and the country as a whole as was the case with the 1990s IPPs affair.

There is a great deal of confusion regarding the real price of the power acquired from the rental power projects. Government officials are giving very mixed signals. At times it is denied that the electricity from the rental power projects would be more expensive than that delivered by current IPPs.[47] In other instances it is admitted that it is a costlier option compared to IPPs.[48]

A quick overview of one of the rental power projects can give an idea of the economic implications the rental power episode is going to lead to. The 150MW 'Sumundri Road' project is being rented at 3.9 cents/kWh. The electricity price is going to depend on oil prices in the international market. Against a furnace oil price of Rs26,000/ton, which is almost half of the pre-economic recession price in the summer of 2008, the electricity price is going to be 10.3 cents/kWh. As of the mid-2009 exchange rate, in Pakistani currency the price of electricity WAPDA would pay is around Rs11.2/kWh. After taking losses into account, WAPDA would end up having this electricity at over Rs14/kWh. In July 2009, the Minister for Water and Power informed the media that currently the average selling price of electricity is Rs5.37/kWh against the average generation cost of Rs8.37/kWh.[49] Thus, as per current selling price, the loss WAPDA is annually going to incur from the 'Sumundri Road' project alone is going to be over Rs8.5/kWh. Assuming 80 per cent capacity factor, the net annual deficit from this project alone is going to be over Rs9 billion.

Some of the new projects are being reported to have been signed at tariff as high as 16–20 cents/kWh, though the Minister for Water and Power has so far admitted the highest tariff being offered to be equal to USCent 13.5/kWh.[17,50] He has informed a Senate committee that the tariff of rental power plants would be linked to oil prices. Hence, no guarantee can be given that the rates will not go up.[51] Assuming that the minister's statement of 13.5 cents/kWh is more reliable compared to that of others of 16–20 cents/kWh (though the likelihood of being so is slim) and again keeping fingers crossed that the oil price does not go up (though the likelihood is very little), still the 2,250MW of rental power would annually bring a net deficit of Rs135 billion to the country. Someone has to pay the price for such expensive electricity whether it is the poor common man, or WAPDA or the country or it could be a collective suffering.

Some segments of pertinent authorities have also admitted that the rental power plants are not only expensive in tariff but also are less efficient in operation in comparison to exiting IPPs. The Private Power Infrastructure Board (PPIB) has also appreciated these concerns. The PPIB

officials have been quoted to have briefed the Board as: 'Tariff for rental
projects is higher than the IPPs by 0.76 cents to 1.63 cents per unit. Being
used, rental projects also have low efficiency as compared to IPPs,
resulting in higher fuel cost'.[52]

Meanwhile, the Asian Development Bank has declared that 'the
planned rental power plants are ineffective and expensive.'[53] Government
representatives, when asked about such a judgement on the part of
such a prominent independent body, could not deny it though they
disagreed in its interpretation. WAPDA/PEPCO officials have also
acknowledged that the proposed rental power plants are ineffective and
expensive.[54] In a meeting on energy efficiency a PEPCO official has stated
that due to the ongoing crisis the department was installing 'the most
inefficient and expensive rental power plants.'[55]

Most of the rental power plants are to run on oil. According to the
PPIB, of the total 6,233MW of new projects being sought under the
rental power and IPPs programme, 3,595MW are going to be oil-based.
A further 910MW of projects being dual fuel are also going to substantially
rely on oil.[32] The effectiveness of the rental power programme would
remain subject to sufficient availability of fuel, something which has not
happened during the last couple of years. A senior WAPDA official
informed the author that, in 2008, the demand for furnace oil in the
power sector was 30,000 tonne/day against which the supply never
exceeded 21,000 tonne/day. He further believe that in 2009, the demand
is expected to be over 36,000 tonne/day.[56] The situation is inevitably
going to lead to a multitude of stresses. As past experiences suggest, such
a massive quantity of oil would not be made available to have all the
power plants run at a maximum capacity factor. Even if the oil can be
purchased, the transportation and distribution infrastructure, as many
senior officials claim, is already overloaded. Reports suggest that in the
wake of the additional thermal power capacity being pursued, a growth
of US$1/barrel in oil prices in the international market would increase
the import bill by US$100 million. The push for more oil imports thus
would result in an even higher trade deficit. As a matter of fact, the
electricity crisis has aggravated mainly because of this very issue—due to
the ongoing circular debt the power plants, be they WAPDA's, KESC's or
IPPs', have struggled to operate on full capacity because of the lack of
fuel.

The rental power programme is also bound to lead to an unhealthy
impacts on the already weak economic condition of WAPDA. The
department's debt burden would once again sharply rise. Bearing in mind

the substantial rise in electricity prices that rental power will inevitably result in, it would defeat the purpose in the first place since the masses would not be able to afford the electricity even if it is available for purchase. The higher tariff structure would also promote corruption and electricity thefts.

Another major implication of the rental power programme is that it would worsen the already imbalanced energy equation in terms of the respective share of thermal power and hydropower. In a healthy scenario, hydropower, which is an indigenous energy resource, should have the lion's share as used to be the case during the 1960s and 1970s. The new wave of thermal power plants in the form of rental power and IPPs is going to further truncate the share of hydropower in the national electricity supply mix.

Thermal power, other than the local coal-based, would greatly remain a foreign resource of energy. It is against the energy security of the country to shift the base load onto a foreign and unreliable resource. Unfortunately this is already the case. The situation must not be aggravated by bringing in more electricity in the supply mix from oil and gas rather than from indigenous coal and hydropower.

Serious reservations are also being raised by various corners on the behind the scene wheeling and dealing—there are reports of nepotism and corruption in the rental power project deals. Though the government is upbeat about the transparency in the bidding process, concerned circles have pointed out that loopholes have been deliberately left in that they claim have led to corruption in the form of post-tender concessions.[57] The Federal Minister for Water and Power, Raja Pervez Ashraf, an upbeat supporter and indeed one of the main architects of the rental power programme, is widely reported to be involved in hefty corruption over this connoversial programme.[67] Transparency International has also expressed concerns over the allegations of corruption in the rental power programme. According to Transparency International such selective concessions are a violation of transparent award of contracts.[58,59,60] The Ministry for Water and Power and other concerned departments have been formally contacted in this regard.[61]

Unfortunately, the government has approved the rental power programme without evaluating its financial implication. The finance minister, Shaukat Tareen, in September 2009, admitted that 'the government was yet to evaluate the financial burden of this programme and that the services of the Asian Development Bank would be requested at some point to look into it.'[62,63] This acknowledgement indeed speaks volumes of the haphazardness and dearth of commitment on the part of government in the whole rental power programme.

Reports in the media also suggest that the said finance minister has actually been protesting against the rental power programme. In a Cabinet meeting he expressed his concerns with forceful and fact-based arguments warning the Cabinet of the huge financial setback this programme is going to inflict. He even considered tendering his resignation because he did not want to be part of such an unhealthy move. He, however, withheld it only after Prime Minister Yousaf Raza Gilani conceded to some of his demands including incorporation of some sort of transparency measures towards the award of the rental power contracts.[64]

The rental power programme is thus an extremely ill-advised and unviable option that the current regime is actively pursuing. The balance of its pros and cons suggests it to be a suicidal move, especially when other far better options are available. The long-term financial damage this misadventure is going to inflict will far outweigh the benefits it would deliver. Scrapping the rental programme would be indeed a service to the nation.

## 6.9. Pragmatic Alternatives to the Rental Power Programme

Evidence suggests there was no real need for such a haphazard rental power/IPP programme. WAPDA officials have even been reported to claim that the installed power generation capacity is sufficient to meet the current requirements but is not being fully capitalized in order to create an artificial shortfall so that a demand can be created for new power plants.[65] A number of other options that are more pragmatic and sustainable and can help bridge the immediate gap between demand and supply at far more economical terms are available as follows.

- Firstly, the installed power generation capacity is not being duly capitalized on. Between the summer and winter months, the hydropower generation capacity fluctuates by as much as 60 per cent—from peak generation capacity of 6,400MW in the summer it slides to around 2,600MW in winter. This fluctuation is an essential characteristic of hydropower and one of the major reasons for developing thermal power initially was to provide a backup to this fluctuation. The current crisis has largely exacerbated due to under-utilization of existing thermal power plants. Estimates suggest that during the summers of 2008 and 2009 thermal power plants underperformed by around 4,000MW leading to acute electricity shortfall. By having the installed thermal power plants run on full throttle the current deficit can be lessened by over 80 per cent. A very senior energy official expressed his frustration at the decision to have new thermal power plants set up at such a high tariff structure when the existing ones are running at capacity factors below 60 and even below 50 in some cases. He was of the view that the existing power plants must run at over 80 per cent capacity factor before the need is felt for new plants.

- Secondly, the circular debt needs to be resolved in order to ease pressure on the involved stakeholders so that the installed power generation capacity can be availed as much as possible. As a matter of fact the circular debt has been one of the main reasons behind the acute shortage of electricity as is being observed over the last couple of years. Unless this problem is addressed, the existing power plants would continue to struggle to run on the optimum level of performance.

- Thirdly, rather than going for rental power, a far economical option would be to revamp WAPDA's old thermal power stations. Officials claim that a number of WAPDA's old power stations can be upgraded/renovated to produce around 3,000–4,000MW as a possible quick and far cheaper solution.[66] Some of these potential power stations include Shahdara, Faisalabad, Multan, Jamshoro, and Guddu.

- Fourthly, with a stringent check and balance programme system leaks  can be controlled. Roughly 1,500–2,500MW of additional capacity can be made available by addressing this problem alone. System losses that ideally should be 6–7 per cent are nearly 23 per cent in WAPDA and over 40 per cent in KESC. In some WAPDA's areas, however, the losses are also over 35 per cent. A major chunk of these losses come from electricity thefts that can be relatively easily curtailed. The technical losses that occur due to poor and inefficient transmission and distribution infrastructure can also be improved by appropriate investment.

- Fifthly, a considerable level of electricity can be saved by implementing a meaningful energy conservation and management programme. Pakistan is very low at energy productivity. As a rule of thumb there is a margin of over 20 per cent saving in electricity consumption across all sectors. Energy saving is like energy generating and is the cheapest possible solution to energy shortfalls. The issue has been discussed in detail in Chapter 7.

These solutions, if truly implemented, can provide a cushion for at least the next three to four years. Meanwhile, more pragmatic and sustainable solutions can be sought by exploring potential avenues including coal, hydropower, and renewable energy. This route can reasonably provide quick stability to the weak electricity scenario. There are thus a number of options available to relatively quickly address the prevalent electricity load-shedding which are far more economical and sustainable than the utterly unnecessary and detrimental rental power programme; however, potential personal gains and kickbacks would have to be compromised upon.

## REFERENCES

1. Syed Tanzeem Hussain Naqvi, Ex-Chairman KESC, Interview, Pakistan, May 2009.
2. An ex-senior WAPDA official, Interview, Pakistan, May 2009.
3. *Express*, 21 August 2009.
4. Owen Bennett-Jones, *Pakistan: Eye of the Storm*, Yale University Press, London, 2002, pp. 244–245.
5. *Daily Express*, 4 December 2009.
6. *The News*, 4 December 2009.
7. *Hasbe haal*, Dunya TV, 5 December 2009.
8. Transparency International News Item, http://www.transparency.org.pk/news/urdu per cent20press per cent20releases/geonews per cent206 per cent20sept per cent2009.jpg (accessed on 7 December 2009).
9. *Daily Express*, 13 August 2009.
10. Ex-Member WAPDA, Interview, Pakistan, May 2009.
11. Ex-Acting Chairman WAPDA, Interview, Pakistan, May 2009.
12. 'Furore in Senate over power crisis', *Dawn*, 25 July 2009.
13. Ex-Member WAPDA, Email correspondence, July 2009.
14. Shamsul Mulk, Ex-Chairman WAPDA, Interview, Islamabad, May 2009.
15. Dr Shahid Masood, *Jang*, 29 July 2009.
16. Khwaja Asif MNA in *Bolta Pakistan*, AAJ TV, 21 July 2009.
17. Kamran Khan, *The News*, 1 August 2009.
18. Kamran Khan, *The News*, 5 August 2009.
19. 'Government, PML-Q engage in blame game over power crisis', Irfan Ghauri, *Daily Times*, 8 August 2009.
20. 'Corruption in Pakistan Increases: Transparency International', *Daily Times*, 18 November 2009, http://www.transparency.org.pk/news/newsnov09.htm#173
21. BBC Urdu, 18 November 2009.
22. *Daily Express*, 19 November 2009, http://express.com.pk/epaper/Article.aspx?newsID=1100774284&Date=20091119&Issue=NP_LHE
23. Hamid Meer, Daily *Jang*, 19 November 2009.

24. Dr Pervez Butt, Ex-Chairman Pakistan Atomic Energy Commission, Interview, Islamabad, May 2009.
25. *The News*, 16 September 2009.
26. *Express*, 3 October 2009.
27. A UK-Based Energy Consultant, Telephonic Interview, March 2009.
28. One of the senior most and founding officials of AEDB, Notes from the meeting, Pakistan, May 2009.
29. Mian Manzoor Ahmed Watto, Federal Minister Industries, Production and Special Initiatives, Proceedings of an energy forum, Lahore, May 2009.
30. One of the senior most officials in ENERCON, Notes from the meeting, Islamabad, June 2007.
31. Capital Talk, GEO TV, 24 September 2009.
32. Former Chairman Planning Commission, Interview, Islamabad, May 2009.
33. Charles Ebinger, *Pakistan: Energy Planning in a Strategic Vortex*, Indiana University Press, 1981.
34. Press Release No. 322, Press Information Department, Islamabad, 26 June 2009.
35. Raja Pervez Ashraf, *Kal Tak*, Express TV, 14 July, *Express* (Newspaper) 15 July 2009.
36. Khursheed Shah rules out end to load-shedding by Dec, GEO TV, 21 May 2009.
37. *Jang*, 20 July 2009, http://www.jang.com.pk/jang/jul2009-daily/20-07-2009/mulkbharse.htm
38. 'Ministers' guessing makes masses suffer', *The Nation*, 22 May 2009.
39. Government of Pakistan website, http://www.cabinet.gov.pk/(accessed on 7 December 2009).
40. Medium-Term Development Framework (2005-2010), Planning Commission, Govt. of Pakistan, May 2005.
41. Economic Survey of Pakistan 2008-2009, Government of Pakistan, Islamabad.
42. PPIB website, http://www.ppib.gov.pk/(accessed on 7 December 2009).
43. *Dawn*, 22 August 2009.
44. *The News*, 27 August 2009.
45. *AAJ News*, 4 August 2009.
46. *Dawn*, 8 August 2009.
47. Rental power plants not costly: Raja Pervez Ashraf, Traders Media, 25 July 2009, http://news.tradingcharts.com/futures/6/6/127187266.html (accessed on 7 December 2009).
48. Raja Pervez Ashraf, *Capital Talk*, GEO TV, 30 July 2009.
49. 'Power tariff to increase by Rs3 per unit', *Daily Times*, 26 July 2009.
50. *Dawn*, 22 August 2009.
51. 'Will rental power plants resolve the crisis?', Ashfak Bukhari, *Dawn*, 13 July 2009.
52. 'PPIB admits rental plant's tariff higher', Mushtaq Ghumman, *Business Recorder*, 23 July 2009.
53. FDM Focus, 6 July 2009, FDM Capital Securities (PVT) LTD.
54. Mushtaq Ghumman, *Business Recorder*, 4 August 2009.
55. 'Will rental power plants resolve the crisis?', Ashfak Bukhari, *Dawn*, 13 July 2009.
56. Senior WAPDA official, Interview, Pakistan May 2009.
57. BBC Urdu, 18 November 2009
58. *Daily Express*, 19 November 2009, http://express.com.pk/epaper/Article.aspx?newsID=1100774284&Date=20091119&Issue=NP_LHE (accessed on 7 December, 2009).
59. Daily *Jang*, 19 November 2009.
60. Press Release, Transparency International, 3 August 2009.

61. Transparency International's letter to the Minister for Water and Power, Dated 24 July 2009.
62. *Express*, 16 September 2009.
63. *Urdu point*, 15 September 2009.
64. Inside story of Cabinet meeting ADB to audit rental power projects, Rauf Klasra, 11 September 2009.
65. *Express*, 3 October 2009.
66. Syed Tanzeem Hussain Naqvi, Ex-Chairman KESC, Capital Talk, GEO TV, 30 July 2009.
67. *Dawn*, 8 August 2009.

# 7

# Sustainable Energy Options

In pursuant to Chapter 6, this chapter provides solutions to the energy problems facing Pakistan in a robust and sustainable fashion. It describes the potential strengths of the country's energy portfolio. The prominent indigenous resources that can be tapped to provide affordable and sufficient energy on a long-term basis have been discussed herein.

## 7.1. ENERGY CONSERVATION

Energy conservation, also referred to as energy conservation and management, is crucial to promoting energy sustainability. The inefficient infrastructure in developing countries consumes much more energy per unit of economic output than that in the developed industrialized countries. The situation with Pakistan is not any different. According to the Planning Commission of Pakistan, the energy utilization per unit of GDP in Pakistan is more than double to that of the world average and more than five times that of Japan and the UK.[1] With the overwhelming energy challenges facing Pakistan in general and the intense shortfall of electricity in particular, apart from setting up new power generation plants, it is imperative to embark on a meaningful and coherent energy conservation programme in order to use the available energy more productively.

### 7.1.1 WHAT IS ENERGY CONSERVATION?

Energy conservation is the practice of reducing the amount of energy required to accomplish a task. By saving energy, apart from delivering financial gain, energy conservation also leads to environmental benefits, human comfort, and personal and national security. For individuals and organizations, energy conservation can reduce costs and promote economic and environmental sustainability. Through increased efficiency, for industrial and commercial users, it results in increased profits. On a larger scale, energy conservation is considered to be an integral part of national energy policy across the world. It could help control energy costs, and reduce the need for new power plants and energy imports. The reduced energy demand can provide more flexibility in choosing the most preferred methods of energy production. It can also facilitate the replacement of conventional energy resources with renewable ones. As a matter of fact saving energy is like generating energy. Energy conservation is often the most economical solution to energy shortages. Saving electricity through energy conservation is usually much more economical than producing it from conventional power plants.

An energy conservation and management programme can have several layers—it can be accomplished in a number of ways and at various degrees depending upon the nature and size of application. It also does not require very specialized knowledge and expertise to incorporate an initial level of energy conservation. In its simplest form, it starts free of cost. Examples here could be switching off appliances such as lights, air-conditioners, fans, and heaters when not required and a sensible setting of the thermostat. It is noteworthy that majority of the energy lost through buildings, even in developed countries, is through infiltration and drafts. At the second level, it could be a low-cost practice, for example, usage of fluorescent lights or energy saver bulbs to cut down the lighting load, shading the south-facing windows and walls in order to reduce the cooling load, and proper calibration and maintenance of equipment to ensure they run at an optimal level. At the third level, it could require relatively more investment, for example, incorporation of insulation to control heating and cooling losses. The last and the most expensive level could be a major overhauling of the existing system/equipment or even replacement of aging and ill-productive equipment with new and more efficient one. Examples in this regard include the implementation of a regular maintenance plan for equipment, replacement of single-glazed windows with multi-glazed windows, replacement of conventional boilers with heat recovery ones, and incorporation of heat exchangers to extract energy from waste heat. It is important to bear in mind that whatever energy conservation measures are adopted, they normally pay themselves back several times over their lifetime.

### 7.1.2 Scope of Energy Conservation

It has been seen even in developed countries that despite modern and efficient infrastructure, there is still a considerable margin for energy saving through the implementation of energy conservation and management measures—reports and case studies indicate that in the domestic, industrial, and commercial sectors, energy conservation practices can easily save more than 15 per cent of the total energy being consumed. This being the saving potential in developed countries, Pakistan has much greater scope for energy conservation practices. According to ENERCON, 25 per cent of the total energy consumption can be potentially saved as suggested in Table 7.1.[2] Considering the current electricity and gas prices in the country, energy conservation can definitely save hundreds of rupees over a year even for the smallest domestic consumer. For large-scale industries that have extensive use of energy, the consequent saving could be in tens of millions of rupees. The subsequent financial relief can thus be reflected in lower operation/ production costs, consequently making products and services more competitive in the domestic as well as international markets. Energy conservation practices find their effectiveness in all sectors, i.e. domestic, industrial, transport and commercial.

**Table 7.1: Energy saving potential in Pakistan in various sectors**

| Sector | Saving potential (%) |
|---|---|
| Industry | 25 |
| Transport | 20 |
| Agriculture | 20 |
| Building | 30 |
| Average | 25 |

#### 7.1.2.1 Industrial Sector

In Pakistan, the industrial sector incorporates significant energy losses that reduce its level of overall operational productivity. Energy extensive equipment such as boilers and compressors often lack proper calibration and maintenance. Even in developed countries such as the USA, proper regulation and maintenance of compressors can save over 20 per cent of the energy consumption.[3] In Pakistan, production and assembly lines run low on productivity. The industrialist is not aware of the financial losses being incurred as a result of inefficient practices. There is little appreciation of energy saving practices. Even the most modern of industries do not have an internal energy auditing and monitoring policy in place which is the key to energy conservation and management. The owners as well as the staff—engineers, technicians and other support staff—have neither the vision to realize the essence of energy conservation nor the training and qualifications to implement it.

### 7.1.2.2 Domestic Sector

The domestic sector is the largest consumer of electricity accounting for 46 per cent of the total electricity consumption in the country. In terms of natural gas consumption, it is the second largest consumer with a share of 16 per cent.[4] A substantial proportion of the total energy load in the domestic sector goes into space conditioning, i.e. cooling in summer and heating in winter. Other major energy-consuming activities include cooking, water heating and lighting. In the absence of any trends to manufacture and sell energy-efficient products, the markets are full of inefficient appliances. Consumers are not aware of the fortune these energy expensive items are costing them in terms of the running cost which consists primarily of the price of the energy consumed. To a great extent, the energy consumption of a building is defined the day it is designed—phenomena like natural ventilation, daylighting and insulation determine the cooling, heating and lighting requirements of a building over its lifetime. In Pakistan these features are hardly taken into account at the design/architectural stage of even the most lavish and modern of the buildings, especially in the domestic sector. The usual practice is to have all the emphasis upon the superfluous architectural features, especially on buildings' external envelope which result not only in more maintenance but also increased energy losses.

### 7.1.2.3 Commercial Sector

The commercial sector that normally consists of retail stores, offices, restaurants, schools and other workplaces has energy applications similar to the ones seen in the domestic sector. Space conditioning is again the single biggest consumption area, followed by lighting. Both of these are generally the most wasteful components of commercial energy use. Buildings, both domestic and commercial, can substantially reduce their energy cost by implementing thoughtful designs in terms of incorporation of daylighting and natural ventilation and by switching to energy efficient appliances.

### 7.1.2.4 Transport Sector

The transport sector consumes nearly 52 per cent of the total petroleum products and thus has a major contribution to make towards the success of an energy conservation programme.[4] The role of the transport sector in Pakistan's energy consumption base has become even more prominent over the last decade or so with an exponential increment in the number of private vehicles on road. It has added stress not only on petroleum imports due to increased demand for fuel oil but has also added pressure on local supplies of gas since a great number of vehicles have switched to gas based fuels. There is a desperate need to address the issue and the possible solution could be revamping the public transport system and making arrangements to improve vehicle fuel consumption. The existing public transport system in Pakistan offers very little to citizens who want an efficient, affordable and comfortable means of commuting. Serious investment would need to be made by the government to bring the train and road transport services up to the mark. Owing to poor quality of engine maintenance and widely sold unoriginal lubricants and impure fuels, engine fuel consumption is very poor. Better and strict standards need to be developed on all fronts and stringently implemented.

### 7.1.3 ENERGY CRISIS AND ENERGY CONSERVATION

The ongoing energy crisis in Pakistan has exacerbated to such an extent that its immediate solution is not an easy option anymore. With the emergence of the problem in 2006, it was clear that the most pragmatic solution, multi-gigawatt capacity addition based on local coal and hydropower, would require a few years provided that bold and concerted steps are taken on a war footing. The new government, having been sworn into office in February 2008, initially warned that it might take three years to completely address electricity load-shedding.[5] Thus, the situation still demands that ways and means be devised in the interim period to meet the electricity deficit which had soared to over 40 per cent the same year. The challenge is to get through the crisis without suffering irreparable damage. One of the most vital solutions, in this respect, lies in a collective national effort to utilize the available lot of energy more wisely and productively through having a robust energy conservation and management programme in place. The two key elements of such an effort should be: energy saving and a voluntary change in lifestyles.

The starting point would be to change existing energy usage trends that are inherently extremely inefficient. With minimal effort, well over 10 per cent of the national electricity consumption can be reduced by applying only the first level of energy conservation, that is, a change in attitude. It is simple, instant and effective and all it requires is abandoning unnecessary consumption of energy. Cooling and heating requirements of different types—for example, air conditioning, refrigeration and space heating—are integral parts of modern age . domestic, industrial and commercial activities. Research shows that by controlling cooling or heating by 1°C, around 7 per cent of the heating or cooling load can be reduced. Also, leaving lights and appliances on even when they are not being used, a common practice across all sectors, needs to be addressed. Similarly, many businesses such as shops dealing in cloth and garments, jewellery, cosmetics, home appliances and electronics are usually extravagantly lit. It is commonly observed that shops that could do with two or three 40-watt tube-lights to meet a reasonable level of luminance use as many as 15 to 20 tube-lights. Not only does this increase power consumption, it also generates heat and makes the environment uncomfortable. Likewise, in industrial applications, the idle running time of production lines and machines can be reduced by incorporating motion sensors. A further economy of 10 to 15 per cent can be achieved by introducing the second and third levels of energy conservation practices, especially in industry. One of the most important initiatives can be replacement of conventional (incandescent) lights with fluorescent lights/ energy savers—the latter can provide 60 to 80 per cent energy saving as shown in Table 7.2. A substantial proportion of the gap between demand and supply can be met just through these energy conservation and management measure. To do that, public education is essential. With the help of effective electronic and print media campaigns the government can convince and motivate the masses.

**Table 7.2: Efficacy of various light sources**

| Light source | Efficacy (lumen/watt) |
|---|---|
| Candle | 0.1 |
| Kerosene oil lamp | 0.3 |
| Original Edison lamp | 1.4 |
| Modern incandescent lamp | 8–22 |
| Tungsten Halogen lamp | 16–20 |
| Standard Fluorescent lamp | 35–80 |
| Compact Fluorescent lamp | 40–75 |
| Mercury lamp | 30–60 |
| Metal halide lamp | 70–115 |
| High pressure sodium lamp | 45–130 |
| Induction lamp | 48–85 |

The second part of the solution lies in a change in lifestyles. It would begin with the acknowledgement that the country is facing a national disaster and every citizen has to chip in to overcome it. Of present, there is not enough electricity to meet both necessities and luxuries. The nation has to draw a clear line between necessities (lighting, fans, TVs, computers, etc) and luxuries (air-conditioners, microwaves, etc), and will have to compromise on the latter in order to meet the former. Markets and commercial places can substantially reduce their electricity consumption by changing their working hours. To capitalize on daylight as much as possible, an early start and early end would be advisable rather than having opening hours from afternoon until late at night. Similarly, academic institutions, operation theatres and medical stores, and agriculture tube wells deserve to be supplied with electricity to a far greater extent than gigantic signboards and street lights. Use of air-conditioning, a sign of a luxurious lifestyle, needs to be curtailed.

Bearing in mind that a typical domestic air conditioner normally consumes more electricity in an hour than a ceiling fan does in over 24 hours (as shown in Table 7.3) the use of air conditioners should be curbed except in sensitive applications such as hospitals and research centres. The choice is between using air conditioners for a few hours and then doing without electricity for the rest of the day during the peak summer months or avoiding air conditioners and other luxury gadgets but having round the clock electricity available to meet fundamental needs.

Here it is worth giving the example of Denmark that is amongst the best rated welfare states in the world and also enjoys energy prosperity.

Over the last thirty-five years, Denmark has seen its gross national energy consumption come down despite an over 50 per cent increment in economy.[6] The secret to this remarkable success is the responsible attitude towards energy conservation on the part of the entire nation. For example, very few households use microwave ovens (considering them an unnecessary luxury gadget). In Pakistan on the other hand, despite much poorer economic conditions across the board, luxury gadgets are very common, thus reducing the amount of energy left for necessary applications.

### Table 7.3: Power rating of typical domestic appliances

| Appliance | Power rating (Watts) |
| --- | --- |
| Air conditioner (split) | 1,200–1,500 |
| Air conditioner (window) | 2,500–4,000 |
| Blender | 300 |
| CD player | 20–40 |
| Ceiling fan | 60–120 |
| Computer | 200 |
| Iron | 1,000 |
| Microwave | 1,000–2,500 |
| Motor pump | 1,000 |
| Refrigerator | 180–300 |
| Television | 70–150 |
| Vacuum cleaner | 400–700 |
| Washing machine | 600–800 |

A collective national effort is required to see the energy conservation programme yield tangible results. In doing so, however, the greatest responsibility rests with the policy and decision-makers to lead by example—first and far most importantly, the ruling elite that enjoys the most privileged lifestyles would have to curtail their lavish routines. It is time for the elite to take bold initiatives like abandoning the use of central air conditioning systems in their palace-like offices and residences and extravagant use of air and road transport at the cost of public money. If the elite start saving energy the common man will follow suit.

These recommendations can not only avoid the collapse of a bankrupt energy infrastructure but also ensure its progress. No one is going to remain immune from the crisis, even those who can afford different gadgets such as generators to partially offset the reduced power supply will still feel the heat one way or the other. The bottom line is, in order to safely get through the current energy crisis the nation has to differentiate between its necessities and its luxuries.

Energy conservation would not only offer a financial reward to individuals but would also offer relief to the national grid. The net financial benefit of energy conservation in Pakistan is estimated to be over US$3 billion per year.[2] Once a robust energy conservation programme has been developed it must be diligently implemented. In doing so, a stick-and-carrot strategy can be adapted particularly with major consumers to deliver tangible results.

## 7.2. COAL

Coal is an important form of fossil fuels which currently meets around 25 per cent of the global primary energy requirements.[7] It is broadly classified into four main types—anthracite, bituminous, sub-bituminous, and lignite. Anthracite coal is the hardest and has more carbon, which gives it higher energy content. Lignite is the softest and is low in carbon but high in hydrogen and oxygen content. Bituminous and sub-bituminous are in between. Coal in general is less efficient and more polluting than its other fossil fuel family members, oil and gas. Coal, however, is more economical as compared to oil and gas. Also, in terms of resource potential, coal has a categorical advantage over them. According to the Energy Information Administration's 2008 statistics, the reserves-to-production ratio both for oil and gas is estimated to be around sixty years worldwide, while the same ratio for coal is 200 years.[8]

### 7.2.1 GLOBAL STATUS OF COAL

Coal is an established and leading part of the world's electricity generation mix contributing a staggering 41 per cent to the total generation as shown in Figure 7.1.[9] Like other technologies, coal has also come of age. Gone are the days when coal power plants used to operate at 20 per cent efficiency. With technical advancements and improvements, the thermal efficiency of modern coal power plants has been greatly enhanced. Much higher pressure and temperature conditions for steam, coupled with advanced materials (i.e. usage of composite alloys in the highest temperature regions of the super-heater, re-heater, turbine and pipe-work) has allowed modern coal plants to operate at an efficiency level of over 35 per cent. State of the art coal plants in China have a thermal efficiency of above 40 per cent. In view of the ongoing research and development and best practiced boilers and turbines, the European Union has set a target to develop the next generation of coal power plants with an efficiency level of 50 to 55 per cent.[10] These factors will ensure a respectable share for coal in future global energy scenarios.

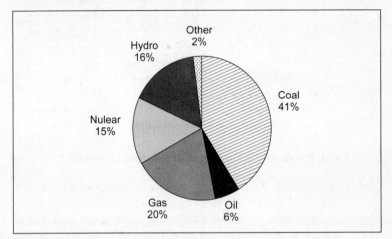

Figure 7.1: Total World Electricity Generation by Fuel type, IEA 2008

According to the latest EU and UK energy directives, by 2030 it is estimated that nearly 1,400GWe of new coal-fired capacity will be built worldwide, with two-thirds of the new capacity in developing countries.[11] Coal-fired power plants are expected to provide about 38 per cent of global electricity needs in 2030. Coal is a key player in the energy markets of a large number of countries. South Africa, Poland and China, for example, respectively produce 94 per cent, 93 per cent and 81 per cent of their electricity from coal. Table 7.4 highlights top ten countries in the world in terms of share of coal in electricity generation.[9] Interestingly, not all of these countries are self-sufficient in coal.

**Table 7.4: Top 10 countries in the world in terms of share of coal in electricity generation, IEA 2009**

| Country | Share of coal (%) |
|---|---|
| South Africa | 94 |
| Poland | 93 |
| PR China | 81 |
| Australia | 76 |
| Israel | 71 |
| Kazakhstan | 70 |
| India | 68 |
| Czech Rep | 62 |
| Morocco | 57 |
| Greece | 55 |

## 7.2.2 COAL RESERVES OF PAKISTAN: THE UNTAPPED ASSET

Coal can substantially help Pakistan overcome its energy challenges. It is an indigenous and abundantly available resource that can provide cheap energy. Coal can make a healthy contribution to the national electricity supply mix. The total coal reserves of Pakistan as reported by the Geological Survey of Pakistan (GSP) are estimated to be around 185 billion tonnes. Of these, nearly 175 billion tonnes are located in the Thar Desert, as discovered in 1992. The distribution of coal reserves in Pakistan has been shown in Figure 7.2.[12] In terms of quality the coal found in Pakistan falls in a range between bituminous and lignite. Presently, the brick kilns industry is the leading consumer of coal, accounting for about 56 per cent of the total, followed by the cement industry as indicated in Table 7.5.[14] Pakistan's attitude towards this precious resource has so far been utterly disappointing. Reports, for example, suggest that Pakistan's coal reserves are twice that of India's yet the former's annual production of coal is only around 1 per cent of that of the latter's.[13] The humble production of indigenous coal, as shown in Table 7.6,[14] implies that coal reserves in the country are virtually untapped.

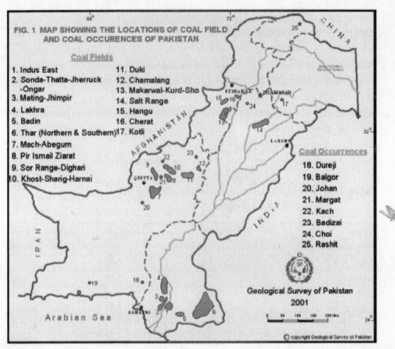

Figure 7.2: Location of coal fields in Pakistan

## Table 7.5: Consumption of coal in Pakistan (%)

| Year | Household | Power production | Brick kilns | Cement industry |
|---|---|---|---|---|
| 1997-98 | 0.1 | 11.0 | 89.0 | 0.0 |
| 1998-99 | 0.0 | 12.0 | 88.0 | 0.0 |
| 1999-00 | 0.0 | 11.0 | 89.0 | 0.0 |
| 2000-01 | 0.0 | 5.1 | 70.2 | 24.7 |
| 2001-02 | 0.0 | 5.7 | 58.5 | 35.9 |
| 2002-03 | 0.0 | 4.2 | 53.3 | 42.5 |
| 2003-04 | 0.0 | 3.0 | 42.7 | 54.2 |
| 2004-05 | 0.0 | 2.3 | 49.5 | 48.2 |
| 2005-06 | 0.0 | 1.9 | 54.7 | 43.3 |
| 2006-07 | 0.0 | 1.8 | 55.7 | 42.5 |

The power sector has neglected to use coal for power generation. One of the downsides of the IPPs programme, for example, in the 1990s was missing out on coal. In an attempt to avert the approaching energy crisis, the government decided to take thermal generation on board through the private sector, and emphasis was placed on oil and gas based projects rather on coal-based ones. Coal is a fuel that is domestically available in abundance compared to gas which is limited, and oil which has to be imported. Owing to the fact that coal would have been a far more cost effective and secure option, the adopted approach is hard to justify. Over the last couple of decades, successive governments have ignored coal, whereas, much of the country's current energy problems could have been avoided had this resource in a timely and meaningful fashion explored.

**Table 7.6:** **Production and consumption of coal (thousand tonnes)**

| Year | Production | Imports | Consumption |
|------|-----------|---------|-------------|
| 1997-98 | 3,159 | 960 | 4,119 |
| 1998-99 | 3,461 | 910 | 4,371 |
| 1999-00 | 3,168 | 957 | 4,125 |
| 2000-01 | 3,095 | 950 | 4,045 |
| 2001-02 | 3,328 | 1,081 | 4,409 |
| 2002-03 | 3,312 | 1,578 | 4,890 |
| 2003-04 | 3,275 | 2,789 | 6,064 |
| 2004-05 | 4,587 | 3,307 | 7,894 |
| 2005-06 | 4,871 | 2,843 | 7,714 |
| 2006-07 | 3,643 | 4,251 | 7,894 |

Vague estimates have been made, by the concerned departments, on the scope of coal reserves available for meeting the country's energy requirements. According to the Geological Survey of Pakistan (GSP), for example, these resources are sufficient to meet the country's energy needs for at least two centuries. Irrespective of the accuracy of these estimates, such an enormous amount of coal definitely holds great potential for bringing about a positive change in the country's energy scenario for several decades. However, despite its rich resource base, the electricity supply mix of the country has not yet seen any notable shift towards coal. All that coal has contributed thus far is a mere 150MW in the total generation capacity of the country (amounting to over 20,000MW), representing a humble share of less than 0.8 per cent. A few years ago, there was talk of a proposed 1,000MW coal-based power project in conjunction with a Chinese company. The project, however, could not materialize due to conflict over the tariff.[15]

Emerging media reports suggest that Pakistan is planning to actively seek international assistance to develop its Thar coal project for power generation. China has also expressed keen interest in the project as seen during a meeting between the prime minister of Pakistan and president of the China Coal Technology and Engineering Corporation Group (CCTEG) in October 2009.[16] With pragmatic planning the Thar coal project can ensure a prosperous energy future for the country.

It would be significantly more advantageous to utilize coal through gasification rather for direct production of electricity. Through gasification, apart from generating electricity, coal can also be used for production of gas, oil, fertilizer and other chemicals. Production of electricity through gasification also offers environmental benefits over direct production from coal. To make the most of the available potential, Pakistan would have to seek international cooperation to develop a coal gasification plant. This would need an investment of billions of dollars but estimates suggest it can bring savings to the country many times over its service life while paying itself back within a matter of four to five years. Reports suggest that while a considerable amount of work has been undertaken in terms of geological surveys of mines and assessments of the quality of the coal, further tests have to be carried out before its suitability for electricity production through gasification can be firmly established. The results of the tests conducted thus far, however, are reported to be satisfactory.[13]

Coal can offer huge strategic and economic benefits to Pakistan. It can not only help the country meet its electricity and gas needs with ease but can also make a considerable contribution towards meeting its oil requirements. By providing a large amount of indigenous and cheap energy, it would improve the energy security of the country. Coal can help Pakistan turn around from its current position of energy deficiency to energy prosperity. By contributing copious and affordable energy, it would provide vital support to industrial, commercial, and agricultural activities. In terms of financial benefit, it would substantially eliminate import of petroleum products such as oil, gas, coal, fertilizer and chemicals. It would also enable Pakistan to export a number of coal by-products such as fertilizers and chemicals. Reports suggest that coal based power generation of 1,000MW could save foreign exchange equivalent to $495.31 million annually in the form of fuel only and could create 20,000 new jobs.[17]

It is time for the policy and decision-makers to realize that it is inevitable to bring coal into the equation without any further delay. There has been much rhetoric on this issue for more than a decade now. It is time that actions must speak louder than words and that pragmatic initiatives are taken to see the project through. The conflict over right of the ownership of the Thar coal reserves between the central and provincial authorities, which has also hampered development of the project,[18] must be amicably resolved in the best interests of all stakeholders including the hapless Pakistanis.

## 7.3. NUCLEAR POWER

Nuclear power currently contributes to around 2.4 per cent of the total installed electricity generation capacity in the country. The Government of Pakistan in its Medium Term Development Framework (2005–2010) has planned to increase nuclear capacity from 462MW at present to 8,862MW by 2030 as highlighted in Table 7.7.[19,20] Globally nuclear power, however, is under considerable pressure for the following reasons:

- *Cost*—Nuclear power suffers from the fact that plants are usually built with varying designs. Customized designs result in high capital costs, driving up the cost of electricity. Costs of decommissioning aged nuclear reactors could also make nuclear power an expensive option.
- *Radioactive waste*—Nuclear power has serious environmental concerns. Radioactive gases produced during the operation of nuclear power plants need to be contained. Permanent storage of spent radioactive fuel is the most crucial concern to which so far there has not been a universally accepted solution.
- *Safety*—Safety of nuclear power plants is another critical issue. In the backdrop of the typical radioactive nature of involved materials, it is of the utmost importance to ensure safety of operations so as to avoid accidents.
- *Proliferation of weapons material*—For wider acceptability and growth of nuclear power, it is vital to prevent the proliferation of material that could be diverted for use in nuclear weapons.

**Table 7.7: Power generation capacity addition plan of Pakistan in MW**

|  | Nuclear | Hydro | Coal | Renew-able | Oil | Gas | Net addition | Total |
|---|---|---|---|---|---|---|---|---|
| Existing (2005) | 462 | 6460 | 160 | 180 | 6400 | 5940 |  | 19540 |
| Addition |  |  |  |  |  |  |  |  |
| 2010 | – | 1,260 | 900 | 700 | 160 | 4,860 | 7,880 | 27,420 |
| 2015 | 900 | 7,570 | 3,000 | 800 | 300 | 7,550 | 20,120 | 47,540 |
| 2020 | 1,500 | 4,700 | 4,200 | 1,470 | 300 | 12,560 | 24,730 | 72,270 |
| 2025 | 2,000 | 5,600 | 5,400 | 2,700 | 300 | 22,490 | 38,490 | 110,760 |
| 2030 | 4,000 | 7,070 | 6,250 | 3,850 | 300 | 30,360 | 51,830 | 162,590 |
| Total | 8,862 | 32,660 | 19,910 | 9,700 | 7,760 | 83,760 | 162,590 |  |

Despite these challenges the GOP has plans to develop nuclear power in an exponential manner in future. Increased access to nuclear power technology would remain a sensitive issue for Pakistan for a number of other reasons apart from the aforementioned. The general perception is that several countries including the United States, Israel, and India do not appreciate Pakistran holding nuclear technology. It is Pakistan's capability to develop nuclear bombs which is of prime concern for these countries. At least three senior security officials who requested to remain anonymous have also expressed their apprehensions on similar lines. There are also growing apprehensions that the turbulent geo-political situation in the region in general and in the country in particular is part of a greater international agenda to deprive Pakistan of nuclear technology.[21] It is, therefore, obvious that in order to achieve the set nuclear power targets to any reasonable level, Pakistan would need to put a great deal of effort in terms of pragmatic geo-political manoeuvring and resistance against international pressures. The country would also need to overcome its internal geo-political and economic problems as quickly as possible. Even if the set targets are successfully met, the contribution made by nuclear power in the total supply mix is going to remain modest.

## 7.4. Hydropower

Hydropower is one of the most efficient and economical forms of energy. It is also one of the most ancient forms of energy that mankind used on a mass scale. Mechanical use of hydropower, for example, was started thousands of years ago by the Egyptians and Greeks for irrigation and milling of grain. Its use for production of electricity dates back to the nineteenth century—on 30 September 1882, the world's first hydroelectric power plant began operation in Appleton, Wisconsin (USA).[22] Hydropower is renewable, abundant, environment friendly and technically mature. It is also regarded as the most economical form of electricity.

Hydroelectric power stations are classified as the most efficient power plants as they can have an operational efficiency of up to 90 per cent. Hydropower can be used in an extremely diverse range of sizes and designs—generation capacity can range from a few watts to giggawatts (GW). Table 7.8 presents classification of hydropower projects with regard to their size. With an average life span of 50 to 100 years, hydropower projects are long-term investments that can easily be upgraded to take advantage of the latest technologies. Hydropower has the advantage of having long viability and very low operation and maintenance costs—it has the lowest operating cost and the longest plant life compared with other large-scale power generation technologies.[23] Water from rivers is a domestic resource that is not subject to fluctuations in fuel prices; therefore, hydropower fosters energy independence and energy security.

**Table 7.8: Classification of hydropower capacity in terms of size**

| Type | Size | Applications |
|------|------|--------------|
| Large | >100MW | Feeding large electricity grids |
| Medium | 15–100MW | Feeding a grid |
| Small | 1–15MW | Feeding into grid |
| Mini | 100kW–1MW | Stand alone schemes or feeding into grid |
| Micro | 5kW–100kW | Provide power to small community or rural industry in remote areas |
| Pico | < 5kW | |

Hydropower is a major contributor to world energy supplies. With a gross installed capacity of 740GW, it provides nearly 17 per cent of the world's total electricity demands and around 90 per cent of the total electricity produced from renewable resources.[24] There are many countries in the world where hydropower plays a predominant role in the electricity supply mix. In more than twenty countries it produces over 90 per cent of the electricity generated.[25] Norway, for example, produces 99 per cent of its electricity from hydropower while Brazil produces 92 per cent, Iceland 83 per cent, Austria 67 per cent and Canada 70 per cent.[26] It is also worth noting that the biggest individual power generation systems are hydropower-based. Itaipu Dam, for example, is the world's second largest power generating plant that is housed on the Parana River between Brazil and Paraguay. Its generation capacity is 12.6GW that is supported by 1,350 sq km of reservoir area. Working at a load factor of up to 85 per cent, it annually generates around 100 billionKWh of electricity that meets 95 per cent of Paraguay's and 25 per cent of Brazil's total power requirements.[27] China's Three Gorges Dam, which became operational in 2008, is the world's largest hydropower project. It is also regarded as the largest power plant on Earth. From the total installed capacity of 18.2GW, in 2009 it produced around 84.68 billion terawatt hours (TWh) of electricity.

### 7.4.1 Strategic Importance of Hydropower

Hydropower is one of the most important sources of energy Pakistan can count on. For the country, hydropower is by far the most economical source of electricity. According to WAPDA, in 2005–06, the average annual electricity production cost from hydropower was less than 8 per cent of that from thermal power—the respective figures from the two sources stood at Rs0.3/kWh and 3.8/kWh as indicated in Table 7.9.[28,29] The 2008 statistics also suggest that hydropower is an extremely cheap option to produce electricity as compared to other forms of fossil fuels as highlighted in Figure 7.3.[30]

**Table 7.9: Electricity generation cost in 2005-06, by fuel type**

| Energy Source | Cost/kWh | |
|---|---|---|
| | Rupees | US cents* |
| Hydro | 0.3 | 0.5 |
| Thermal | 3.8 | 6.3 |
| Nuclear | 2.7 | 4.5 |

*2006 exchange rate, Rupees 60 = 1$

Despite such a distinctive financial edge over other forms of electricity sources, not enough has been done to sufficiently tap the available hydropower potential in Pakistan. Over the last three decades, a sluggish approach towards orchestration of large-scale dams has caused the share of hydropower to plunge in the national electricity supply mix—its contribution in the total electricity generation mix has decreased from 60 per cent in 1962–63 to less than 33 per cent in 2008–09.[31] The consequent vacuum has been filled by thermal power that now contributes to nearly 65 per cent of the total installed capacity of the country.

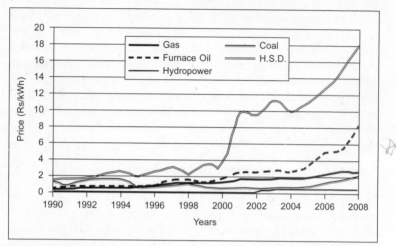

Figure 7.3: Comparison of electricity prices from hydropower and thermal power plants

Here it is vital to understand that hydropower is an indigenous and renewable resource while oil (a key player in thermal power generation) is by and large a foreign one since Pakistan meets more than 85 per cent of its oil demands through imports.[4] This categorical shift from hydropower to fossil fuels thus implies that the country has become substantially dependent upon imports to meet its energy requirements. In other words, it has seriously compromised on its energy security. In the wake of the ongoing geo-political and military conflicts in the world, especially in and around South Asia, the dependency upon foreign energy resources is not a comfortable situation to be in.

Another downside of the shift from hydropower to fossil fuels is the enormous fiscal burden. Reports suggest that within a matter of four years, between 2004 and 2008, due to the steep rise in international oil prices the petroleum import bill has increased by nearly 300 per cent—from around $3 billion to $11.5 billion in the respective years.[29,32]

Hydropower also has a strategic significance for the country. At the time of the partition of the British India, no arrangements were made to appropriately distribute the water resources between Pakistan and India. The situation with Pakistan was a lot more delicate compared to India since the former was to get almost all of its water from the rivers flowing through the latter as highlighted in Figure 7.4.[34]

The vague situation over water resources resulted in an Indo-Pak water dispute as India without any intimation disconnected the supply of water to the canals in Pakistan on 1 April 1948. It was a serious blow to Pakistan whose food and agriculture needs mostly relied on the fertile areas that were directly being affected by the Indian act.[33] Upon Pakistan's protest and negotiations with India, the supply of water was restored after a couple of months. The situation between the two countries over the issue, however, remained turbulent until a settlement was made in the form of the Indus Water Treaty in 1960.

From the outset of the Treaty, Pakistan embarked on an impressive hydro-base development programme. In principle, it was to be of dual purpose: to store water for irrigation and to generate power. Consequently,

Figure 7.4: Indus River System. Courtesy STRATFOR.com

around 76 per cent of the existing hydropower generation capacity sits on the subsequently developed water reservoirs. Pakistan aims to develop new hydro projects with the same rationale, to generate power as well as to maximize availability of irrigation water.

The future of hydro projects, however, depends upon the secure supply of water from the rivers flowing through the Eastern boarders. Safeguarding the supply of this water is a matter of life or death for the agricultural base of the country and is of no less importance for the sustainability of the power sector and the national economy. Every drop of water from the three Western rivers—Indus, Jhelum and Chenab—as assigned to Pakistan under the Indus Water Treaty, needs to be acquired without any interference from India. Unconditional access to this water is a matter of survival for the country. In order to stop India from capturing this water, as it has been doing for many years, Pakistan needs to take an unyielding stance and must employ every possible means, diplomatic or otherwise. The action must be meaningful and without any further delay.

Water storage capacity also needs to be improved so that it could be effectively capitalized for power generation and irrigation. It can be made feasible only by building as many dams as possible. Currently, Pakistan, at most, can store water for only 30 days. Comparatively other countries have built dams to store water to meet their requirements for over a year. Pakistan in recent years has significantly and repeatedly suffered from its less than satisfactory water storage capacity—often compromises have been made both upon the agricultural and power sector requirements resulting in enormous implications not only for the concerned sectors but also for the national economy. It is therefore extremely crucial for the country to go for the development of large as well as small dams to optimize its water storage capacity. More dams are imperative not only for the sustainability of the energy and agriculture sectors but for the national development. Another subsidiary yet vital benefit dams would offer is the provision of a shield against the impacts of natural calamites like drought and flooding.

## 7.4.2 THE WAY AHEAD

Estimates suggest that Pakistan's total identified potential for hydropower is around 42GW out of which only 15 per cent, amounting to nearly 6.4GW, has been exploited so far. In order to address the energy challenges facing the country and to ensure a sustainable energy future multi-fold exploitation of hydropower is imperative. There are at least seven potential hydropower projects with capacity in multi-giggawatts (GW). These include Bhasha (4,500MW), Bunji (7,100MW), Dasu (4,320MW), Kalabagh (3,600), Kohala (1,100MW), Patan (2,800MW) and Thakot (2,800MW). Apart from these, there are a number of other projects with capacity in hundreds of megawatts such as Neelam-Jhelum (950MW), Munda (750MW) and Akhori (600MW) as given in Table 7.10. Furthermore, WAPDA has also identified a number of other projects worth a collective capacity of more than 2,400MW as shown in Figure 7.5.[35]

**Table 7.10: Estimated installed and generation capacity of some of the identified projects**

| Project | Installed capacity (MW) | Generation capacity (GWh) |
|---|---|---|
| Bunji | 7,100 | 24,088 |
| Bhasha | 4,500 | 18,000 |
| Dasu | 4,320 | 21,300 |
| Kalabagh | 3,600 | 11,400 |
| Thakot | 2,800 | 15,200 |
| Patan | 2,800 | 14,095 |
| Kohala | 1,100 | 4,800 |
| Neelum Jhelum | 969 | 5,150 |
| Munda | 740 | 2,407 |
| Akhori | 600 | 2,155 |
| Dubar Khwar | 130 | 595 |
| Allai Khwar | 121 | 463 |
| Golen Gol | 106 | 436 |
| Khan Khwar | 72 | 306 |

Notwithstanding initial work in the form of feasibility or pre-feasibility reports which was undertaken on almost all of these potential projects years (and in some cases decades) ago, construction of any of these is yet to be initiated. Apart from these major reservoir-based projects there are also a number of potential small to medium scale run-of-river sites. From the rivers and richly available streams, the Northern Areas have a considerable potential for pico to small scale projects—estimates suggest that up to 350MW of power projects can be materialised in this fashion.[36] Small water streams can be locally and even privately capitalised to set up pico to micro level projects that can generate electricity for a home, set of homes or a whole village. Across the world, in areas not connected to

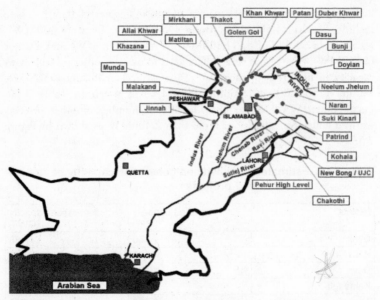

Figure 7.5: Identified sites for hydropower generation

national grid, it is a common and cost effective practice to have private pico-sized hydropower projects to generate electricity. Photograph 7.1, for example, shows a private 60W turbine that meets electricity needs of a remote home in Scotland.

The energy problems facing the country cannot be addressed without fully utilizing its hydropower potential. Pakistan needs to learn lessons from the ongoing hydropower development across the world particularly in the neighbouring countries. Every potential project should be capitalized upon. To ensure the development of hydropower, meaningful efforts, however, need to be made to safeguard the country's water resources flowing from Eastern borders. It is equally vital that the political differences of the Kalabagh be resolved so that such an important and advantageous project can be streamlined for the wider benefit of the country.

Figure 7.6: A pico-level hydropower system in the Scottish
Highlands

## 7.5. SOLAR ENERGY

### 7.5.1 SUN: THE ULTIMATE SOURCE OF ENERGY

The sun is a source of energy for the earth. It is the earth's tilt towards
the sun that creates the seasons. Through photosynthesis and
biodegradation the sun helps plants to grow and ecosystems to complete
their natural cycles. The sun is a huge ball-shaped cloud of hot gases held
together by gravity. It is made up mostly of hydrogen and helium. Solar
energy is created deep within the core of the sun. Extremely intense
conditions—temperatures of over 15 million Celsius and pressure of
nearly 250 billion atmospheres—lead to a nuclear fusion reaction in
which pairs of hydrogen nuclei are fused into helium nuclei. Around 700
million tons of hydrogen is converted every second to generate about 695

million tons of helium and 5 million tons of energy in the form of gamma rays.[37]

The sun has been consistently emitting energy for nearly five billion years and is expected to continue doing so for another five billion years. It is 146 million km from earth due to which only a small fraction of solar radiation reaches the planet. In spite of this, the daily average of the solar energy available to the planet is well over the total amount its 6.5 billion inhabitants would consume in twenty-five years.

The sun also sources several other forms of energy on the planet. Wind power, for example, is a function of the sun's impact on atmospheric movement as it creates wind patterns. It is estimated that around 1 to 2 per cent of the solar energy reaching the earth is converted into wind energy.[38] The temperature differences around the globe caused by the sun make the wind travel. The sun heats the regions of the earth nearest to it, around the equator, more than the rest of the world. Because hot air is lighter than cold air, this air rises and spreads from the equator to the north and south. This system is called the trade wind system and is one of the most important of the global wind systems. Hydropower is also a function of solar energy—the sun is the prime influence on the natural water cycle that constitutes of evaporation of water from oceans, rivers and lakes, creation of rain and snow and melting of ice that makes rivers flow into oceans and lakes. The sun also plays a major role in the development of tidal power. Tides occur twice a day and are caused by the gravitational effect of the moon and the sun on the world's oceans. Similarly, bioenergy, the extract of biomass, is also a derivative of solar energy. Biomass is an organic material that is available on a renewable basis. Plants absorb the sun's energy in photosynthesis. In this process, the sun's energy is converted into and stored as chemical energy in the form of a sugar. The quantity of sugar molecules increases in green plants during photosynthesis in the presence of sunlight. Fossil fuels also owe their creation millions of years ago to solar energy. The energy stored in fossil fuels came originally from the sun and was captured by plants through photosynthesis.

## 7.5.2 TYPES OF SOLAR ENERGY TECHNOLOGIES

Solar energy is one of the most promising renewable resources. It is abundant in nature and is acknowledged to be vital and plentiful enough to meet many times the entire world's energy demand as shown in Figure 7.7. Solar energy has the potential to play a very important role not only

in providing most of the heating, cooling, and electricity needs of the
world, but also to solve global environmental problems. Solar energy can
be exploited through solar thermal and solar photovoltaic (PV) routes for
various applications. While the solar PV technology enables direct
conversion of sunlight into electricity through semiconductor devices
called solar cells, solar thermal technologies utilize the heat energy from
the sun for a wide range of purposes.

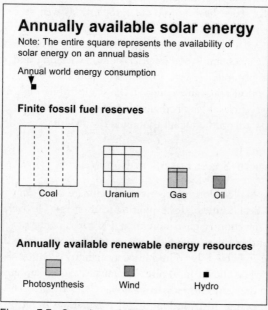

Figure 7.7: Overview of flobal energy demands and
potential of various energy resources

Solar photovoltaic can produce power at the point of demand in both
rural and urban areas. Solar PV electricity is an equally significant energy
option for developed and developing countries. Because of the cost of
transmission lines and the difficulty of transporting fuel to remote areas,
developing countries are increasingly turning to solar energy as a cost-
effective way to supply electricity. With a fifth of the world's population
still without electricity, most of whom live in developing countries usage
of solar PV modules is rapidly increasing as the demand for electricity
spreads throughout the world. Photovoltaic cells have been in use in
spacecraft since the 1950s. However, with the energy crisis of the early

1970s, a steadily growing terrestrial industry has developed. Initially, it supplied PV cells mainly for remote area applications where conventional electricity is expensive. Nonetheless, the industry is now in an explosive period of growth where the subsidized urban-residential use of photovoltaics is providing the main market. The global PV industry has grown at a phenomenal rate since 1995.

Solar thermal technologies are quite diverse in terms of their operational characteristics and applications—they include fairly simple technologies such as solar space heating and solar cooking as well as complex and sophisticated ones like solar air conditioning and solar thermal power generation. Solar thermal technologies have also a broad bandwidth in terms of their economic standing. Solar water heating and solar space heating, for example, are very cost effective and are regarded among the most economical renewable energy technologies while high temperature technologies such as solar thermal power generation and solar air conditioning are on the higher economic bandwidth.

### 7.5.3 Scope of Solar Energy in Pakistan

The geographic location, topography and climate conditions of Pakistan make it an ideal candidate for exploiting solar energy. On average, almost all parts of the country have more than 300 sunshine days in a year. The average monthly solar irradiation at various locations across the country is presented in Table 7.1.[39] The annual availability of 1,900–2,200KWh/m² of energy, as shown in Figure 7.8, ranks Pakistan amongst the rich countries in the world in terms of solar energy potential.[40] The figure also indicates that the distribution of solar radiation is fairly consistent throughout the country. The available level of solar radiation makes the climatic conditions of Pakistan highly favourable for solar energy applications such as solar photovoltaic, solar thermal power, solar water heating, solar desalination, solar crop drying and solar cooking.

**Table 7.11: Average monthly irradiation values for Pakistan, kWh/m² day**

| Month | Karachi | Quetta | Multan | Lahore | Islamabad | Peshawar |
|---|---|---|---|---|---|---|
| January | 131.8 | 113.7 | 105.1 | 90.4 | 87.0 | 90.4 |
| February | 131.3 | 128.9 | 117.6 | 111.2 | 109.6 | 115.2 |
| March | 173.9 | 162.8 | 155.0 | 151.6 | 133.5 | 149.8 |
| April | 185.0 | 201.7 | 187.5 | 180.0 | 183.3 | 179.2 |
| May | 198.1 | 235.9 | 203.2 | 198.9 | 209.3 | 214.4 |
| June | 187.5 | 238.3 | 190.0 | 196.7 | 194.2 | 220.8 |
| July | 150.7 | 214.4 | 186.0 | 162.8 | 181.7 | 199.8 |
| August | 144.7 | 207.5 | 184.3 | 167.9 | 176.5 | 180.0 |
| September | 250.8 | 192.5 | 168.3 | 165.0 | 162.5 | 160.0 |
| October | 162.8 | 169.6 | 143.8 | 137.8 | 135.2 | 137.8 |
| November | 130.8 | 127.5 | 116.7 | 103.3 | 96.7 | 135.8 |
| December | 121.4 | 105.9 | 95.6 | 87.8 | 69.8 | 90.4 |

### 7.5.3.1 Solar Photovoltaic

Access to electricity remains one of the most important developmental issues for a substantial proportion of the population in Pakistan. The issue mainly exists in villages and remote areas across the country where the national grid has limited penetration. In some cases, local socio-cultural trends make it virtually impractical to extend the grid to every inhabitant.

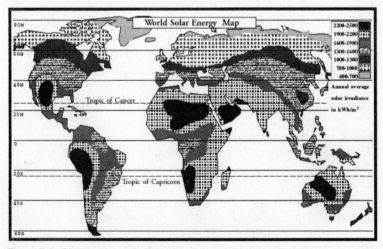

Figure 7.8: Global solar radiation map of the world

For example, in rural areas of Balochistan, NWFP, Cholistan and Thar, a substantial proportion of the population lives in small villages (consisting of a few houses). These villages (or pockets of houses) are widely scattered and also are many miles away from the nearest point of grid. Extension of electric grid for miles to provide electricity to a few homes is simply financially impractical for a developing country like Pakistan.

Solar photovoltaic (PV) can be a very useful technology to deliver electricity in these cases. Off-grid or stand-alone PV systems produce power independently of the utility grid. It is worth noting that the typical remote nature of the scattered population makes the technology the by default choice—in many cases solar photovoltaic would become the most value-engineered and cost effective solution to have electricity. At some off-grid locations, as near as one-quarter mile from the power lines, stand-alone PV systems can be more cost effective than extending power lines. Direct-coupled systems need no electrical storage because they operate only during daylight hours, but most systems rely on battery storage so that energy produced during the day can be used at night. Some systems, called hybrid systems, combine solar power with additional power sources, such as wind or diesel. Communal use of stand-alone PV systems would be a very viable option in many areas. For the mentioned, small remote villages, solar PV systems can be effectively employed to deliver electricity to meet fundamental needs; a central water pump and TV; and a set of 2–3 energy saver lights and a fan for each home. Solar home systems similar to the ones being developed by Grameen Shakti in Bangladesh, as discussed in section 5.4.2.2.1, also possess significant prospects both in urban and rural areas across the country.

Solar PV systems can make a notable contribution in overcoming Pakistan's electricity issues. However, the government has thus far tended to neglect the technology.

### 7.5.3.2 Solar Water Heating

Solar water heating, one of the oldest and the most successful applications of solar energy, utilizes solar energy to heat water in a cost effective way and also without producing any harmful emissions into the environment. Solar water heating, besides its domestic role, has a wide array of applications within the industrial sector (e.g., food and beverages, processing, and textile industries) and the commercial sector (e.g., swimming pools, laundries, hotels, and restaurants). In many parts of the world, water heating accounts for as much as 15 to 25 per cent of the total energy consumed in the domestic sector. In the United States and United Kingdom, for example, water heating, respectively, consumes 18 per cent and 23 per cent of the domestic energy. Estimates suggest that nearly 10 per cent of the total primary energy in Pakistan is consumed in water heating.[41]

A solar water heating system essentially consists of a collector and a water storage tank. The collector absorbs solar radiation and transfers it to the water stored in the tank. Residential and commercial applications often require hot water that is at a temperature of less than 60°C. In industry the required hot water temperature, however, could vary significantly depending upon the type of activity especially within the textile sector where it often needs to be near the boiling level. Modern solar water heaters can accomplish these temperatures. However, taking into account various factors such as unpredictable weather conditions (rain or overcast sky) and a solar heating system's size limitation in case of high demand, solar water heaters require a conventional heating system as a backup. A typical domestic solar water heating system can provide up to two-thirds of the total hot water requirements cutting down on fossil-fuel energy costs and also reducing the associated environmental impacts.

Solar water heating is a technically mature and economically viable technology even for a developing country like Pakistan. The economic payback period of a solar water heating system, like other renewable technologies, is a function of various factors such as system efficiency, local weather conditions (i.e. the level of solar irradiance available), and the price of conventional energy being displaced by it. The initial cost of a solar water heater is higher than the conventional water heating options. A solar water heater because of its almost zero running cost, is much more economical over the lifetime of the system than heating water with electricity, fuel oil, propane or natural gas. Solar water heating under Pakistan's climatic condition can have a payback period of less than three years with a service life of over twenty years.

With the fact that the technology is simple, and easy to manufacture, install and bring into operation there is enormous potential for solar water heating in Pakistan. For industries the benefits of adopting solar water heating technology are manifold. Firstly, in the wake of the ongoing electricity and gas crises, it will provide relief in terms of lesser reliance on already deficient energy resources. Secondly, it will be economically cheaper, and thirdly, it will cut down on the environmental loads associated with water heating.

### 7.5.3.2.1 Solar Water Heating in the Textile Sector

The textile industry is the backbone of Pakistan's economy. Besides making a gigantic contribution of over 60 per cent to the total exports of the country, it also has a share of around 40 per cent in the country's employment pool. Pakistan is amongst the most prominent cotton producing countries in the world. The availability of local cotton has led to a well established textile sector in the country. A large proportion of its cotton products goes into export. Being a successful candidate in the international market, the Pakistani textile industry is continuously seeking modern and high-tech facilities to improve the quality of its products. One of the biggest challenges the textile industry is facing today is how to cut down its environmental burdens to cope with the international standards on the issue.

To sustain its leading role in export markets, the national textile sector has to comply with international environmental protocols. Pakistan's textile exports face tough challenges in the coming years unless focused measures are adopted to address concerns relating to the environment. In fossil fuel-run textile units, toxic emissions into the air and ground water are the major concerns. It is, therefore, very important for the textile industry to adopt environmentally efficient technologies to address any future challenges. At present there are hardly any textile units in the country that have addressed the issue in a sustainable fashion.

Like many other industrial sectors, the textile industry requires a continuous supply of water. One of the major applications of water in the textile industry is in the dyeing process. Water is required not only at normal temperature but also at boiling point. Heating water to such a high temperature makes up a major chunk of the total energy being consumed in a textile unit. Water heating can account for as much as 65 per cent of the total energy used during processes such as dyeing, finishing, drying, and curing. Water if heated through conventional energy sources has environmental impacts in the form of greenhouse gases and other toxic elements released both in air and water. At present almost every major textile group is fitted with its own power plant. These internal power plants are normally run by furnace oil or gas. In either case this is environmentally an expensive choice. Solar water heating is an ideal candidate to partially replace the presently employed water heating technologies. Typical solar water heaters can deliver hot water up to a temperature of 80°C. In cases where hot water is required at near boiling

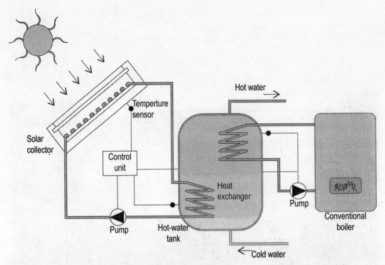

Figure 7.9: Solar water heater coupled with conventional back-up system

temperatures, solar water heaters can be coupled with conventional systems as shown in Figure 7.9.[42]

### 7.5.3.2.2 Solar Water Heating's Wake-up Call for Pakistan

Solar water heating is one of the fastest growing renewable energy technologies. Since 2002 it has been experiencing rapid growth across the world including Asia, the European Union, and North America. Despite the global economic downturn, the international market for solar water heating grew at a remarkable pace in 2008. Statistics suggest that in China, where almost 75 per cent of the world's total capacity exists, the solar water heating market during this year grew by 28 per cent. With an annual addition of 23.4 million square meter of collector area, China's solar water heaters have covered around 108 million square meters of area. In 2008, the European Union's solar water heating market, on the other hand, jumped by 60 per cent.[42,43]

An across the board passiveness in Pakistan on solar water heating is a matter of utmost frustration for concerned circles. It is also one of those vital technologies that AEDB overlooked. Pakistan has not yet taken any notable initiative on it while other countries with a comparatively far less solar potential are benefiting significantly from

Figure 7.10: Solar water heating facility in Denmark with 8000m² collector area

this technology. Figure 7.10, for example, shows a large solar water heating facility in Denmark which is being used to supply hot water for a district heating system. This facility with collector area of 8000m² has offered a payback period of five to six years. On 19 August 2008, when the author visited this site, under overcast conditions and at an ambient temperature of 15°C, the controls were showing output from the solar water heaters at a temperature of 71°C. In Pakistan, that annually receives around three times more solar radiation compared to Denmark, this facility would have offered a much better output and a payback period of around two years.

On top of ensuring wider application of solar water heating, it is also essential to develop the technology locally. Presently, in Pakistan, imported vacuum tube solar water heaters are being marketed. The downsides of this design of solar water heater are its fragility, high cost and import dependency. Compared to that, the aforementioned model being used in Denmark is much more economical, durable and robust and is regarded as one of the best solar water heating designs in the world. Compared to vacuum tube, in terms of technology, this model is not so complicated or expensive to develop locally. Figure 7.11 shows the factory where the solar water heaters shown in Figure 7.10 were produced. The fact that absolutely world-class solar water heaters are being produced in such a

Figure 7.11: Solar water heater manufacturing factory in Denmark

humble setup offers some good food for thought to concerned Pakistani authorities, investors and industrialists. The meaningful exploitation of solar water heating can considerably help the country cut its reliance on  imported and expensive fossil fuels. Without any further delay Pakistan should take solar water heating on board as it offers a win-win situation.

### 7.5.3.3 Solar Thermal Power

Solar thermal power systems produce electricity by capturing the heat from solar radiation. Direct solar radiation can be concentrated and collected by a range of concentrating solar power technologies to provide medium- to high-temperature heat. This heat then operates a conventional power cycle—for example, through a steam turbine or a Stirling engine to generate electricity. Parabolic trough power plant is the most prominent type of solar thermal power plant technology with existing commercial operating systems. The parabolic trough systems consist of large curved mirrors or troughs that concentrate sunlight by a factor of 80 or more onto thermally efficient receiver tubes placed in the trough's focal line. A thermal transfer fluid, such as synthetic thermal oil, is circulated in the

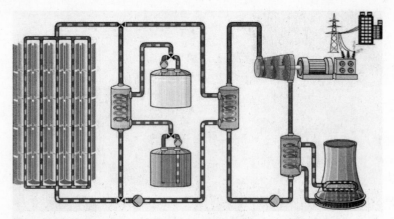

Figure 7.12: External view of the solar water heating manufacturing unit

tubes at focal length. Heated to approximately 400°C by the sun's concentrated rays, this oil is then pumped through a series of heat exchangers to produce superheated steam.[45] The steam is used to produce electrical energy in a conventional steam turbine generator, which can either be part of a conventional steam cycle or integrated into a combined steam and gas turbine cycle, as shown in Figure 7.12.[46] Solar thermal power plants can be designed for solar-only or hybrid operation, where some fossil fuel is used in case of lower radiation intensity to secure reliable peak-load supply.

The solar thermal power market has experienced a relative state of stagnancy since the early 1990s. However, in the backdrop of the global search for sustainable energy solutions new opportunities are now opening up for solar thermal power. Both national and international initiatives are supporting the technology, encouraging commercialization of production. Recently, commercial plans in Spain and the United States have led to a resurgence of interest, technology evolution, and potential investment. Even a number of developing countries, including Morocco, India, Egypt, and Mexico have also planned projects with multilateral assistance. Currently, in these countries, seven solar thermal projects of over 17,00MW of collective capacity are in the pipeline.

Though, of present, solar thermal power is a relatively expensive technology compared to conventional forms of electricity generation systems, the fact that the price of solar thermal technology is reducing while that of the electricity generated from conventional means is rapidly surging implies that in the near future solar thermal power would be a financially viable option. A scenario of what could be achieved by the year 2025, as prepared by Greenpeace International, the European Solar Thermal Industry Association, and International Energy Agency (IEA) Solar PACES projects suggests that by 2025, the total installed capacity of solar thermal power around the world will reach over 36,000MW. It is also projected that by 2040 more than 5 per cent of the world's electricity demand may be satisfied by solar thermal power.[45]

Deserts are rich in solar energy and have a great role to play in the provision of sustainable energy in future. The European Union is working on a collaboration programme with a number of countries from the Middle East and North Africa (MENA) to establish large scale concentrated solar thermal power plants in the MENA region to supply electricity to Europe. Under the DESERTEC initiative of the EU-MENA (European Union-Middle East and North Africa), by 2050, annually 700 TWh of electricity, generated at 20 different locations from within MENA will be transported to the main centres of demand in Europe. This will contribute to around 15 per cent of Europe's electricity needs.[47]

Pakistan also has a huge potential to generate electricity from its deserts. Pakistan should give serious consideration to this vital technology that can play a major role in meeting the country's future energy demands. It is important to start doing the necessary homework without any further delay. For example, like many other countries, establishing a solar thermal power project, even on a relatively small-scale (i.e. 10–50MW), within the next few years would go a long way in acquiring pertinent technical expertise. It is crucial that Pakistan is technically and financially ready to fully exploit the technology as it becomes financially viable over the next few years.

## 7.5.4 RECENT SOLAR ENERGY INITIATIVES AND A NEED FOR PRAGMATISM

In the backdrop of the intense energy crisis, media reports over the last couple of years have repeatedly suggested that the government is considering utilizing solar energy to run tube wells/water pumps to help the agricultural sector that has been badly affected by the ongoing load-shedding. In January 2010, the Punjab Government also announced its plans for solar water pumps. In this regadrd a formal understanding has been developed with a German company under which initially a few systems would be installed and after a trial period the number of installed systems would be extended to 800,000.

Each solar water pump costs hundreds of thousand of rupees. Even a few thousands solar water pumps would mean an investment of billions of Rupees. Obviously, such initiatives are commendable as long as the pros and cons are carefully weighed. As a matter of fact, all of the renewable energy programmes initiated in the public sector since the 1970s, have been nothing but utterly disappointing and have failed. With such an unenviable track record, one can't help but wonder if lessons have been learnt from the past mistakes.

The authorities must do their homework diligently before embarking on such a demanding project. They have to ask themselves some tough questions, for example:

- Have they looked into the reasons behind the failure of past attempts?
- Have they undertaken a cost and value study of the solar water pumps to be installed?
- Given the insecure environments of villages where tribal and other disputes rage, have they worked out a security plan for the pumps?
- Have they worked out a maintenance programme for the pumps?
- Have they worked out a customer education programme?

If the concerned authorities have not taken care of these issues in a robust and meaningful fashion they should do so immediately, otherwise it is going to be another disaster resulting in the wastage of large sums of public money.

There is also a great need for product standardization and regulation at all level. Since 2008, a large number of companies have been set up in Pakistan to take up the renewable energy business. The major emphasis has been on the marketing of various types of solar energy technologies that are mainly being imported from China. It is a promising and a much needed trend. The downside here, however, has been the fact that most of the people running these business are non-technical and have little understanding of the technologies they are dealing with whatsoever. Consequently, renewable technologies, to a considerable extent, are in the hands of cowboys, as was the case with AEDB. The author has come across the work of such companies that are official consultants to the Government of Pakistan and yet lack the fundamental understanding of the renewable technologies they are marketing.

It is important that the concerned government departments set their directions right and equip themselves with qualified and competent people. They should then regulate the business of renewable energy by developing and implementing robust quality controls and standards. In this regard, dedicated workshops and short courses should also be arranged to train the entrepreneurs, engineers and technicians, and sales and marketing personnel. The renewable energy sector should be protected from the quacks and adventurous businessmen; otherwise the confidence of the people in renewable technologies may receive a severe jolt.

## 7.6. BIOMASS

Biomass is an organic material that is available on a renewable basis. Biomass is derived from a wide range of sources including dedicated energy crops and trees, food and feed crops, agricultural crop wastes and residues, wood wastes and residues, aquatic plants, animal wastes, municipal wastes, and other waste materials. Biomass is one of the oldest forms of energy available to mankind. The energy derived from biomass is called bioenergy. As of 2008, biomass contributes to nearly 11 per cent of the global primary energy supplies. The role of biomass is even more crucial in the developing world—it respectively provides 44 per cent and 21 per cent of the total primary energy requirements in Asia and Africa. Biomass energy extraction procedures are broadly classified into two types: thermal conversion (i.e. combustion, gasification and pyrolysis) and biochemical conversion (i.e. anaerobic digestion, fermentation and transesterification).

### 7.6.1 TRADITIONAL ROLE OF BIOMASS

Biomass plays an important role in the energy mix of Pakistan, contributing to almost 35 per cent of the total primary energy requirements. The country's large agricultural and livestock sector produces plentiful biomass in the form of firewood, crop residues and animal waste, such as bagasse, rice husk, and dung, much of which is currently collected and used outside the commercial economy as unprocessed fuel for cooking and household heating. Table 7.12 provides an estimated consumption breakdown of various non-commercial biomass resources. Wood provides an important source of energy, particularly in rural areas where the majority of households use it for cooking. It is also vital for space heating in certain areas. In Pakistan wood is primarily a non-commercial fuel source but it is also sold on the market. Sugar mills use bagasse for cogeneration purposes and recently have been allowed to sell surplus power to the grid up to a combined limit of 700MW.[48] Apart from this, biomass-based fuels have not managed to break into the commercial market.

**Table 7.12: Non-commercial biomass energy consumption by fuel type**

| Fuel type | Share (%) |
|---|---|
| Firewood | 54.2 |
| Bagasse | 16.5 |
| Dung cakes | 15.5 |
| Cotton stick/rice husk | 6.4 |
| Shrubs | 5.6 |
| Sawdust | 1.3 |
| Charcoal | 0.3 |
| Weeds | 0.3 |
| Tobacco sticks | 0.1 |

## 7.6.2 BIOGAS

Animal, human, and vegetable waste can be converted into biogas to provide both a decentralized electricity source and a fuel for cooking, heating, and lighting. It is cleaner and healthier for cooking than dung cakes, and the energy yield from biogas is greater than that obtained from burning the original dung as shown in Table 7.13. Biogas plants are popular across the world—estimates suggest that around 16 million households rely on biogas plants for cooking and lighting needs.[49] In Pakistan too, biogas pilot projects have been launched in the past. During the 1970s, for example, nearly 4,000 family and community based biogas digesters were constructed to help villagers utilize dung more efficiently.[50] However, after a promising start the use of these digesters has almost ceased due to a number of factors such as lack of customer training, absence of a maintenance plan, socio-economic trends, and withdrawal of external subsidies. Ironically, only a small fraction of the installed biogas plants are currently in operation. It is important to promote biogas systems so that the precious biomass resource could be utilised in a more efficient and productive manner. Biogas systems are cheap to install and are efficient and versatile in application. They can considerably help address energy problems at the micro-level.

In addition, municipal solid waste produced by a large urban population is presently openly dumped, which could instead be disposed of in proper landfill sites or incinerated to produce biogas (60–80 per cent of which consists of methane) or electricity. Despite repeated claims by pertinent authorities in recent years, there have not been any meaningful initiatives taken to capitalise this important source of energy.

**Table 7.13: Comparison of the energy content of various biomass fuels against Methane and Hydrogen**

| Fuel | Energy content (kWh/kg) |
|------|------------------------|
| Firewood | 4.9 |
| Straw | 4.17 |
| Sugar cane residues | 4.72 |
| Dung cake | 4.4 |
| Charcoal | 8.3 |
| Biogas | 11.5 |
| Bagasse (dry) | 4.5 |
| Molasses | 4.0 |
| Ethanol | 7.5 |
| Biodiesel | 9.2 |
| Methane | 15 |
| Hydrogen | 39 |

### 7.6.3 BIOFUEL

Travelling and transportation are essential features of human life. Today, societies spend huge amounts of energy on both passenger travel and freight transport. Over the last one hundred years, travelling and transportation has mainly been fuelled by oil. There are growing concerns about the long-term sustainability of oil since reserves are rapidly diminishing. Pakistan, importing over 85 per cent of its oil, urgently need to tackle the growing challenge. The way ahead is exploitation of indigenous energy resources. Biofuel is one possible candidate to supplement transportation fuel. Biofuel is the fuel derived from biomass (either in the form of living organisms or the waste they produce). Biofuel offers many advantages over conventional oil. It is a domestic resource, thereby reduces reliance on imported oil. Also, it is renewable, environment friendly, biodegradable and non-toxic. Biofuel can help Pakistan substantially cut its petrol import bill, diversify supply energy mix and increase energy security. It also exhibits great micro-economic advantages. For example, farmers can not only become self-sufficient in their energy requirements but can also earn handsome revenue by selling it in open market.

Biofuel can be broadly classified into two types: bioethanol and biodiesel. As an alternative fuel biofuel is finding superb growth in many parts of the world. In 2006, the global biofuel production rose by 28 per cent, reaching to 44 billion litres—bioethanol grew by 22 per cent and biodiesel rose by 80 per cent. On 24 February 2008, biofuel hit another landmark when a commercial flight flew between London and Amsterdam using biofuel—one of the Boeing 747 aircraft's four engines ran on fuel comprising a 20 per cent biofuel mix of coconut and babassu oil and 80 per cent of the normal jet aviation fuel.[51]

Bioethanol is used in gasoline (spark ignition) engines and is made through the fermentation process. It is mainly produced by the sugar fermentation process, although it can also be developed by the chemical process of reacting ethylene with steam. Ethanol fuel blends are usually 10 per cent ethanol and 90 per cent petrol. Modern car engines require no modifications to run on this composition. However flex-fuel vehicles can run on up to 85 per cent ethanol and 15 per cent petrol blends. Biodiesel is used in diesel (compression ignition) engines and is made through a variety of chemical processes. Most importantly it is produced through transesterification process in which glycerine is separated from the biomass oil to deliver biodiesel. Biodiesel can easily be made from any fat (i.e. animal fat), tree/crop oil or vegetable oil (i.e. soy, canola, sunflower, castor and palm) or even a common waste product such as used cooking oil.

In recent years, Pakistan took initiatives to promote biofuel. The emphasis, however, has been on bioethanol coming from molasses, a by-product of sugar with the Pakistan Sugar Mills Association (PSMA) being closely involved in the advancement process. But in 2007, only six out of more than seventy sugar mills in the country had facilities to transform raw molasses into fuel quality ethanol. With the current production level of sugarcane crop, Pakistan has a potential to produce over 400,000 tons of ethanol. Nonetheless, less than one-third of it is being currently produced. The state of affairs is such most of the raw material, molasses, gets exported either as it is or in the form of industrial alcohol (an intermediate stage between molasses and ethanol) at a very low price.[52] A full-throttle exploitation of the aforementioned potential to displace equivalent amount of imported petrol (in terms of energy content) can offer very healthy economic relief to all stakeholders including the government, PSMA, farmers and the common man.

The fears that increased pursuance of biofuel may lead to displacement of food crops do not hold water in the proposed case. Statistics suggest that so far less than 0.1 per cent of the total potential of the molasses based bioethanol is being used as alternative fuel. Thus, a 1000-fold increment is manageable without any adverse impacts on food crops. Furthermore, efforts could be made to increase the sugarcane yield and also to introduce other energy crops such as sugar beet. Waterloged land, estimated to be around 7 million acres, with appropriate techniques such as gypsum treatment, can also be used for growing low quality energy crops. There is also tremendous potential to produce bioethanol from biomass waste and municipal waste. On top of bioethanol there is also an overwhelming potential for biodiesel production. One of the prospective biodiesel sources worth quoting here is castor bean. It is a self gown plant seen in many parts of Pakistan particularly in arid and semi arid areas. Here it is noteworthy that in terms of energy crop (i.e. seed production per hectare and oil content) castor seed is a far better choice as compared to other crops presently employed in Europe and USA such as corn, rapeseed, sunflower, and soybean as highlighted in Table 7.14.

Castor oil (derivative of castor bean) is regarded as one of the best substances to produce biodiesel because it is soluble in alcohol and does not require heat and consequent energy requirements as other vegetable oils do in transforming them into biodiesel. Detailed figures and mappings for castor bean production in Pakistan are not available. Castor oil is very much an untapped resource in Pakistan. With a little attention it can be converted into a healthy biodiesel resource for the country. Similarly, Jatropha is another potential source of biodiesel that can be promoted. Again, Jatropha can be cultivated on vastly available barren land without posing any threat to food security.

**Table 7.14: Comparison of potential energy crops for biodiesel production**

| Crop | kg oil/hectares |
|------|----------------:|
| castor beans | 1,188 |
| corn (maize) | 145 |
| mustard seed | 481 |
| rapeseed | 1,000 |
| sesame | 585 |
| soybean | 375 |
| sunflowers | 800 |

Despite the government's initiatives, the bioethanol led biofuel promotion programmes, as yet, have just been of cosmetic value. A typical example is that of the pilot project launched in 2006 as part of which three petrol stations (one each in Karachi, Lahore, and Islamabad) introduced ethanol-petrol blend in a ratio of 1:9. Ironically, the track record suggests that mostly such initiatives evaporate within their embryological stages falling well short of being in a position to make any meaningful impact. To make the bioethanol initiatives tangible, rationale policies will have to be made and efficiently implemented. There is a wider perception that the bioethanol programme should not be under the mandate of the ministry of petroleum and natural resources. Bearing in mind that all over the world, there are conflicts of interest between rival technologies—such as fossil fuels, renewables and nuclear power—the bioethanol programme should have an autonomous mandate, independent of the influence of oil and gas stakeholders. The present practice—export of the bulk of raw material (molasses and industrial alcohol)—is a far less lucrative affair and should also be discouraged. In order to make a real breakthrough the biofuel policies should be redesigned in consultation with all stakeholders such as PSMA, oil and gas companies, industrialists, investors, farmers, agriculture bodies and civil society. Even automobile companies should be convinced to introduce flex-fuel vehicles. Financial incentives, where appropriate, should be offered.

### 7.6.4 Forest Rehabilitation

Pakistan is rapidly losing its already less than satisfactory forest stock. Amongst the scientific and environmental circles across the world, deforestation is considered to be one of the most important environmental concerns. Pakistan needs to run crash forestation programmes to give itself any chance to maintain a sustainable biomass energy resource. Forest-growth is also vital for the ecological balance, as well as development of the agriculture and food sectors.

Unlike the existing annual forestry campaigns that are only of cosmetic value, these programmes should deliver tangible results. However to do that, in the first place, the powerful timber and deforestation mafias have to be dismantled. By employing modern techniques and with the right strategy, it is possible to double the national forest stock within a decade or so. In this respect a collective national effort on the part of all stakeholders including pertinent government and private sector bodies, NGOs and developmental organizations, civil society, and masses is required. Lessons are to be learnt from the successful forest management programmes currently being implemented in various countries.

## 7.7. Wind Power

Wind power is the electricity produced by wind turbines that utilize the natural power of the wind to drive a generator. Wind power is one of the fastest growing renewable technologies in the world. Within the recent past, the annual market for wind has continued to increase at the staggering rate of over 25 per cent following the 2005 record year in which the market grew by 41 per cent. Over 27GW of wind power was installed in 2008, led by the US, China and Spain, bringing world-wide installed capacity to 120.8GW. The top five countries in terms of installed capacity are the US (25.4GW), Germany (23.9GW), Spain (16.7GW), China (12.2GW) and India (9.6GW) as shown in Table 7.15.[53]

**Table 7.15: Top 10 leading countries of the world in terms of installed wind power capacity**

| Country | Installed Capacity (GW) |
| --- | --- |
| United States | 25.4 |
| Germany | 23.9 |
| Spain | 16.7 |
| China | 12.2 |
| India | 9.6 |
| Italy | 3.7 |
| France | 3.4 |
| United Kingdom | 3.3 |
| Denmark | 3.2 |
| Portugal | 2.8 |

With the creation of the Alternate Energy Development Board (AEDB) in 2003, Pakistan attempted to take a significant initiative towards the development of a strong wind power base as discussed in detail in Section 5.4.2. Commercially exploitable wind resource is considered to exist in the southern parts of Pakistan, especially along the coastal areas. The 1,046 km long coastal belt in some areas such as Keti Bandar and Gharo is reported to have monthly average wind speeds reaching 7–8 m/s at a height of 50m as shown in Figure 7.13. Here it is worth explaining that the power available from a wind turbine is a function of the cube of the

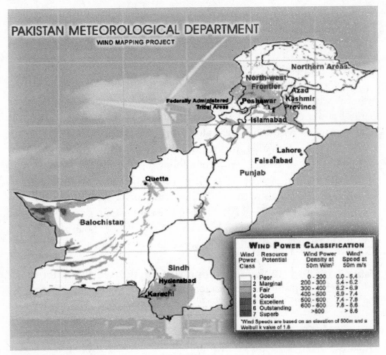

Figure 7.13: Wind power map of Pakistan at a height of 50 m

wind speed, the rate at which air flows past a point above the earth's surface.

Pakistan has been a late starter in wind power. Over the last seven years, since Pakistan has been apparently in hot pursuit of wind power, countries across the world have made substantial progress. Spain, for example, having doubled its wind power base, has become the third largest country in the world in terms of installed capacity. Similarly, over the same period India has doubled its installed capacity, reaching over 9.6GW. Having developed a local wind turbine manufacturing base India has also become an exporter of wind turbines.

Pakistan, on the other hand, has seen only disappointment in terms of wind power. It is a disgraceful situation that against the original target of 700MW by 2007, only 6MW of capacity has been installed as of early 2010. As per media reports, for the very reason the founding chairman of AEDB was sacked in 2008. Firing the chairman, however, did not resolve the problem because substantial damage had already been inflicted to the cause of wind power development. Again, no lesson has been learnt from the past mistakes that have been discussed in detail in Section 5.4.2.

Interestingly, hybrid wind-diesel power systems were in place in Europe in the late nineteenth century. Wind turbines with hydrogen backup were also operational as early as 1904. Bearing in mind that more than a hundred years ago there were no such high-tech scientific and technological gadgets that modern industries enjoy today, the achievement is phenomenal. Pakistan has not made due developments in wind power. If Pakistan were to make effective and sustainable progress, it should have prioritized the indigenous production of wind turbines. Without access to sophisticated technologies, what the Europeans accomplished over a century ago only through handy workmanship, Pakistanis could also have done in recent years had this been genuinely encouraged. As a matter of fact, a manufacturing company in Gujranwala developed 2.5kW wind turbines in the 1980s. Rather than being appreciated and encouraged by pertinent authorities for this achievement the manufacturer was asked for financial kickbacks if he wanted to win business contracts. Thus, the manufacturer was forced to scrap the wind turbine manufacturing project. Had this project been given due support, it could have been now making world-class wind turbines of MW scale.[54]

Like other renewable technologies, wind power is also an expensive choice that requires around $2 million/MW. To have 1,000MW (though the original target was to develop 2,000MW) of wind power by 2012, apart from totally relying on imports of wind turbines, Pakistan also inevitably requires huge cooperation on the part of foreign investors/ donors.

In recent years the intensity of challenges for Pakistan, however, has substantially increased. A few years ago, vital technology transfer options were offered to AEDB but only to be rejected. The situation has now changed—the chances of technology transfer and foreign investment in Pakistan's renewable sector have skewed. not only that, despite the ongoing economic downturn, the prices of wind turbines are on the rise—reports emerging from the international renewable energy market suggest that within the next few years, the cost of wind turbines is expected to double, partly due to growing material cost, stresses on global supply chain and to a certain extent monopolization of technology.[55] Another damaging factor is the continuous devaluation of the Pakistani Rupee which keeps making imports ever more expensive.

For real progress in the area of renewable energy in general and wind power in particular, it is imperative to revamp all of AEDB. The Board needs to be run by dedicated, qualified and competent professionals with an emphasis on the development of an indigenous technology-base. Interestingly, the key behind the success of both of the aforementioned countries, Spain and India, is their indigenous production. Consequently, these countries are not only meeting their own rapidly growing demands but are also exporting wind turbines all over the world. Pakistan could also have utilised this resource had a similar strategy been adopted right from the beginning in 2003.

Given the challenges and opportunities, the optimum strategy for the country is to seek technology transfer and to go for indigenous production at a relatively smaller scale, i.e. 250kW to begin with. The key to success is to start with small-scale and simple designs and to gradually scale them up, both in terms of size and quality. That is how all successful renewable energy companies have evolved and established themselves. Going against this strategy is bound to have numerous implications. This is by far the best choice although it would be a little more time taking and laborious route that in the beginning may only deliver relatively less sophisticated and small-scale turbines. Nevertheless, it would enable Pakistan to gradually establish expertise and a technical base to produce highly competitive turbines of MW-scale within a period of six to eight years. It is also important to bear in mind that unless indigenous production of wind turbines is underway one of the main objectives of wind power, 'energy independence', will remain denied.

## REFERENCES

1. Energy Security Action Plan, Planning Commission of Pakistan, 2005.
2. ENERCON, http://www.enercon.gov.pk (accessed on 12 December 2009).
3. UE Systems, http://www.uesystems.com/energy_waste.asp (accessed on 12 December 2009).
4. Pakistan Energy Year Book 2008.
5. *The Nation*, 6 May 2008, The Indonesian Embassy Islamabad, http://server.kbri-islamabad.go.id/index.php?option=com_content&task=view&id=4568&Itemid=43 (accessed on 12 December 2009).
6. *Dawn*, 7 October 2008, http://www.dawn.com/2008/10/07/ed.htm (accessed on 12 December 2009).
7. International Energy Agency statistics 2008.
8. Energy Information Administration statistics 2008.
9. Coal and Electricity, World Coal Institute, http://www.worldcoal.org/coal/uses-of-coal/coal-electricity/(accessed on 12 December 2009).

10. *Dawn*, 2 February 2008, http://www.dawn.com/2008/02/02/op.htm (accessed on 12 December 2009).

11. Advanced Power Plant Using High Efficiency Boiler/Turbine, Department of Trade and Industry, UK, 2006.

12. Mineral/Energy Resources, Geological Survey of Pakistan, http://www.gsp.gov.pk/ resources/seminars2.htm (accessed on 12 December 2009).

13. *Nawa-i-Waqt*, 16 August 2009.

14. *Economic Survey of Pakistan 2007–08*.

15. Thar Coal Authority asked to make bankable feasibility study, *Daily Times*, 27 July 2008, http://www.dailytimes.com.pk/default.asp?page=2008\07\27\story_27-7-2008_ pg5_3 (accessed on 12 December 2009).

16. *Dawn*, 13 October 2009.

17. *Daily Times*, 27 July 2008.

18. Ashfak Bokhari, Thar coal project and energy crisis, *Dawn*, 27 July 2009.

19. Medium Term Development Framework (2005–2010), Planning Commission, Govt. of Pakistan, May 2005.

20. Parvez Butt, Pakistan's Nuclear Power Needs and Future Options, Presentation for South Asian Strategic Stability Institute, Brussels, 17 November 2006.

21. BBC Urdu, 30 October 2009, http://www.bbc.co.uk/urdu/pakistan/2009/10/091030_ anti_usanger_sen.shtml (accessed on 12 December 2009).

22. M. El-Sharkawi, Electric Energy: An Introduction, CRC Press, 2005.

23. Hydropower and the World's Energy Future, International Hydropower Association, UK, 2000.

24. Centre for Energy, Canadian Centre for Energy Information.

25. German Energy Agency, http://www.renewables-made-in-germany.com/en/wasserkraft/ (accessed on 12 December 2009).

26. M. Asif, 'Price of neglecting hydropower', *Dawn*, 5 March 2008.

27. Volker Quaschning, *Understanding Renewable Energy Systems*, Earthscan, UK, 2005.

28. Data provided by WAPDA, Email correspondence.

29. M. Asif, 'Sustainable Energy Options for Pakistan', *Renewable and Sustainable Energy Reviews* 13, 2009.

30. Data extracted from the Electricity Marketing Data, National Transmission & Despatch Company, 2008.

31. Electricity Marketing Data, National Transmission & Despatch Company, 2008.

32. Drop in global crude prices: Country's oil import bill tumbles 17.04 per cent, *Daily Times*, 25 July 2009.

33. Mr Shams ul Mulk, Former Chairman Pakistan WAPDA, Interview, Pakistan, May 2009.

34. STRATFOR.com, http://www.stratfor.com/files/mmf/7/3/7311fc94bd002e2cf 680d548088d1514bade8c02.jpg (accessed on 12 December 2009).

35. Water and Power Development Authority (WAPDA), www.wapda.gov.pk (accessed on 12 December 2009).

36. *The Nation*, 11 August 2009.

37. http://www.solarviews.com/eng/sun.htm (accessed on 12 December 2009).

38. Paul Gipe, *Wind Power*, James & James, London, 2004.

39. T. Muneer and M. Asif, 'Prospects of Solar Water Heating for Textile Industry in Pakistan', *Renewable & Sustainable Energy Reviews*, 10, 2006, 1-23.

40. M. Asif, 'Sustainable Energy Options for Pakistan', *Renewable & Sustainable Energy Reviews*, 13, 4, (2009) 903–909.

41. M. Asif and T. Muneer, 'Life Cycle Assessment of Built-in-Storage Solar Water Heaters in Pakistan', *Building Services Engineering Research & Technology*, 27, 1, 2006.
42. M. Asif and T. Muneer, Solar Water Heating for Domestic and Industrial Applications, Encyclopedia of Energy Engineering and Technology, CRC Press, New York, 2007.
43. Market Report for China Solar Water Heater—2009, Evergreen, http://www.solar-water-heater-china.com/en/news/Market-report-for-china-solar-water-heater-2009-5.html (accessed on 12 December 2009).
44. David Appleyard, Solar Water Heating Industry Review 2009, *Renewable Energy World*, 21 September 2009.
45. Concentrated solar thermal power—now!, Report by European Solar Thermal Industry Association and Greenpeace, 2005 http://www.greenpeace.org/raw/content/international/press/reports/Concentrated-Solar-Thermal-Power.pdf. (accessed on 12 December 2009).
46. M. Asif and T. Muneer, 'Solar Thermal Technologies', Book for the Encyclopaedia of Energy Engineering and Technology, CRC Press Inc, New York, 2007.
47. Gerhard Knies, EU-MENA solar power partnership for energy, water and climate security, Trans-Mediterranean Renewable Energy Cooperation, 2008, http://www.europarl.europa.eu/intcoop/empa/committee_econ/docs21_01_2008/kniessolarpower_en.pdf (accessed on 12 December 2009).
48. Policy for Development of Renewable Energy for Power Generation, Government of Pakistan, 2006.
49. Robert Hathaway and Michael Kugelman (eds.), *Powering Pakistan*, Oxford University Press, 2009, p. 151.
50. Charles Ebinger, *Pakistan: Energy Planning in a Strategic Vortex*, Indiana University Press, 1981.
51. M. Asif, Winning the oil endgame, *Dawn*, 7 May 2007.
52. M. Asif, Valuable but untapped, *Dawn*, Opinion, 16 April 2008.
53. http://www.our-energy.com/news/wind_power_global_installed_capacity.html (accessed on 12 December 2009).
54. Interview with the Company Director, Gujranwala, May 2009.
55. Renewable Energy World, January–February 2010.

# Glossary of Terms

**Barrel:** Unit of oil equivalent to 42 American gallons, 35 Imperial gallons or 159 liters

**Bioenergy:** Energy produced from biomass (organic materials)

**Bioethanol:** Type of biofuel that is used in spark ignition internal combustion engines

**Biofuel:** Liquid fuel derived from biomass materials

**Biodiesel:** Type of biofuel that is used in compression ignition internal combustion engines

**Biogas:** Gas produced during biological degradation (decomposition) of biomass

**Biomass:** Organic material, such as wood, crops and other agricultural wastes that can be used to produce energy

**Boiler:** A vessel or tank in which heat is produced from the combustion of fuels such as natural gas, fuel oil, or coal to generate hot water or steam for applications ranging from building space heating to electric power production or industrial process heat

**Carbon Dioxide:** A colorless, odorless, non-poisonous gas that is a normal part of the ambient air. It is compound of Carbon and Oxygen and is one of the most prominent greenhouse gases in the atmosphere

**Calorific value:** The amount of heat delivered by a unit mass of a fuel (or unit volume in the case of a gas) when it is completely burned.

**Climate Change:** Changes in the earth's climate, especially those triggered by global warming

**Coal:** Solid form of fossil fuel composed mostly of carbon, with traces of hydrogen, nitrogen, sulphur and other elements

**Crude oil:** Unrefined petroleum. It is the liquid form of fossil fuels

**Daylighting:** The practice of lighting an area with day-light

**Eco Footprint:** A measure of human demand on the Earth's ecosystems. It compares human demand with planet Earth's ecological capacity

**Efficacy:** Ability to produce a desired effect. It's like efficiency and is used to measure the output of a lamp in lumen/watt

**Electricity:** Form of energy that is generated by flow of electrons

**Energy:** The capacity or ability to do work. It is most commonly expressed in Joules (J)

**Energy Conservation:** The practice of saving energy to reduce the impact on the environment and to reduce costs

**Fossil Fuels:** Fuels that come from the long-term decomposition of plant and animal matter from millions of years ago such as coal, oil and natural gas

**Fuel Cell:** Electrochemical conversion device that converts the energy of a fuel directly to electricity and heat, without combustion

**Global Warming:** Warming of the earth's surface temperature reportedly caused by the emission of greenhouse gases that trap the sun's heat in the earth's atmosphere

**Generator:** Machine or engine that produces electricity. It converts mechanical energy into electrical energy by electromagnetic induction

**Greenhouse Gases:** Gases that contributes to greenhouse effect by absorbing infra-red radiation in the atmosphere such as Carbon Dioxide ($CO_2$), Methane ($CH_4$), Nitrous oxide ($N_2O$) and Chlorofluorocarbons (CFCs)

**Human Development Index:** It is an index of human progress introduced by the United Nations Development Programme (UNDP) to rank countries by human development or quality of human life

**Hydropower:** Electrical energy produced from flowing water. Kinetic energy of water is used to rotate a turbine that in turn drives a generator to produce electricity

**Industrial Age:** The time of the industrial revolution during the late eighteenth to early nineteenth century when there was a rapid development in technology allowing for increased production through mechanization and large-scale production

**Kilowatt-hour:** Common unit of electricity consumption that is equal to the use of 1000-watt of power in one hour

**Lignite:** A low-grade, brownish-black type of coal

**Lumen:** The System International unit of luminous flux, a measure of the perceived power of light

**Mega Watt:** Unit of (electric) power, equal to one thousand kilowatts or million watts

**Millennium Development Goals:** These are eight developmental goals that 192 United Nations member states and 23 international organizations have agreed to achieve by 2015

**Nuclear Power:** Electricity generated by a power plant with turbines that are driven by steam generated in a reactor by heat produced from the fission of uranium atoms

**Photosynthesis:** A process in which plants utilize sunlight to produce energy while converting carbon dioxide into oxygen

**Photovoltaic:** Solar cells that directly convert sunlight into electricity

**Power:** Power is the rate at which work is done

**Primary Oil:** The oil that flows out due to the differential pressure as hole is drilled

**Radioactive Waste:** Contaminated waste left over from nuclear power plants

**Renewable Energy:** Energy produced from inexhaustible natural resources such as solar energy, wind power and biomass

**Reserve to Production Ratio:** The number of years the reserves of a particular petroleum/mineral resource will last at the current annual production rate

**Reverse Engineering:** Process of taking apart an object (usually a device or machine) to see how it works in order to replicate it or enhance its performance

**Solar Energy:** Energy derived from the sun either in the form of thermal energy or electricity

**Solar Thermal Systems:** Solar energy systems that collect or absorb solar energy for useful purposes

**Thermal Power Plant:** Power station in which electricity is produced through the use of heat energy

**Tidal Power:** A form of hydropower that produces electricity from the movement (ebb and flow) of tides primarily triggered by gravitational force of moon

**Turbine:** Machine having rotors or blades that spin when driven by a flowing substance such as steam, gas, water or wind. It transforms the kinetic energy of the flowing substance into mechanical energy

**Voltage:** Measure of the electrical pressure or force between two points that causes current to flow

**Watt:** Unit of power or electricity that is equal to one joule per second

**Wind Mill:** Traditional machine that converts the energy of the wind into mechanical output for various applications such as grinding of grain

**Wind Turbine:** Modern machine that captures the energy of the wind and transforms it into electricity. It is the modern version of wind mills

**Wind Power:** Electricity produced from wind. Electricity produced by a generator that is driven by mechanical energy extracted from the kinetic energy of wind

**Work:** Effect of a force on an object carrying it through a certain distance. Work is expressed in Joules.

# Index